Faith of Our Fathers:

Scenes from Church History

Edited by Mark Sidwell

Bob Jones University Press, Greenville, South Carolina 29614

Library of Congress Cataloging-in-Publication Data

Faith of our fathers : scenes from church history / edited by Mark Sidwell.

Includes bibliographical references.
ISBN 0-89084-492-5 (pbk.)
1. Church history.   I. Sidwell, Mark. 1958-
BR145.2.F35   1989
270—dc20   89-36674
                                                                          CIP

Faith of Our Fathers:
Scenes from Church History

Edited by Mark Sidwell

NOTE:
The fact that materials produced by other publishers are referred to in this volume does not constitute an endorsement by Bob Jones University Press of the content or theological position of materials produced by such publishers. The position of Bob Jones University Press, and the University itself, is well known. Any references and ancillary materials are listed as an aid to the student or the teacher and in an attempt to maintain the accepted academic standards of the publishing industry.

Cover: *Wittenberg, October 31, 1517,* by Eyre Crow,
   Bob Jones University Collection of Sacred Art
Photograph by Unusual Films
Cover designed by Moses Yong Ah Wan.

©1989 Bob Jones University Press
Greenville, South Carolina 29614

ISBN 0-89084-492-5
Printed in the United States of America.

20   19   18   17   16   15   14   13   12   11

Table of Contents

The Early Church

The Medieval Church (590 to 1517)

The Modern Church (1517 to the Present)
The Reformation

The Church in the Age of Reason

Introduction

Jewish writer Jesus ben Sirach (c. 190 B.C.) spoke of those "whose righteousness hath not been forgotten." "Their bodies are buried in peace," he said, "but their name liveth for evermore." Such men "were the glory of their times."

This book is an attempt to note those men and women who were the "glory of their times," the heroes of the Christian Church. Such a theme is, surprisingly, not often a goal of most church histories. English historian Joseph Milner, in the introduction to his church history, criticized those historians who "gave a much larger proportion to the history of wickedness than to that of piety in general." He noted later in his introduction, "A history of the perversions and abuses of religion is not properly a history of the Church; as absurd were it to suppose an history of the highwaymen that have infested this country to be a history of England." In his own work, Milner wrote, "Nothing but what appears to me to belong to Christ's kingdom, shall be admitted: genuine piety is the only thing I intend to celebrate." Regardless of whether Milner succeeded in achieving his lofty aim, his goal was certainly praiseworthy and serves in part as the ideal for this book.

The usual method of introducing church history is the survey. In broad strokes, a survey summarizes and outlines the main persons, movements, and events of the history of Christianity. Brevity and generalization characterize the survey as the author strives to compress centuries of history into comparatively few pages. The survey is a useful tool for studying church history, but it has its limitations as well. Often, an author must omit illuminating details because of the constraints of book size and the sheer breadth of the subject. Figures quickly stroll out on stage, as it were, take a bow, and exit never to be seen again.

This collection is an attempt to provide some of the depth often missing in surveys. If church history may be likened to a broad, deep stream, then this work takes soundings of the depths at certain strategic points. A survey, by contrast, attempts to encompass the whole stream but rarely dips below the surface. Obviously, one should not consider an anthology of this type and a survey to be antithetical; the two should be read in conjunction for a fuller view of church history. (See "Suggestions for Further Reading" on pages 22-24 for suggested church history surveys.)

The present book arose in response to a perceived need in Christian circles—particularly for school teachers, pastors, and others who address audiences. History teachers realize that a strict teaching of facts without illustration is the surest way to put a class to sleep. A collection such as this provides some of the stories and anecdotes that can enliven the subject. In particular, the articles collected here provide material that can awaken the student to the richness of his Christian heritage.

For pastors and those who give devotionals, the need for illustrations is a constant problem. Although church history is an abundant source of material, surveys normally lack detail, and books of illustrations often either sound contrived or are inaccurate. By reading these articles, the Christian is able not only to draw upon church history for illustrations but also to understand the illustrations in context and therefore be able to present them more accurately.

The format of the book is designed to provide at least some overview of church history and to underscore the principle-oriented thrust of the articles. The book divides into four sections, the first containing general articles and the other three devoted to the Ancient Church, the Medieval Church, and the Modern Church respectively. The first and last of these chronological periods are further subdivided. An introduction to each section summarizes the chronology and main themes of the respective era.

Each article focuses on one person or topic. The majority of the articles are biographical, discussing either an individual who is himself of great importance to history, such as Martin Luther, or who represents a notable theme of church history, such as Thomas Chalmers and the Christian reaction to the Industrial Revolution. The book does not use biography exclusively, however, because many vital subjects are best treated topically, such as the article on Christian art. A brief paragraph introduces each article. The paragraph discusses the place of the subject in church history and highlights the main principle taught or theme developed in the article.

The articles themselves, as implied above, discuss their subjects with certain principles or lessons in mind. Each seeks to describe its subject and explain why the subject is important to church history. Most of the articles originally appeared in *FAITH for the Family* magazine, although several were written especially for this anthology. A list of the contributors to this collection along with a brief description of each is found at the end of the book.

In the first section of the book and at the close of each article are "Suggestions for Further Reading." The works in these lists have been selected with the general reader in mind. The works mentioned are usually nontechnical and popular in style. A few more technical works are included, usually reference works. Inclusion in the suggested reading lists does not constitute unqualified endorsement of the contents of such works or of other works done by the authors or publishers. Annotations are sometimes attached to the suggestions to help guide the reader in his selections.

The editor hopes that this anthology will provide an interesting and inspirational introduction to church history. If spiritual gifts are to be used for edifying the body of Christ, then writing should also serve to edify. Church history should not simply entertain; it should glorify God. Joseph Milner summarizes well this idea: "To see and trace the goodness of God taking care of his Church in every age by his providence and grace, will be, to the devout mind, a refreshment of the most grateful nature."

General Articles

Although we generally organize church history chronologically, some themes cut across history's lines of chronology. For example, disciplines such as historical theology, the history of missions, and the history of hymns draw from all periods of the history of the Church. Likewise, the study of topics such as the philosophy of history and the lessons of history touch on all eras.

Despite the fact that they do not always fit into our chronological schemes, these broad themes present useful opportunities for studying church history. Themes allow us to view church history in miniature, as it were, by presenting a portion of each era as it is reflected in a narrow subject. The result is a kind of cross section of church history. The articles on the history of Christian art (pp. 12-16) and the role of women in church history (pp. 17-21) are examples of this approach.

The philosophy of history is perhaps less exciting than other topics, but it is essential to the Christian's understanding of history. The first article in this section, on the lessons of history (pp. 6-11), is a practical yet profound demonstration that there is meaning in history, especially for the believer. Ultimately, finding meaning in history is the goal of the Christian. As Perry Miller wrote in describing the Puritan view of history, "History is a memorial of the mercies of God, so that posterity may know them, remember them, and hymn His praises."

Church History Teaches . . .

by Edward M. Panosian

If there be any truth to the idea that "those who do not learn from history are doomed to repeat it," then history must certainly hold lessons for the diligent to discern and to grasp. The Christian who views history as a source of inspiration and edification should be particularly eager to learn those lessons and to profit from them. Consider, for example, the five Scriptural principles that the following article finds validated through the study of history.

It is fashionable to deny that history "teaches" anything; yet there is ample opportunity for any observant person to find fundamental principles and patterns in history. The Bible-believer who studies the history of the Church of Jesus Christ cannot but be impressed with certain basic and recurrent truths concerning that Church.

The Whetstone of Persecution

One compelling fact of history is that the Church has always had its strongest, most effective, and most incisive message when it has been most opposed to and by the world system. Persecution, not accommodation, has been the whetstone of the sword of the gospel. When it has been at odds with the world, the Christian testimony has grown in the world. When the heathen were persecuting and trying to destroy the people of God in the fifth century, Augustine stated, "The same stroke which crushed the straw separated the pure grain which the Lord had chosen." What men intended for evil, God used for good.

Purification and separation of truth from error have always resulted from the pressures of those who oppose the truth, never from the tolerant appeals of error. This, to be sure, is only logical. Those who see no difference between themselves and those who claim to follow the Lord Jesus Christ—whether in speech, action, appearance, or attitude—are not likely to see any need to accept the message that Christians proclaim. It was the superior moral quality of the lives of second- and third-century believers that could not be gainsaid by the heathen. The anonymous *Epistle to Diognetus* (Diognetus being an inquiring heathen of the second century), called a "pearl" of post-apostolic Christian literature, illustrates this principle. A portion of chapter five reads,

> The Christians are not distinguished from other men by country, by language, nor by civil institutions. For they neither dwell in cities by themselves, nor use a peculiar tongue, nor lead a singular mode of life. They dwell in the Grecian or barbarian cities, as the case may be; they follow the usage of the country in dress, food, and the other affairs of life. Yet they profess a wonderful and confessedly paradoxical conduct. They dwell in their own native lands, but as strangers. They take part in all things, as citizens; and they suffer all things, as foreigners. Every foreign country is a fatherland to them, and every native land is a foreign. They marry, like all others; they have children; but they do not cast away their offspring. They have the table in common, but not wives. They are in the flesh, but do not live after the flesh. They live upon earth, but are citizens of heaven. They obey the existing laws, and excel the laws by their lives. They love all, and are persecuted by all. They are unknown, and yet they are condemned. They are killed and are made alive. They are poor and make many rich. They lack all things, and in all things abound. They are reproached, and glory in their reproaches. They are calumniated, and are justified. They are cursed, and they bless. They receive scorn, and they give honor. They do good, and are punished; when punished, they rejoice, as being made alive. By the Jews they are attacked as aliens, and by the Greeks persecuted; and the cause of the enmity their enemies cannot tell.

Counterfeit Christians

This makes a second principle clear: Satan's master device of opposition to God and to the people of God has been by counterfeit, not by contest. If persecution only strengthens what you are persecuting, then another approach is required; the idea "if you can't lick 'em, join 'em" is not of recent origin. Imitation may be the sincerest form of flattery, but when used to deceive and to deter men from God's truth, it is the most subtle form of fatality. Satan set the pattern for deceit with his temptations in Eden and after Christ's forty days in the wilderness. The god of this world offered and promised what the God of Heaven had purposed, but without God and contrary to God's means and will. The Devil and his demons have been doing so ever since.

The goals and dreams of the humanists of our time—whether they are "liberals" (in this context "infidels" or "without Biblical faith"), evolutionary sociologists, myopic politicians, or naturalistic humanitarians—are little different from those which God's Word makes clear as His purpose for man. They seek and promise peace by human contrivances; the Prince of Peace offers peace in the heart of every blood-washed believer and someday for all the earth when He shall reign in righteousness and peace. They seek the acknowledgment of brotherhood among all men; the Scripture teaches two brotherhoods—that of sinners, who "are of [their] father, the devil," and that of Biblical saints, the brotherhood of believers in every age. Man's ideal conceptions of justice, equality, prosperity, and the "good life" are noble, but the fallacious foundations (natural evolution, inherent goodness, and the ability to develop toward individual and universal perfection) defy his dreams.

The world's religions, ancient and modern, attempt the same counterfeit of the truth. Many of them retained elements of the original universal knowledge of the true God; Romans 1:20 says, "For the invisible things of him from the creation of the world are clearly seen, being understood by the things that are made, even his eternal power and Godhead; so that they are without excuse." But the same passage teaches that they corrupted and perverted that knowledge because of their unwillingness to retain the true God in their knowledge. "Professing themselves to be wise, they became fools, and changed the glory of the uncorruptible God into an image made like to corruptible man, and to birds, and fourfooted beasts, and creeping things" (Rom. 1:22-23). Heathen religions—whether typical of ancient ritual and modern philosophy or of ancient philosophy and modern ritual—contain some truth, but any truth that denies Him who is the Truth becomes damning error. Truth mixed with error is the most fatal form of error; it is not truth.

Water is an excellent illustration of this fact: two identical glasses of water are offered—to one has been added a small, but lethal, quantity of an odorless, colorless, tasteless poison. The water was no less pure or wholesome than the water in the other, but if a person knows what has been added to the one, he no longer refers to it as a glass of water. It is poison; the alien addition has contaminated every molecule of the pure. Likewise, a person does not plead the virtue of all the good, clean water in the glass of poison; rather he warns against even one sip, because "a little leaven leaveneth the whole lump" (I Cor. 5:6). Yet how often is today's Christian unwittingly conditioned to be appreciative of the good in mixtures of good and evil and thus tolerant of the evil. A brief reflection should make it clear that we should be conditioned to look for and point out the evil in such a mixture and "touch not the unclean thing" (II Cor. 6:17).

The Diligent Minority

A third observation of the acts of the Christian Church through the centuries is that the people who do the work of God are usually a minority. Popularity and numerical prosperity have never been the domain of the faithful. The omnipotent God seems to delight in showing Himself strong by moving among few men, so that thoughtful people cannot doubt that *God did it*. Gideon's 300 warriors were not victorious because they had superior manpower. The Apostle Paul was not sponsored on his missionary journeys by the National Council of Synagogues with the blessing of the Provincial Council on Communications. Luther, at the Imperial Diet in the city of Worms in 1521, was not exactly popular with the ecclesiastical rulers of his day; he was one man, but he was a man of God.

The underground Church, the trail of truth preserved through the centuries by *some* of the groups outside the established church, was often persecuted, overtly and covertly, and never enjoyed the favor of ecclesiastical, political, social, economic, or intellectual prestige. The faithful remnant in each age were an affront to the compromising and corrupted majority and, like their divine Founder, were despised and rejected of men. But through this remnant came the preservation and transmission of the true Word of God. Through a revival of emphasis on truths preserved by a long line of these faithful ones came the Reformation.

God Uses Men

In the third lesson is a hint of the fourth. Not only are God's people in a minority; they are led, also, by individual men. God does not use institutions or organizations or denominations primarily; He uses men. Institutions, organizations, and denominations may be, and have sometimes been, useful tools, but their usefulness has depended on the fidelity of the men who guide them. There is a sterling quality to faithful men. A Gideon, a Paul, or a Luther willing to carry out God's orders becomes invincible before his enemies, who are God's enemies. Someone has well said that an institution is the lengthened shadow of a man. How often have once-spiritual institutions declined to a shadow of the principles and purposes of the men who were their founders. Only as men, individual men, chosen and used of the Lord, are faithful to Him in the leadership of others—in the family, in the Christian institutions of learning, in the churches, in the nation—can those institutions prosper and be blessed.

God's Work, God's Way

Because individual men are instruments of God for the blessing or the chastening of His people, it is necessary that they "strive lawfully." The lesson from the past, both from the Scriptures and from the subsequent historical record, is that the Christian must be wary of using Satan's weapons to do God's work. He who will not give His glory to another, in whom we live and move and have our being, by whose word of power all things are sustained, insists that His work be done in His way. Christians in this generation—and the world watching them—have seen too much unlawful striving in the interest of "good" goals. Too often men's opinions and human "wisdom," when they are contrary to Biblical principles, have dictated "better" methods. But where God has spoken, the phrases "in my opinion," and "I think" are irrelevant and rebellious and invite God's judgment.

Those who have read of Uzza's being smitten dead by God for using his hands to steady the ark of God (when the oxen pulling the cart stumbled) have marvelled at God's severity (I Chron. 13). Was not Uzza doing a good work in protecting the ark? Perhaps, but the God of the ark had clearly commanded how the ark was to be transported and by whom (Num. 4). If the ark had been carried as God had commanded, it would not have been necessary to disobey God again in "protecting" the ark. One sin produced another; neither was necessary. God, whose words of promise and blessing are sure and true, is no less sure and true in His words of command and warning.

How often today is conviction supplanted by compromise, courage by convenience, and God's demands by man's devisings. How often people prefer crowds to character, quantity to quality, and popularity to purity. Only the man of character will see crowds under conviction, only the quality of spiritual courage will produce a quantity who will stand in the day of testing, and only the purity of obedience will be popular with Heaven.

Lessons to Live By

These five lessons which church history teaches match the five fingers on a hand. Yet these five are strong fingers which, when manipulated together, make a hand well practiced to wield the weapons of spiritual warfare. Realizing that the Church is strongest when most opposed to and by the world, that Satan's master plan is to counterfeit the truth, that God's people are usually a minority, that God uses individual men to do His will, and that Christians must avoid using Satan's weapons to do God's work—the soldier is ready to do battle for God, to fight the good fight of faith.

Suggestions for Further Reading

Jeremy C. Jackson. *No Other Foundation: The Church Through Twenty Centuries.* Westchester, Ill.: Cornerstone Books, 1980. (An interpretative book that attempts to relate the lessons of church history to modern life.)

The Christian Teaching of History. Greenville, S.C.: Bob Jones University Press, 1981. (A pamphlet of fourteen pages that briefly but succinctly discusses some of the more important aspects of a Christian approach to history. Also available as Chapter 7 in *Christian Education: Its Mandate and Mission,* from Bob Jones University Press [1992].)

A Christian View of Religious Art

by Bob Jones

At the conclusion of this article, the author writes, "We cannot reject a study of religious art unless, at the same time, we condemn an awareness of history." The history of religious art is obviously as much a part of church history as, for example, the history of missions or the history of doctrine. What Christians often do not realize is that the history of Christian art is also a reflection of the social, political, and religious influences that have affected the history of the Church. In this article Dr. Jones, a connoisseur of sacred art, discusses how the Christian should approach the study of religious art so that he might best profit from it.

Today many Sunday schools give the pupils little folders or pamphlets presenting children's adventure stories with a moral or spiritual twist. Undoubtedly such literature has some value, but I do not think that these pamphlets are as instructive as the Sunday school lesson sheets that were commonly given to the pupils fifty years or more ago. These presented Bible stories in simple language for children and were beautifully illustrated with Biblical scenes, oftentimes reproductions of famous religious paintings by great artists. To many in my generation, this was the first introduction to religious art; and, as a whole, it was an introduction to *good* religious art.

Most nonliturgical churches shy away from pictorial representation of Bible characters and scriptural scenes as if this were something dangerous and, therefore, to be avoided. As a result, there has been a cultural and spiritual impoverishment which, taken together with the increasing use of cheap religious music and the neglect of sound doctrinal and literary hymnody, may be a contributing factor to the shallow Christianity of our day.

During the Reformation many regarded art of any sort in the church, whether painting or sculpture, as Romanist and idolatrous;

and some good, sincere Christians hold the same view today, quoting, "Thou shalt not make unto thee any graven image, or any likeness of any thing that is in heaven above, or that is in the earth beneath, or that is in the water under earth" (Exod. 20:4). Does the Scripture, however, indeed forbid representing in art a sacred object, heavenly creature, or religious theme? The answer is a clear-cut no.

What the Bible does forbid is any kind of representation for the purpose of worship. We are not to make graven images or likeness of anything in heaven above or in the earth beneath for the purpose of bowing to or worshiping them. Indeed, God gave clear-cut commands for making images and depicting sacred themes in connection with the furniture and decoration for the tabernacle and the temple. The ark of the covenant, the most sacred and holy of all the religious furniture, was to be surmounted by golden figures of cherubim bending above the ark. Heavenly creatures were to be embroidered in the hangings. Among other things, embroidered pomegranates were to decorate the garments of the high priest. All of these representations, whether in the form of images or embroideries, had a spiritual symbolism and purpose.

It is understandable that someone may feel that it is impossible to represent God the Father, who is Spirit, and that to try to do so is presumptuous. We might ask, however, who, unless he'd had a vision, had ever seen a cherub; yet God commanded that these heavenly creatures be represented among the holy furnishings and decorations.

The history of Christian art in western Europe goes back to the time of the Roman Empire itself. Religious symbols were carved in the rock of the catacombs. Following the proclamation of Christianity as the state religion, scenes and religious personages in mosaic and fresco appeared on the walls and ceilings of churches; and the practice continued through the dark ages with the addition of stained glass windows and carved figures of stone and wood.

With the coming of the Renaissance, a new realism took over and holy or angelic figures were represented in a more human fashion. Scenes from both the Old and the New Testaments were favorite subjects for Renaissance and Baroque artists. Miracles (both Scriptural and legendary) and scenes from the lives of the saints were commissioned, oftentimes by a religious order desiring to have its history and traditions represented in its church or monastery chapel. In order to distinguish between various saints, each was represented by a special attribute associated with his life—for example, Peter is often depicted carrying keys, and Paul, the sword with which he was beheaded. Sometimes ecclesiastical figures were identified not only by their outstanding attribute but also by their clothing. The first martyr, Stephen, chosen by the church of Jerusalem as a deacon, was represented in the Catholic vestments of the deacon—a far cry indeed from the fact of history but which, coupled with the two or three stones on his head or in his hand, identified his martyrdom quite clearly to the beholder.

Religious art, in the beginning, had as its purpose the teaching of Scripture or legend to the simple worshiper who could neither read nor write. Religious art was not intended solely for decoration; it was a teaching medium whereby Biblical truth or ecclesiastical tradition could be imparted. No Biblical Christian has any brief for Catholic heresy, legend, and the follies of Papist deceits. Prior to the Reformation, however, organized religion in western Europe was represented solely by the Roman Catholic church, and any religious art was Romanish art. Any thoughtful modern student understands this, and this art helps him to understand Romanism with all of its tyranny, bigotry, and false teaching.

However, not only art but almost all of the religious writings of the period were produced by Romanist theologians. Some of these, in spite of the dross of Romanish deception and tradition, reach a very high level of spiritual insight and love for Christ as, for example, does Bernard of Clairvaux's great hymn, "Jesus, the Very Thought of Thee," which is still used by those Protestants who have not sold out to "junk" music.

A whole artistic tradition developed which had no basic foundation in Scripture or in history but which embodied certain basic spiritual and moral lessons. For example, in the fifteenth century, cherubim were often painted in red and seraphim in blue—red represents the cherub's love, and blue, the seraphim's knowledge. Later, cherubim were represented as young children or sometimes simply as infant heads with a pair of wings, intending to convey to the viewer the holy innocency and purity of the angelic creatures and their freedom from the lusts and limitations of the flesh.

The three wise men before the cradle of the infant Christ were traditionally depicted as being of different ages and nationalities— one young, one middle-aged, and one elderly; a European, an African, and an Asiatic. As far as this portrayal is from fact (they were all Persian or Babylonian astronomers or astrologers and not kings, as traditionally shown), the symbolism of the representation embodied a universal truth that Christ meets the needs of men of every nation and of every age and condition of life. However much a fundamentalist Christian may deplore inaccurate representations of Biblical scenes, he can at least understand the purpose behind the representation and the Biblical truths which the artist tried to convey, even though the representation itself is not strictly true to the Biblical account or goes beyond the oftentimes brief Scriptural facts presented in connection with the incident.

Prejudice and lack of understanding may cause good people to object to artistic representation. Sometimes Christians become extremely agitated when they see a Baroque or Renaissance picture of Christ with His hair to His shoulders. This aspect of the representation of our Lord may be reasonably accurate, even though the artist was not himself aware of the fact. Throughout history painters have usually represented Biblical characters in something approximating the costume and hair styles of the painters' own time or in some fantastical dress which they felt represented an ancient or Oriental costume.

The latter interpretations are particularly apparent in the Manneristic works of the sixteenth-century artists. Shoulder-length hair, however, was the common hair style among most Jewish men in the time of our Lord. Some argue that because the Roman emperors wore rather closely cropped hair at this period, the custom had been adopted throughout the Roman world. This idea is very far from the truth—at least outside of Italy. In Judea and Galilee the Herodians, who wished to flatter Caesar, aped everything Roman from dress and hair style to love for pagan games and Roman literature. Not so with the average Jew who despised Rome and everything connected with it. Hair even to the shoulders was not "long hair" in Biblical times. Hair which we would consider long today was the customary masculine length among Jews.

The Scriptural injunction against a man's having long hair is directed against that which is "unisex" or gives the impression of a man's trying to be like, look like, or dress like a woman. In the time of our Lord a Jewish woman's hair was never cut, but was bound up and veiled; therefore, hair that was cropped to the shoulders or above carried no impression of femininity in Bible times. The Biblical principle, therefore, is that men should look like men and women like women. Today women cut their hair to their shoulders (and sometimes far shorter than that); and if men do not have fairly close-cropped hair, there is going to be no difference between men's and women's hair styles. This lack of distinction is what Scripture condemns.

No man can understand the history and development of any culture unless he studies the art and manners of that culture; similarly, no man can fully understand the development of the history of western Europe who does not know something about its art with its aims and traditions. The Counter Reformation, for example, produced the great Baroque canvases of Rubens and the dramatic and ecstatic works of such men as Guercino, Guido Reni, and Lanfranco in Italy, and Murillo in Spain. These works, some of them commissioned directly by churchmen, were governed by explicit rules set down by the Council of Trent for depicting sacred scenes. The pictures, by sheer beauty and dramatic force, were designed to stifle the Lutheran teachings and impress the viewer with the spiritual authority, power, and wealth of a totalitarian church. A hint of the Charismatic tendencies which crept into the Church in seventeenth-century France appears in some of the works of the French artist Philippe de Champaigne.

Religious art depicts more than religious scenes and Biblical subjects. It teaches us much about the religious and political history of Europe during those centuries when politics and religion were so interwoven that it is impossible to understand one without a knowledge of the other. We cannot reject a study of religious art unless, at the same time, we condemn an awareness of history. Recognizing that religious art provides valuable historical information, Christians may cultivate an appreciation of religious art as a means of understanding history and of broadening their artistic horizons.

Suggestions for Further Reading

Leland Ryken, ed. *The Christian Imagination: Essays on Literature and the Arts.* Grand Rapids: Baker, 1981.

Martyrs, Missionaries, and Mothers: Great Women in Church History

by Rebecca Lunceford Foster

In recent years historians have shown a greater interest in the role of women in history. Unfortunately, the histories resulting from this renewed appreciation have not always praised women whose lives conformed to the standards of God's Word. Indeed, for some historians, a woman's rejection of divine standards is reckoned a virtue. In contrast to this tendency, the author of this article uplifts women whose faith, character, and behavior exemplify Christian truth. As you read the article, note the last paragraph in particular. The truly great women of church history are those who conform to the ideal picture presented in Scripture: "Many daughters have done virtuously, but thou excellest them all. Favour is deceitful, and beauty is vain: but a woman that feareth the Lord, she shall be praised" (Prov. 31:29-30).

The Christian woman of today can learn much from the lives of her predecessors. Historically, women have played an important part in the Church. They have gone with courage to martyrs' deaths; they have served as faithful wives and helpmeets to support the ministries of great men of God; they have faced the dangers of the mission fields with their husbands and often alone; they have been some of God's truest prayer warriors; they have reared sons and daughters to God's glory; and they have worked tirelessly to serve the Church and the needy world. In short, women have been greatly used by God while remaining obedient to the Scriptural teachings in regard to women's service.

The list of Biblical women who have served God is a long one: in the Old Testament, Eve, Sarah, Miriam, Ruth, Esther, and the widow who fed Elijah; and in the New Testament, Mary the mother of Jesus, Elizabeth, Martha and Mary of Bethany, Mary Magdalene and the other women who served the Lord during

His earthly ministry, Lydia, Priscilla, Lois and Eunice, and many others. All these are part of the heritage of any Christian woman. But there are others, some well-known, some obscure, whose lives are recorded in the pages of church history. The list is nearly endless, but even a few examples show the impact a godly woman's life can have.

During the earliest persecutions of the Church, women went to the arena and the stake with their fathers, brothers, and husbands. Perpetua is one of the best-known of the many women who suffered and died under the Roman persecutions. Vibia Perpetua was a young married woman in her twenties, the mother of an infant son. We have no record of her husband's life; he may have died, or deserted her when she became a Christian. The Romans arrested her together with her maid, Felicitas, who was expecting a child. Several men were arrested, condemned, and martyred with them.

In spite of pleading by her father to recant, Perpetua and her companions remained true. Her letters from prison and the records of others testify to her faithfulness. "Can one call anything by any other name than what it is? So neither can I call myself anything else than what I am, a Christian." At her questioning by the procurator, she said, "I cannot forsake my faith for freedom," and a short time later went to the arena to face a wild steer, singing a hymn and trying to help Felicitas when she was gored. When the animal did not kill her, she asked for her brother, encouraged him to be faithful to Christ, and returned to the arena where she was beheaded.

Other women died as bravely, and still others faced danger to themselves and to their families with equal courage. It is not always an easy task to be the wife of a man whose service to God calls him to controversial and dangerous positions. Indeed, some of the wives of the great Reformers had to face the same conflicts in withdrawing from the Roman Catholic church as did their husbands.

One such woman was Katherine von Bora, who was to become the wife of Martin Luther. A nun who had come under the influence of Lutheran teachings and been saved, she escaped with eight others from the convent in a merchant's cart and went to Luther at Wittenberg. When Luther was faced with a wagonload of escaped nuns, he exclaimed, "This is not my doing; but would to God I could, in this way, give liberty to enslaved consciences and empty the cloisters of their tenants."

Luther knew that since their families would not support the runaway nuns, they needed either professions or husbands to provide for them. For eight of the nuns, husbands were quickly found. But God had a special plan for Katherine. She had no intention of marrying the first candidate who came along, and on at least one occasion, she refused a gentleman whom Luther suggested. Instead, she told Luther's aide, Nicholas von Amsdorf, that she was not unreasonable and would gladly marry either Amsdorf himself or Martin Luther. The idea was a surprise to Luther but one that he felt was of God, and soon the ex-priest and the ex-nun were married.

During the years that followed, Luther's "dear Katie" reared his children, supported his ministry, and shared his danger. Besides the monumental task of running a large sixteenth-century household, Katherine Luther undertook responsibilities that would have broken a lesser woman. She threw open her house to the homeless, including former monks and nuns who had nowhere else to go. She set up a hospital in her home, attending to the sick herself. With wisdom and good humor, she encouraged and supported the sometimes-difficult Luther, helping to meet his emotional and spiritual needs as well as the physical. So great was her husband's regard for her that he wrote, "I would not change my Katie for France or Venice, because God has given her to me, and she is true to me and a good mother to my children."

Other women are remembered for the influence they had on their children. Monica, the mother of Augustine, was a godly woman whose prayers for her wild son were answered when he was saved and went on to become one of the great scholars and apologists of the Christian faith. Susanna Wesley was another famous mother, whose sons John and Charles were shining testimonies to her example and training.

Still other women devoted their musical talents to God's service. Women such as blind Fanny Crosby and her English contemporary, Frances Ridley Havergal, have provided some of our most loved and familiar hymns. "Take my voice and let me sing / Always, only, for my King," Miss Havergal wrote in one of her famous hymns, and the words could be her autobiography.

The mission field, too, has been an arena for women serving God. Many have gone with their husbands to face deprivation and danger in distant places. The great Baptist missionary, Adoniram Judson, was blessed with three courageous and godly wives, each of whom labored with him in Burma. Ann Judson, the first American woman to go to the mission field, spent fourteen years working with her husband, helping as he translated the Scriptures and printed tracts, opening a school for Burmese girls, comforting, aiding, and suffering with her husband when he was imprisoned. Only a few months after they were finally released and had set up a new mission work, Ann died at the age of thirty-seven. Her faith in the midst of great trial is evidenced by a statement in her journal: "God is the same when He afflicts as when He is merciful, just as worthy of our entire trust and confidence."

Seven years later, Judson married Sarah Hall Boardman, the widow of another Burma missionary. Sarah had remained alone for three years after her husband's death, working with her son among the wild mountain tribes of Burma. After her marriage to Judson, she bore eight children—six of whom survived—and continued her work translating tracts into the native languages, writing hymns, and aiding her husband. Eleven years later, in 1845, exhausted by childbearing and a disease contracted in Burma, she died en route to the United States.

Soon after his arrival in Boston, Judson contacted Emily Chubbock, a Christian writer, to ask her to write a biography of Sarah. As they worked together on the book, friendship grew into love, and when Adoniram Judson returned to Burma in 1848 Emily was with him. In addition to bearing the hardships of the work in Burma, Emily reared the three of Sarah's children who were still young enough to need her as well as one of her own. Five years after she left Boston, she returned, a widow with four children in her care; and three years later, at the age of thirty-seven, she died of tuberculosis. Many of the great men who went out as pioneering missionaries expressed gratitude for their faithful and courageous wives; Adoniram Judson was triply blessed.

Two other missionary wives—a mother-daughter pair—are worthy of note. Mary Smith Moffat went with her husband Robert to Africa, facing great hardships as they built a great work at Kuruman, in South Africa. After years of seemingly fruitless labor, they at last began to see results. Mary wrote back to England, "Our gracious God has been very condescending to spare the lives of His unworthy servants to witness some fruits of missionary labor."

The Moffat's eldest daughter, Mary, found her childhood in Africa good training, for she married David Livingstone, who called her "the main spoke in my wheel." In spite of her lengthy separations from her husband, Mary Livingstone faced suffering and sorrow with courage as great as her mother's.

There were many others, too—women who accompanied their husbands to the mission field and women such as Mary Slessor who went alone when there was no man to do the work that must be done.

Over and over again, the history of the Church tells the story of God's working through faithful women who lived and worked and died to further the gospel. The lessons of their lives should speak to modern women. It is all too easy for us to listen to the voice of the world telling us that doors are closed to us because we are women and that we should expend our energies in fighting for a kind of "liberation" that brings neither joy nor blessing. The lives of women of the past point us to the many doors of service that are as open to us as they were to them. Indeed, we are blessed with better education, better health, and greater opportunities to prepare for the same tasks they faced. Proverbs 31:30 tells us that "a woman that feareth the Lord, she shall be praised." The women of God who have gone before us deserve that praise; we ought to learn from them.

Suggestions for Further Reading

Edith Deen. *Great Women of the Christian Faith.* New York: Harper and Brothers, 1959.

Mary Hammack. *A Dictionary of Women in Church History.* Chicago: Moody, 1984.

Ruth Tucker and Walter L. Liefeld. *Daughters of the Church.* Grand Rapids: Zondervan, 1987. (A self-proclaimed "history of women in the church" which professes to balance "traditionalist" and "feminist" approaches.)

Suggestions for Further Reading

For those interested in pursuing the subject further, this essay provides a brief introduction and guide to the enormous amount of literature in the field of church history. The books described are intended to provide the nonhistorian with the most accessible and readable works. Therefore, many scholarly works have been omitted, and popular works have been given preference. Those works of special interest to orthodox Christians are emphasized.

In the foremost place must come the works of nineteenth century American church historian Philip Schaff (1819-1893). His *History of the Christian Church* (8 vols. 1910; reprint Grand Rapids: Eerdmans, 1981) is impressive in its depth of scholarship and learning but is also written in a flowing, readable style. In addition, Schaff was generally conservative and presents few views objectionable to most orthodox Christians. Furthermore, he is exhaustive as far as he goes (the eight volumes go only halfway through the Reformation) and covers nearly every topic that the reader might wish to research. Another valuable work of Schaff's is *Creeds of Christendom* (3 vols. 1931; reprint Grand Rapids: Baker, 1983). The first volume contains a thorough history of all major Christian creeds, and the other two volumes reproduce the creeds themselves.

There are many surveys of church history to choose from. The two standard seminary texts are Kenneth Scott Latourette, *A History of Christianity* (New York: Harper and Brothers, 1953) and Williston Walker, et al., *A History of the Christian Church* (4th ed., New York: Charles Scribner's Sons, 1985). Both are thorough (Latourette's being the more exhaustive) but theologically liberal. The standard evangelical survey is Earle E. Cairns, *Christianity Through the Centuries* (Rev. ed., Grand Rapids: Zondervan, 1981). Cairns is complete, though less thorough than Latourette or Walker, and takes a generally orthodox position. Another recent popular work is Tim Dowley, ed., *Eerdmans Handbook to the History of Christianity*

(Grand Rapids: Eerdmans, 1977). It is probably the most eye-pleasing survey, with its color photos and appealing lay-out, and is generally conservative. The use of multiple authors, however, results in an uneven quality in writing. Another work that Christians should consider is S. M. Houghton, *Sketches from Church History* (Edinburgh: Banner of Truth Trust, 1980). Although, as its title suggests, it is not thorough, the book is warm in its evangelical emphasis, and it focuses on genuine instead of nominal Christians. A work that teachers might examine is B. K. Kuiper, *The Church in History* (Grand Rapids: Eerdmans, 1951, 1964). Kuiper wrote his book as a text for Christian high schools, and a teacher's guide for the book is also available.

Two collections provide a good sampling of the original sources of church history. Henry Bettenson, *Documents of the Christian Church* (New York: Oxford Univ. Press, 1943) is the older work and is often reprinted. Ray C. Petry and Clyde L. Manschreck, *A History of Christianity* (1962; reprint Grand Rapids: Baker, 1981) is larger and perhaps more useful.

Books on historical theology, or the history of doctrine, are often useful but prove to be difficult reading. For example, W.G.T. Shedd, *A History of Christian Doctrine* (9th ed., 3 vols. 1889; reprint Minneapolis: Klock and Klock, 1978) and William Cunningham, *Historical Theology* (1862; reprint Edinburgh: Banner of Truth Trust, 1960) are standard, orthodox works but are rather heavy for the casual reader. Justo L. González, *A History of Christian Thought* (3 vols. Nashville: Abingdon, 1970-1975) is more recent and more readable but is also far more liberal. Geoffrey W. Bromiley, *Historical Theology, An Introduction* (Grand Rapids: Eerdmans, 1978) and Louis Berkhof, *The History of Christian Doctrine* (1937; reprint Grand Rapids: Baker, 1975) are more conservative modern surveys. A different approach is taken by Harold O.J. Brown, *Heresies* (Garden City, N.J.: Doubleday, 1984). Brown surveys church history as it revolves around the doctrine of Christ. His work is marred, however, by an unnecessary attack on fundamentalism.

A few standard reference works are helpful to the study of church history. The best dictionary for the orthodox Christian is J. D. Douglas, ed., *New International Dictionary of the Christian Church* (Rev. ed. Grand Rapids: Zondervan, 1978). Also good is Elgin Moyer and Earle Cairns, *Wycliffe Biographical Dictionary of the Church* (Chicago: Moody, 1982). The standard work for church historians in general is *The Oxford Dictionary of the Christian Church* (2nd ed. London: Oxford Univ. Press, 1974). Another interesting work, particularly useful for the teacher, is Robert C. Walton, *Chronological and Background Charts of Church History* (Grand Rapids: Zondervan, 1986). Another interesting resource is the magazine *Christian History*. Each issue is devoted to a single person, such as Martin Luther or John Calvin, or a single topic, such as Christian views of money or Russian church history. The articles are well written, colorfully illustrated, and highly informative.

It is difficult to select only one or two books for the different eras of church history, but most Christians will find the following works helpful. For the Old Testament era, Leon Wood, *A Survey of Israel's History* (Grand Rapids: Zondervan, 1970) is very good; and for the intertestamental period, see Charles F. Pfeiffer, *Between the Testaments* (Grand Rapids: Baker, 1959). F. F. Bruce has written two outstanding works on the ancient period, *New Testament History* (New York: Doubleday, 1971) and *The Spreading Flame* (1958; reprint Grand Rapids: Eerdmans, 1979). The latter, on the history of the early post-New Testament church, is a particularly fine and readable work. Also see Rousas J. Rushdoony, *Foundations of the Social Order: Studies in the Creeds and Councils of the Early Church* (Fairfax, Va.: Thoburn Press, 1978) for a conservative, strongly Reformed interpretation of the early Church.

On the Middle Ages, William Ragsdale Cannon, *History of Christianity in the Middle Ages* (1960; reprint Grand Rapids: Baker, 1983) is a solid if uninspiring work. G.S.M. Walker *The Growing Storm: Sketches of Church History from A.D. 600 to A.D. 1350* (Grand Rapids: Eerdmans, 1961) is more evangelical in outlook.

For the Reformation, the standard textbook has been Harold J. Grimm, *The Reformation Era, 1500-1650* (2nd ed. New York: Macmillan, 1973), but it is a secular approach to the era. More Christian in outlook is R. Tudor Jones, *The Great Reformation* (Downers Grove, Ill.: InterVarsity Press, 1985). Readers might also consult the works of nineteenth century Swiss church historian J. H. Merle D'Aubigné. (See pp. 155-56.) They are often available in reprint, though often with uncomfortably small print. (See also p. 105.)

For the post-Reformation era, two adequate surveys are Gerald R. Cragg, *The Church and the Age of Reason, 1648-1789* (Grand Rapids: Eerdmans, 1960), and Alec R. Vidler, *The Church in an Age of Revolution, 1789 to the Present Day* (Grand Rapids: Eerdmans, 1961). More interesting is A. Skevington Wood, *The Inextinguishable Blaze: Spiritual Advance in the Eighteenth Century* (Grand Rapids: Eerdmans, 1960), but it concentrates almost entirely on Great Britain. A theologically conservative survey is Roy A. Suelflow, *Christian Churches in Recent Times* (St. Louis: Concordia, 1980).

The Ancient Church
(To A.D. 590)

Traditionally, the era of the Ancient Church dates from the time of Christ to the beginning of the pontificate of Gregory I ("the Great") in 590. The birth, life, ministry, death, and resurrection of Christ not only begin this period, but they are also the central events of history. From Jesus' small band in Palestine, the Church grew and spread throughout the known world. With growth came increased opposition and outright persecution within the Roman Empire. Ultimately, the Emperor Constantine converted to Christianity (312)—it is argued how sincerely—and within a century that religion had become the official faith of the Empire. Yet, less than two centuries after Constantine, the Empire had fallen, and Europe moved into the Middle Ages.

Several themes and characteristics mark this era. In addition to the importance of evangelism and persecution, as mentioned above, the period saw the labors of those men who became known as the "Church Fathers." To the modern reader, the very title conjures up images of old, white-bearded men in long robes writing dusty-dry theological treatises. Others, perhaps, look askance at the Fathers because of the unmerited authority that Roman Catholics give to their writings. The Fathers themselves, however, were mostly devout Christians who simply grappled with the practical problems of life and who wrote for the edification and defense of the Church. Some of their writings are admittedly banal and erroneous. Other works are much sounder and even brilliant. If viewed without the halo of sanctity with which tradition has crowned them, the Church Fathers are believers whose works give the modern Christian insight into the life and history of the early Church. As for their value in interpreting Scripture, we might do well to consider the statement of Swiss reformer Ulrich Zwingli, who wrote, "I study the doctors [Fathers], with the same end as when we ask a friend: How do you understand this passage?"

Faith of Our Fathers: Scenes from Church History

This section of the book subdivides into three periods. The first, "Old Testment and Intertestamental Period," is admittedly not really *Church* history. But the New Testament emphasizes, particularly in Matthew's Gospel and the Epistle to the Hebrews, that Christianity makes no sense apart from its roots in Judaism. Understanding the history of God's people before the coming of Christ can only aid in the study of the history of His people after His advent.

The second period, "New Testament Era," supplements the record of Scripture. Of course, the Bible is a completely accurate record and contains all truth necessary for salvation and Christian living. Historical background, however, enriches the study of Scripture and can help deepen the believer's understanding and appreciation of the Bible.

The final section, "The Early Church," covers that five-hundred-year period which saw the gradual growth, eventual triumph, and—sadly—increasing corruption of the Church. In addition to the work of the Fathers, this period also saw many of the important early doctrinal controversies. In response to heretical teaching, orthodox theologians summarized and stated the Biblical doctrines concerning the Trinity, the deity and person of Christ, and more. In works such as the Apostles' Creed, the Nicene Creed, and the Athanasian Creed, we have both the fruit of their labors and carefully balanced Scriptural statements of the true faith.

The Mideast Connection: Archaeology and the Old Testament

by Dan Olinger

As Christians we do not need the evidence of secular history to prove the reliability of our faith. Our trust is in God and His infallible Word. Nonetheless, because we know that the Biblical record is completely true, we realize that the study of ancient history often cannot help confirming the Bible. Such study can also shed light on some passages of Scripture. In the following article, the author discusses some of the most famous archaeological confirmations of the Bible's truth and shows how a knowledge of history can enrich the study of Scripture.

"I besieged and conquered Samaria, and led away as booty 27,290 inhabitants of it." These are the words of the Assyrian emperor Sargon II, the man who sent his general, Sennacherib, to bring God's judgment upon the backslidden Northern Kingdom of Israel in 722 B.C. Nearly all Christians know that much of the Old Testament is history; they also believe that this history is true. What they may not know is that secular historical records confirm much of the history God has given us. Though we would believe God's account even if every "scholar" in the world scoffed at it, it is interesting nonetheless to see God's Word confirmed by those who would rather not believe it.

The Nuzi Tablets

In 1925, on a site near the Tigris River in northern Iraq, archaeologists discovered the ancient city of Nuzi. With it they found a wealth of social records that tell us much about the customs prevailing during the time of Abraham and before. For example, one tablet describes the adoption of a man named Wullu by someone named Nashwi, who needed an heir. Wullu would be the legal heir unless Nashwi later had a natural son. This record explains perfectly why Abraham adopted his slave, Eliezer of Damascus, as a sort of "conditional heir" (Gen. 15:2-4). Another tablet records a court decision obligating a barren wife to provide a substitute to bear children to her husband. This is exactly what Sarai (16:1-2) and Rachel (30:1-3) did. The same tablet also says that if the barren wife later bore children, the offspring of the substitute could not be sent away. This may well be the reason that Abraham needed a divine vision before he would reject Ishmael (21:11-13). Finally, another tablet points out that the family idols were the symbol of inheritance rights and that natural sons would receive these idols before adopted sons would. Rachel's theft of her father's idols (31:19) was her attempt to steal the inheritance from her brothers (31:1). That is why Laban made such an extensive search for them (vv. 19-23).

This is not to say, of course, that the patriarchs lived according to Nuzi's laws, but the Nuzi tablets reveal to us that some family practices in Genesis were common throughout the Middle East.

The Sumerian King Lists

Many liberals have scoffed at the great ages recorded in Genesis, but the Sumerian King Lists provide evidence that Methuselah's 969 years may not be so far-fetched after all. One king in the list, Ubartutu, is said to have reigned 18,600 years; another, A-lulim, 28,800 years; and yet another, Alalgar, a whopping 36,000 years (*Biblical Archaeologist,* Spring 1980, pp. 69-70). This is not to say that we accept these figures as accurate; they certainly are not. But usually such traditions in the ancient Near East were based to some degree on fact; it is very likely that the great ages in the king lists point to a time when men lived far beyond the modern threescore and ten. And the Biblical figures are much more believable, even to the infidel, than are these obvious exaggerations.

The Ebla Tablets

Perhaps the most exciting recent find is the city of Ebla, southwest of Aleppo, Syria. This city was apparently a major commercial center about 2500 B.C., four hundred years before Abraham. A fire in its library baked hundreds of clay tablets and preserved them for modern students. Because the find is so recent, there is much yet to be translated and published. The situation is further complicated by political controversy over the ownership of the finds. But what little has been published is quite exciting indeed; for example, the tablets may mention the cities of Sodom and Gomorrah, never before mentioned outside of the Bible.

A number of its records concern tribute received from other kings; it is interesting to note that Ebla received yearly from one other city, Mari, over half as much in silver and gold as Solomon received yearly from his entire kingdom (666 talents: I Kings 10:14). For years, many liberals had thought that the Biblical writer was exaggerating, since it is hard to imagine anyone's receiving nearly twenty *tons* of gold every year. But the Ebla tablets speak quite matter-of-factly of gold and silver by the ton. (The critics are getting quiet on this point!)

Egyptian Records

There has been a wealth of records of various kinds found in Egypt, many of which confirm Biblical customs and events. For example, many liberal scholars had refused to believe that Solomon really married a daughter of Pharaoh (I Kings 9:16), since before that time Egypt never allowed its princesses to marry foreigners. As a matter of fact, Pharaoh Amenhotep III, a contemporary of Joshua, snubbed a king of Babylon who asked for his daughter; the Pharaoh told him, "From of old a daughter of the king of Egypt has not been given to anyone." But it has been discovered that when Egypt's power began to decline—just before Solomon's time—the Pharaohs began using their daughters as pawns, marrying them off to foreign kings in order to keep peace. There are numerous examples of this practice in secular history; so Solomon's marriage is not in the least inconsistent with historical records.

Several passages in the Old Testament mention a "Shishak, king of Egypt": he gave sanctuary to Jeroboam when the latter fled from Rehoboam (I Kings 11:40), and he later attacked Jerusalem, taking booty but unable to conquer it completely (II Chron. 12). The victory stela, or monument, of Shishak (in Egyptian, *Shishonq*), found at Karnak, Egypt, records his campaign into Palestine and lists the cities that he conquered. Conspicuous by its absence is Jerusalem; he did not claim to conquer it. It is very likely that Jeroboam's later building of Shechem and Penuel (I Kings 12:25) was his *re*building after Shishak's attack; both cities appear on the stela as conquered.

Isaiah 37:9 mentions "Tirhakah king of Ethiopia," who attacked the rear of Sennacherib's army when the latter was besieging Jerusalem. The stela of "Taharqa," found at the ancient Egyptian city of Kawa (in what is now northern Sudan), describes the movement of his army from southern to northern Egypt into position for some major battle. This account squares exactly with the Biblical event.

First Kings 11 records the flight of Hadad, king of Edom, into Egypt to escape Solomon. It says that he grew up in Pharaoh's court (v. 18) and married Pharaoh's sister-in-law (v. 19). She bore him a son, Genubath, who was considered a son of Pharaoh (v. 20). Several different Egyptian records tell of similar occurrences: foreign kings were taken into court and given allowances; many Pharaohs took "wards" and brought them up as their own sons; and occasionally the son of a foreign king was held hostage in the court as a means of ensuring peaceful relations with the king in question. So Hadad's experience was not exceptional.

Often in Scriptural genealogies, names will be omitted: a man will be called the son of his grandfather or great-grandfather. For example, Jehu is called the son of Nimshi (I Kings 19:16; II Kings 9:20) when he was really the son of Jehoshaphat, who was the son of Nimshi (II Kings 9:2). For years liberals looked at these occurrences as classic examples of errors in the Bible. But findings in Egypt and elsewhere tell us that throughout the Middle East such omissions were a common custom, especially if the writer was trying to make a point or to list a genealogy with equal divisions (like the one in Matthew 1; see v. 16). The omissions were perfectly acceptable, and the reader was expected to recognize them as a literary technique. For example, an inscription on the temple of Taharqa (see above) names Sesostris III, who lived in 1880 B.C., as the father of Taharqa, who lived in 680 B.C.! It's not likely that Sesostris waited twelve hundred years to have a son; many generations have been omitted, as was the custom.

Nehemiah speaks often of an Arabian named Geshem, or Gashmu (2:19; 6:1-6). Interestingly enough, his name has been found inscribed on a silver bowl discovered in the Nile Delta. We have learned from this inscription that he was the king of Qedar, now northern Saudi Arabia. Since this land held the main trading route from Asia to Egypt, Geshem was a powerful figure in his day. This fact explains why his words carried so much weight in Nehemiah 6:6.

Assyrian Records

Isaiah 20 describes Tartan's coming from Sargon, the Assyrian ruler, to Ashdod, a city in southern Palestine, and conquering it. Isaiah goes on to talk of Egypt's coming downfall, and the connection between the two events is somewhat unclear. An inscription has been found at Khorsabad, Iraq, however, which sheds much light on the event. Evidently Ashdod had revolted against Assyrian rule, and Sargon sent his "turtan," or high military official, to quell the revolt. The instigator of the trouble fled to

Egypt for asylum, but the Egyptians returned him, hoping to "butter up" the turtan and so to avoid being themselves attacked. Isaiah's prophecy is pointing out the fact that Egypt will be destroyed despite her attempt to placate the mighty Assyrians. Needless to say, his prophecy was fulfilled.

Many of the kings of Israel and Judah are recorded in the Assyrian inscriptions. Ahab's name appears on a bull statue found in Calah, near Nineveh; Shalmaneser II's famous Black Obelisk pictures Jehu paying tribute to the Assyrian monarch; Tiglath-Pileser II (called "Pul" in II Kings 15:19) claims to have collected tribute from Menahem of Samaria ("Sa-me-ri-na-a-a"), as II Kings 15:19-20 records. The same annals of Tiglath-Pileser say, "They [the Samarians] overthrew their king Pekah and I placed Hoshea as king over them." This event is recorded in II Kings 15:29-30.

Perhaps the most interesting account in the Assyrian records is that of Sennacherib's attack on Jerusalem, also mentioned in II Kings 18-19, II Chronicles 32, and Isaiah 36-37. The Bible tells us that in response to Hezekiah's prayer the angel of the Lord killed 185,000 Assyrian soldiers, forcing Sennacherib to return home. Naturally the Assyrian ruler would not wish to record such a stunning defeat. His record of the confrontation says, "I made [Hezekiah] a prisoner in Jerusalem, like a bird in a cage." But he does not claim to defeat him, and he does not say why he was unable to do so.

The Bible says that "we walk by faith, not by sight" (II Cor. 5:7). We do not need secular history to tell us that we can trust the record of the Scriptures, but it should not come as any surprise to us that since that record is true, it is backed up by secular history. As time goes on and more discoveries are made, we can expect more and more confirmation of the truth of the Scriptures, as well as the disproving of supposed "historical facts" that contradict the Biblical record. We have every reason to trust our lives and our souls to the faithfulness of this great and God-given Book.

Suggestions for Further Reading

Howard La Fay, "Ebla, Splendor of an Unknown Empire," *National Geographic,* December 1978, pp. 730-59.

Alan Millard, "Does the Bible Exaggerate King Solomon's Golden Wealth?" *Biblical Archaeology Review,* May/June 1989, pp. 20-34.

Merrill F. Unger. *Archaeology and the Old Testament.* Grand Rapids: Zondervan, 1954.

Howard Vos. *Archaeology in Bible Lands.* Chicago: Moody, 1977.

The Broken Towers of Tyre

by Dan Olinger

The study of fulfilled prophecy has often enriched the devotional lives of Christians. God's promises of blessing or judgment and His ultimate enactment of these promies reveal to us the diverse ways in which He guides history. We could cite many examples of fulfilled prophecy; the Gospel of Matthew, for instance, makes Christ's fulfillment of prophecy a major theme of the book. The following article discusses the story of Tyre—how God pronounced judgment on the city and then, in His wisdom and grace, took over fifteen hundred years to fulfill His prophecy. The history of Tyre is proof of the maxim "Though the mills of God grind slowly, yet they grind exceeding small."

If ever a city had little to fear, it was Tyre. Its situation was ideal: Palaetyrus ("Old Tyre") stood on the shore of the Mediterranean Sea less than forty miles north of Mount Carmel. It was well supplied by aqueducts from the springs at Ras El-Ain, about five miles away. What made it impregnable, however, was its "other half": the island city, a half-mile offshore, with a sturdy wall and two harbors connected by a canal. Since Tyre was the capital of Phoenicia and controlled the sea, the island was all but invulnerable. Its navy could supply it through interminable sieges, and its distance from the shore made it impervious to land armies. Of all cities, Tyre had reason to be smug and proud. And it was.

According to Herodotus, Tyre was founded in 2750 B.C. That date may be much too early, but we are sure that Tyre was well established by Joshua's time (1400 B.C.). It carried on extensive trade with Amenhotep IV of Egypt during the early 1300s. Its traders travelled the known world, and some of the unknown, in search of commercial gains. By 600 B.C. it had established colonies in Greece, Asia Minor, and most of the Mediterranean islands;

it had founded Carthage, Utica, and other cities of Africa and Spain. Phoenicians had circumnavigated Africa under the sponsorship of Pharaoh Necho II of Egypt, had engineered a primitive "Suez Canal," and had explored in the Atlantic at least as far as the Azores, perhaps landing even on the American continent. Phoenician ships brought wealth from every corner of the world: silver, tin, iron, and lead came from Spain and the British Isles; copper from Cyprus; gold, bronze, and slaves from Asia Minor; horses and mules from Armenia; lumber and jewels from Syria and Palestine; linen from Egypt; and gold, jewels, and cattle from Arabia (Ezek. 27:12-24). Tyre's most famous and lucrative product was its purple dye, made from the secretion of the hypobranchial gland of the snails *Murex brandaris* and *Murex trunculus*. Because nearly ten thousand snails were necessary to produce a gram of the precious dye, it brought the highest prices on the market; Pliny reports that the modern equivalent of ten ounces of dye cost as much as one thousand denarii. (A denarius was one day's wage.) Lydia, the seller of purple (Acts 16:14), must have been a wealthy woman indeed. The Tyrians were also skilled artisans, especially in sculpture and engraving, and produced high-quality glass. An Egyptian papyrus of about 1300 B.C states that Tyre was "richer in fish than in sand." Tyre was truly, as Isaiah called it, "a mart of nations" (Isa. 23:3).

Undoubtedly the most famous king of Tyre was Hiram, who lived at the time of David and Solomon. This "lover of David" (I Kings 5:1) supplied him with cedar trees, carpenters, and masons for his house (II Sam. 5:11) and provided for Solomon's temple the artisans to do the fine engraving, carving, and casting (I Kings 5:18) as well as cedar and fir trees for the actual construction (vv. 8-10). He received in return wheat, barley, oil, wine, and twenty Galilean cities (II Chron. 2:10; I Kings 9:11) and made a league with Solomon. He shared with Israel the port of Ezion-Geber on the Red Sea, from which his ships sailed to the Orient to bring back gold and other luxuries (I Kings 9:26-28).

But Tyre's influence was more than commercial: it was the major force behind the spread of Baal-worship in the Mideast. Tyre had three main gods: Baal-Shemen (the sky); Melkarte, also called Baal, Molech, or Hercules (the sun); and Astarte or Ashtoreth (the moon), also called "the queen of heaven" (Jer. 44:25). Tyre's temple to Astarte was well known 175 miles away in Ugarit; the temple to Melkarte featured a pillar of gold and another of green glass which shone in the night by means of a fire kept burning within it. (The Strait of Gibraltar was named for these "Pillars of Hercules.") The outstanding features of this religion were temple prostitution and child sacrifice: the children were either thrown into flames ("tophet," Jer. 7:31) or sewn up in leather bags and thrown from the temple wall. This false religion was actively promoted in Israel by Jezebel, daughter of a Tyrian king, and in Tyre's colonies as well. It was this Tyrian influence on Israel as well as its selling of Israelites into slavery (Joel 3:3, 6) that spurred Ezekiel to call down God's judgment.

Fittingly enough, Ezekiel's name meant "God strengthens"; such power could have come only from God. He was a priest living in exile, and his rough ways remind one of Elijah or John the Baptist. With angry voice Ezekiel called down the judgment of God on His enemies: Ammon, Egypt, Assyria, Edom. But his most scathing denunciations were reserved for the city that was "strong in the sea," the "merchant of the people" (Ezek. 26:17; 27:3); he was adamant in his condemnation of Tyre, the city that had made itself wealthy by its cleverness rather than its might. Many nations, cried the prophet, would make the godless city like the top of a rock, a place for fishermen to spread their nets (26:3-5).

If any Tyrians heard of Ezekiel's prophecies, they must have feared little. Nebuchadnezzar, the dominant leader at the time, was no more to be feared than great rulers of the past, and the Tyrians knew how to deal with such rulers. They had always been under the rule of foreign leaders eager to control their port city, but they found that tribute was an easy way to placate most rulers. An occasional minor rebellion would remind overly strict lords that in the final analysis the Tyrians were their own people. And they had always recovered quickly from the few times they had been directly attacked; even in the last great attack, that of the Assyrian Ashurbanipal in 638 B.C., when Old Tyre had been levelled, they had barely slowed their commerce for the occasion. They had learned that nominal subjection and payment of tribute would bring peace and the accompanying freedom of trade, and trade was what kept Tyre going. In this manner they had dealt with the Pharaohs of Egypt and the kings of Assyria. Nebuchadnezzar and his Babylonian Empire would be no greater challenge.

After Nebuchadnezzar destroyed Jerusalem in 586 B.C., he came up to the coast and besieged Tyre. For thirteen years the siege lasted before Tyre finally capitulated. But even then the wholesale destruction prophesied by Ezekiel did not come. Nebuchadnezzar took a few captives, but the island city of Tyre was still very much in existence. In the eyes of the Tyrians, Ezekiel had been wrong; their gods were greater than the God of captive Israel. As Babylon lost power and was replaced by Persia, Tyre's spiritual rebellion continued. The Tyrians supplied building materials to Zerubbabel's workers for the new temple in Jerusalem, receiving money and supplies in return (Ezra 3:7). But they insisted on selling in Jerusalem on the Sabbath day, until Nehemiah threatened them with bodily harm (Neh. 13:16-21). Their driving concern, clearly enough, was not for religion, but for money.

Under Persia Tyre prospered, supplying fully one-fourth of Persia's twelve hundred ships. Tyrians were instrumental in bridging the Hellespont and in digging a canal across the isthmus of the Peloponnesus in Greece. But then the Greeks destroyed the Persian navy at Salamis, and Tyre was to have a new master.

The greatest Greek ruler was, of course, Alexander the Great. He determined that before he could chase Darius back into Persia he must "close the back door" by conquering Tyre. When the city refused peaceful submission, he began a siege in 333 B.C., first destroying Old Tyre on the mainland. When he saw that the siege would be ineffective, he began a most unusual project. The Greeks, he said, would build a jetty out to the island and turn it into a peninsula. They would use the rubble of Old Tyre to fill in the half-mile of water. His men argued against the idea; Xerxes had made such an attempt and had failed. But Alexander had made up his mind. For seven months his soldiers built up the sea bottom between the shore and the island. To protect his men and to prevent supplies from reaching the island by sea, Alexander enlisted the navies of the other Phoenician cities that he had already conquered. Tyre's island fortress was cut off from help. When the jetty was completed, Alexander ran a battering ram up to the wall and attempted to breach it. Unsuccessful, he attacked the city from all sides by ship, finally breaching the wall and storming the city. Massacre followed: eight thousand men were killed, two thousand of them crucified on the beach and left to decompose; thirty thousand women and children were taken into slavery. The distinctive culture and glory of Tyre were gone forever. But still Ezekiel's prophecy had not been fulfilled. Tyre was not "like the top of a rock"; it sprang back and thrived again under Alexander's rule.

Following Alexander's death, Tyre was ruled by the Egyptian Ptolemies and then by the Romans. In spite of constant battles and at least one severe plundering in A.D. 193, Tyre continued its commerce and rebuilt its city. It possessed one of the largest hippodromes of the Roman Empire; on the island (now a peninsula) was a marble-paved, porticoed thoroughfare; its cathedral, built in the fourth century A.D., featured marble and mosaic floors, bronze doors, and beautiful fountains. Its merchants still dealt in linen, glass, and purple dye. Furthermore, God was being kind to the once-tortured city. Christ Himself visited the area (Matt. 15:21), and many Tyrians travelled to Galilee to see Him (Mark 3:8); Paul visited there on his third missionary journey, at which time there was already a Christian church in operation (Acts 21:3-4). But Tyre's rebellion continued. The neoplatonist Tyrian Porphyry wrote a twenty-one volume work ridiculing Christianity, which hardened many of the educated across the Empire against the "new religion." An eighteen-year-old girl and five Egyptian Christians, as well as many others, were martyred in the hippodrome. In the fourth century Tyre was a stronghold of the Arian heresy, which denied the deity of Christ, claiming that Christ Himself was a created being. The Synod of Tyre, held in A.D. 334, supported Arianism and was later declared heretical. It seemed that whether God judged the city or bestowed grace on it, it only grew harder against Him. It remained wealthy into the Middle Ages; it was well fortified, the local artisans were producing beautiful goods, and the traders were sailing as much as ever. But time was running out; God's Spirit would not always strive with Tyre.

Tyre repelled a four-month siege by the king of Jerusalem in A.D. 1111. Thirteen years later it fell to the warriors of the First Crusade. Then in 1291 it was approached by the Mamelukes, warlike Egyptian Muslims. Whether the Mamelukes had learned from history that sieges were not effective against Tyre, or whether they simply attacked with their usual method, we do not know. All we know is that they did not waste time with a siege. By sheer numbers and brute force, they overran the entire peninsula, bringing with them a kind of destruction never seen by the Tyrians. They massacred Tyrians in even greater numbers than Alexander had. Those they did not kill they sold into slavery or dispersed across the countryside. They destroyed every building they could find; even the beautiful and famous cathedral fell before them, its fluted columns toppling into the sandy soil. But even this destruction was not the full extent of God's judgment. The ruins lay undisturbed for five hundred years before Ahmad al-Jassar of Sidon removed the usable building stones to Acre, where he was building a mosque. This, finally, was the end of Tyre. After centuries of spurning God's longsuffering and ignoring His prophecies of impending destruction, Tyre finally became "like the top of a rock."

Today on the old site there is a small fishing village of about five thousand people, called Sur, but the people bear no relationship to the Tyrians of old. Tyre is dead. On the quiet shore of what was once a bustling harbor, the modern traveller can watch local fishermen spread their nets to dry. "Many nations" (Ezek. 26:3) have finally carried out God's threat.

Suggestions for Further Reading

Nina Jidejian. *Tyre Through the Ages.* Beirut: Dar El-Mashreq Publishers, 1969.

Charles Pfeiffer and Howard Vos. *The Wycilffe Historical Geography of Bible Lands.* Chicago: Moody, 1967. (Pages 185-213.)

The Story of Hanukkah

by Craig Jennings

Christians are sometimes lamentably ignorant of the history of the era between the two testaments, the so-called four hundred silent years. Yet a proper understanding of the intertestamental period is an aid to understanding Biblical history. Probably the most famous and most inspiring story of the era is the account of the Maccabees, the Jewish zealots who fought against pagan tyranny. The Jewish holiday Hanukkah, the celebration of the Maccabees' cleansing of the temple, is a reminder of these heroes and their exploits.

Of all the major Jewish festivals, the only one not established by God in the Old Testament is the celebration of Hanukkah. This eight-day festival, which began in the second century B.C. falls in the month of December, and so to most people Hanukkah is simply the "Jewish Christmas."

Today the Hanukkah festival includes songs, games, gifts to children, various festive meals, and the lighting of the eight-branched candelabrum. Each night of the celebration the family lights one additional candle until all eight are lighted. The synagogue service often includes the chanting of the Hallel (literally, *praise,* referring to Psalms 113-118), public readings from the Torah, prayers, and the lighting of the candelabrum.

While it is true that this "Festival of Lights," as it is sometimes called, has become more of a family-centered holiday (as has Christmas), it has no truly Christian connotations. Born from resistance to political and religious tyranny, Hanukkah stands as a memorial to Jewish courage and resilience.

Following the death of Alexander the Great in 323 B.C., his generals partitioned his huge empire (which included Palestine) into three major divisions. At first the Jews came under Egyptian control, but eventually the Syrian Seleucid dynasty conquered the area in 198 B.C. For a time the Jews offered no serious challenge to this foreign political domination; however, soon after Antiochus Epiphanes IV ascended the throne in 175 B.C., Jewish discontent flared into open revolt.

What sparked the uprising was a decree issued by Antiochus in 168 B.C. which outlawed the Jewish faith. The edict forbade the Jews to observe the Sabbath or any other religious festival, ordered that all sacrifices and the practice of circumcision be terminated, forbade the reading of the Scriptures, and ordered all copies to be burned. Later Antiochus even rededicated the temple in Jerusalem to the Greek god Zeus. Out of fear and weakness many Jews compromised their faith, but others determined to face death rather than surrender their heritage.

The center of resistance was an old priest by the name of Mattathias and his five sons. One day officials who had been sent out by Antiochus to enforce his new edict entered the small town of Modin (modern el Arba'in). Since Mattathias was a revered leader in the community, the king's officials tried to persuade him to offer the first of several public sacrifices to Zeus. Mattathias refused. Another Jew in the crowd stepped forward, however, and offered the pagan sacrifice which the officials had requested. Mattathias and his sons quickly drew their swords and rushed upon the hapless Jew, killing him and several of the king's men.

Father and sons then fled the village, leaving the following challenge from Mattathias, "If any one be zealous for the laws of his country, and for the worship of God, let him follow me." Many responded from all over Judah, and armed resistance began. Following the death of Mattathias, his third son, Judas Maccabeus, assumed leadership. Finally in December of 164 B.C. the rebels under his command recaptured Jerusalem.

Following the capture of the city, the first priority of Judas was to restore the Jewish worship. Priests who had not compromised with paganism cleansed the Holy Place, built a new altar, and rededicated the temple to Jehovah. According to Jewish tradition, Judas Maccabeus then established a celebration in honor of this rededication which today is known as Hanukkah (literally, *dedication*). Josephus describes it this way:

> Now Judas celebrated the festival of the restoration of the sacrifices of the temple for eight days; and omitted no sort of pleasures thereon: but he feasted them upon very rich and splendid sacrifices; and he honored God, and delighted them, by hymns and psalms. Nay, they were so glad at the revival of their customs, when after a long time of intermission, they

unexpectedly had regained the freedom of their worship, that they made it a law for the posterity, that they should keep a festival, on account of the restoration of their temple worship, for eight days. And from that time to this we celebrate this festival, and call it Lights. I suppose the reason was, because this liberty beyond our hopes appeared to us; and that thence was the name given to that festival.

Through the years the celebration of Hanukkah has changed. At first the festival centered in the temple and included sacrifices and feasting. However, with the scattering of the Jews following the destruction of Jerusalem in A.D. 70, Hanukkah became more widely observed and more family-oriented. The medieval Hanukkah custom of giving money to children has become in modern Judaism a theme for fund raising, and in modern Israel the government emphasizes the military victory of Judas Maccabeus more than the religious or social aspects of the celebration.

During Hanukkah season, as the Jews kindle lights which represent "the indistinguishable and ever spreading Jewish faith," Christians can be witnesses of the true Light which came into the world to enlighten hearts and minds through the gospel. In a unique sense, therefore, Christmas is for the believer a true "Festival of Lights."

Suggestions for Further Reading

H. A. Ironside. *The Four Hundred Silent Years.* New York: Loizeaux Brothers, n.d.

Charles Pfeiffer. *Between the Testaments.* Grand Rapids: Baker, 1959.

When Was Christ Born?

by Dan Olinger

Our system of dating (B.C. and A.D.) testifies to the central importance of Christ's incarnation to human history. Even so, some Christians do not understand the meaning of the abbreviations B.C. and A.D. For example, although most people know that B.C. stands for "before Christ," some think that A.D. stands for "after death" (i.e., after Christ's death). Others imagine that the system originated from the Scriptural record and are therefore surprised to read that Christ was born around 4 B.C. The following article clarifies misconceptions such as these as it explains the origin and history of our method of reckoning the years.

In the year A.D. 525 a Catholic monk living in Rome, named Dionysius Exiguus ("the little"), was computing the dates of Easter for the next several years. He decided, however, to break with tradition. Easter tables of that day, following church practice, identified the year as "*x* years after the persecution under Diocletian," the wicked Roman emperor who reigned from A.D. 284 to 305, shortly before Constantine legalized Christianity within the Roman Empire.

It bothered Dionysius that the Church fixed its calendar in reference to an ungodly ruler; so he decided to indicate the date as "*x* years after the incarnation of the Lord." He computed Christ's year of birth as 754 years after the founding of Rome, called that year "A.D. 1," and reckoned all dates from it. ("A.D." stands for *anno Domini,* which is Latin for "in the year of the Lord.") Unfortunately, it was later discovered that his "A.D. 1" was four years after the death of Herod the Great, who not only was very much alive at the birth of Christ but also ordered the "massacre

41

of the innocents" some time after Christ's birth (Matt. 2:16). Dionysius erred by *at least* four years. So today, nearly fifteen hundred years later, we are forced to say that Christ was born four years (or thereabouts) "before Christ." Confusing, isn't it?

Three other Biblical passages confirm the monk's error. Luke 3:23 notes that Christ was "about thirty years of age" at the beginning of his ministry, which was close to "the fifteenth year of the reign of Tiberius Caesar" (v. 1). Tiberius began to reign as co-regent with Augustus in A.D. 11; so his fifteenth year would be A.D. 26, at which time Jesus was "about thirty." Subtracting thirty from this date takes us to 4 B.C. We could safely say that Christ might have been born as early as 5 or 6 B.C.; these dates would allow time for the journey of the wise men and the murder of the infants before Herod's death in 4 B.C., and Christ still would have been only 31 or 32—"about thirty"—in the fifteenth year of Tiberius.

In connection with this verse, John 2:20 records the comments of the Jews at this time that the temple had been "forty and six years . . . in building." The temple of their day, also known as Herod's temple, had been begun in 20 B.C., so their statement points us to A.D. 26, the same date indicated by Luke 3:23.

One final passage confirms these dates in an unusual way. Luke 2:2 states that the census ordered by Augustus just before Christ's birth "was first made when Cyrenius was governor of Syria." Since Cyrenius officially ruled only after the death of Herod, many critics charged Luke with an error here; Cyrenius could not have been governor of Syria and Herod the king of Judea at the same time. But the noted archeologist William Ramsey has shown that Cyrenius was given a special position by Caesar to administer the census around 6 B.C., and that by virtue of that appointment he was called the "governor" of the region. (See Ramsey's *Was Christ Born in Bethlehem?* pp. 243ff). So the date checks out exactly right.

It may sound amusing, if not downright preposterous, to say that Christ was born in 4 "B.C." (before Christ). Many Christians have been confused by the date, and a few have even been offended. But we should remember that the error was with a medieval monk, and not with the Scriptures. They were right all along.

Suggestions for Further Reading

W.P. Armstrong. "Chronology of the New Testament." *International Standard Bible Encyclopedia.* 1:645-47.

William Ramsey. *Was Christ Born in Bethlehem?* 1898; reprint Grand Rapids: Baker, 1979.

More Evidences of His Gracious Hand

by Edward M. Panosian

"The fulness of the time" (Gal. 4:4) is an inspiring concept for the Christian to consider. At the appropriate point in history, God sent His Son to accomplish man's redemption. The time of Christ's birth was not the result of random chance; the events and circumstances were directed by our sovereign God. In this article, the author demonstrates how the time of Christ's incarnation was such a time of "fulness." Furthermore, he shows through consideration of the Reformation era how each movement of God's Spirit is the culmination and outworking of seemingly mundane historical factors. A final section comparing eighteenth-century France and England reveals that such points of history not only build upon previous events but in doing so also reveal the blessing or curse of God. God's sovereignty in history is the theme of this selection.

One remarkable evidence of God's providence is the preparation of the ancient world for the coming of the long-promised Messiah, the Lord Jesus Christ. Just as three languages identified Him on the parchment placed above His head on the cross, so did those same three cultures contribute to what the apostle calls "the fulness of the time" (Gal. 4:4). The Hebrew represented the religious preparation; the Greek, the intellectual; the Latin, the Roman political and technological preparation.

God chose the Jews to preserve the testimony that God is one. While often departing from that fidelity—and repeatedly being judged for it—they yet represented the truth that the many gods of the heathen nations are no gods and that God is Spirit, not fashioned by men's hands, nor visible to men's eyes. This testimony set them apart religiously from their contemporaries.

The Greeks sought human explanations for the phenomena of nature which others had attributed to "the gods." Reason and logic

43

were their tools. Their philosophies attempted to comprehend what others had called the spiritual world. With remarkable facility they emphasized reason and the intellectual capacity of man.

The Romans provided the physical, political setting of order, unity, and power. They created the political world into which Christ came. It was a world unified under one rule, secure and protected under Rome's might, comparatively peaceful internally, speaking one language (or two: Latin and Greek—but all could be understood throughout the empire) and offering one citizenship (while today the rim of the Mediterranean represents many different countries). These made for ease of travel and communication, legal protection of the rights of citizens, and—because Rome was an empire of cities— the rapid publication of new ideas, such as the gospel message, to great numbers of men in one place at the same time. God wonderfully prepared the very means for the propagation of the gospel of Jesus Christ by the Hebrew, the Greek, and the Roman worlds.

Christ's birth illustrates that He uses human agency to accomplish divine purpose. While the prophet Micah (5:2) centuries before had prophesied that the "ruler in Israel," the Messiah, should come forth out of Bethlehem, it was the human decree of Octavian Augustus Caesar which brought Mary and Joseph to that town just when "the days were accomplished that she should be delivered" (Luke 2:6). A pronouncement of a heathen emperor requiring all citizens to return to their own cities to be enrolled or registered for purposes of taxation was used to bring the mother of Jesus to Bethlehem at just the right time. The emperor was doing his own will, unaware that he was a vessel in the Lord's hand for *His* purpose. Surely "the king's heart *is* in the hand of the Lord" (Prov. 21:1).

More than a millennium later, long after the fall of that Roman Empire and after centuries of "dark ages" of papal ecclesiastical dominance, of comparative intellectual and educational ignorance, of economic and social serfdom for masses of Europeans, came another evidence of God's providence. The Renaissance of the four- teenth, fifteenth, and sixteenth centuries in Europe was many-sided. Paradoxically, the very benefits of the Renaissance were accom- panied by a rationalistic humanism, which created a condition virtually requiring a spiritual revival, the Reformation. At the same time, God was using the Renaissance to make possible that very Reformation.

Partially as a result of the Crusades of the eleventh through thirteenth centuries, ostensibly to rescue the holy land shrines from the Muslims, western Europeans renewed contact with the Near East, and its capital, Constantinople, where classical culture had been preserved since Rome's fall. This contact stimulated Europe culturally and commercially. Trade grew between east and west. The science and philosophy of the east filtered westward.

In addition, there was a revived interest in manuscripts of the Greek authors, both secular and religious. Included were Greek manuscripts of the Scriptures, the language in which the New Testament was first written. Scholars compared the Greek texts with the prevailing Latin Bible of the Roman church in the west and perceived differences, not only literary, but also doctrinal.

A fundamental example is illustrated by Acts 2:38, where Luke records Peter's reply to those who, pricked of heart at his preaching on the day of Pentecost, asked, "What shall we do?" Where the Greek is translated, as in our Authorized King James Version, "Repent," the Latin Vulgate Version—as some standard Roman Catholic versions since—says, "Do penance." This is a natural consequence of the inability of the ecclesiastical Latin language to convey that subtlety of meaning present in the Greek word for repentance. Latin was a language of law and government; Greek was more suited to the expression of ideas—"the Greeks had a word for it."

This rediscovery of basic gospel truth by such simple tools as language was a by-product of the Renaissance's challenge to the authority of the medieval Roman church. Reformers of the sixteenth century returned to the authority of the Bible. As basic grammar education became more accessible to the laity, as versions and translations of the Scriptures were prepared in the languages the people spoke—and gradually read—a Reformation resulted which spread over Europe and laid the foundation of modern religious (and political, economic, and intellectual) liberty.

The Reformation began in the sixteenth century in Germany where God protected it in its infancy. Germany was not then a nation. It was a collection of loosely knit states forming the Holy Roman Empire. Its nominal head in the second quarter of the century was Charles V, the Hapsburg heir of many lands and titles. Among the German princes, each of whom headed several German states, political power was jealously held; each considered himself a practical sovereign over his own territory. While the prevailing theory of power required a single political head, the princes only reluctantly yielded to the emperor. He, in turn, was unable to act effectively without their support.

With trouble to the east and to the west of his domain, Charles could ill afford to offend his princes within. In this, then, God protected the Reformation. Simply stated, heaven kept the emperor so busily occupied with the Bourbon French threats to his west and with Muslim Turkish threats to his east that he had little time to deal with Lutheran Protestant "threats" at home. He could not actively oppose his princely supporters of the Reformation, although he was himself strongly opposed to it, without losing their needed support against external enemies. The most he could do at the Diet (Congress) at the city of Worms in 1521 was to declare Luther outside the protection of the law and warn Luther's friends against helping him, whereas earlier emperors—such as Sigismund with John Huss in 1415—had put similar reformers to death.

In God's good providence, that imperial Edict of Worms proved to be no deterrent to God's servant. While anyone could have put him to death on sight and been rewarded by the empire for having done so, Luther lived another twenty-five years and died a natural death. God's man was immortal until he had finished the work God had for him to do.

For a final example of God's intervention into the affairs of man, we look two hundred years beyond, to the eighteenth century, for a marked contrast in the life of England and France. England had embraced the Reformation of the sixteenth century, however weakly and incompletely. France had rejected it, had renounced the Huguenot cause from the throne, had reluctantly granted a toleration of that cause for a time, and by 1685 had revoked that toleration.

Both countries in the eighteenth century suffered spiritual declension with the growth of forms of rationalism—the English with deism, the French with naturalism. Yet God's dealing with each was different. John and Charles Wesley and George Whitefield brought to England a wave of spiritual refreshing, a revival of heart religion, as men responded to the clear preaching of the Word of God. France experienced, by the close of the same century, a bloody and destructive revolution that ultimately exchanged one form of tyranny for another.

England had honored the Word of God and was granted the blessing of revival. France had rejected God's people and made them exiles, and France suffered revolution. Again heaven had vindicated the principle that obedience brings blessing, while disobedience brings judgment.

These observations can be made only by looking back with the eyes of faith. While God is working, even the believer cannot always see the evidence of His working; he must simply know that God is working. The believer must remember both that "now we see through a glass, darkly" when we would discern God's hand, and that He uses men and circumstances as He accomplishes His eternal purpose.

Josephus

by Richard Garrett

The name of Josephus is vaguely familiar to most Christians, but many are not exactly sure who he is. Josephus is, in fact, one of the most important historians in the history of the Church; yet he was not a Christian but an unconverted Jew. This fact is but one of several paradoxes concerning this unusual man. His contribution to our knowledge of New Testament times makes his work an invaluable resource. As this article demonstrates, however, Josephus's life is just as varied and absorbing as his numerous writings.

Historian or flatterer? Military commander or pacifist? Jew or Roman citizen? Patriot or traitor? Visionary or realist? Beloved or hated?

Josephus was all of these. He was, perhaps, the ultimate paradox of the first century, a dichotomous product of that turbulent time when Christianity was beginning to supplant Judaism and Rome's voice started to outstrip her virtues.

Josephus, the author of *The Antiquities of the Jews* and *The Wars of the Jews,* was the only major writer to provide a contemporary, sequential, historical account of the period in which the Church was formed. One of his references, for instance, is used to date the birth of Christ. His alleged apprenticeship with the Essene sect has also been carefully examined for possible insight into the group which preserved the famous Dead Sea Scrolls.

There was a time in England when almost every house boasted of two books—a Bible and the works of Josephus. Modern criticism engulfed the Jewish historian in the wake of the Bible-destruction attempts of the nineteenth century, but recently (true to his survivalistic character) Flavius Josephus has been making a "comeback" among Christians, both scholars and laymen. Here is his intriguing story.

Joseph ben Mattias (his Jewish name) was born the year after Pontius Pilate had been recalled from Judea, A.D. 37. His was a priestly family, with Hasmonean royal blood on his mother's side.

We are dependent on his autobiography for details of his life, and Josephus describes himself as a precocious child. At fourteen, "the high priest and principal men of the city came . . . frequently to me . . . in order to know my opinion about the accurate understanding of points of the law." At sixteen, he decided to make intensive studies of the three dominant sects of Judaism—the Essenes, the Sadducees, and the Pharisees; after trying each, he would "choose the best."

For three years he attached himself to Banus, an aesthete who lived in the desert. Some people conjecture that Banus might have been a follower of John the Baptist.

At nineteen, Josephus joined the Pharisees, and remained their devotee the rest of his life. Therefore, he never examined the third group, the socialite Sadducees.

When he was twenty-six, in A.D. 64, Josephus journeyed to Rome. Along the way, like Paul, he was shipwrecked. His account helps verify Acts 27:37, in which 276 persons were said to be aboard Paul's ship. Critics have charged that no first-century boat could hold so many, but Josephus says six hundred were on his vessel!

The visit to Rome impressed the young man with the apparently invincible might of the Emperor and his legions, an impression that was to affect every action he took thereafter.

When Josephus arrived home, the Jews were preparing to revolt against the oppressive Roman rule. "I foresaw," he lamented, "that the end of such a war would be most unfortunate to us. But I could not persuade them; for the madness of desperate men was quite too hard for me." Fearful, he went into semi-hiding, hoping the advance of Roman general Florus would quell the smoldering revolt. But the Jewish rebels, surprisingly, routed the Twelfth Legion in the pass at Beth-horon and the revolt erupted full-scale.

Opportunist Josephus, extolling his fine education, efficiency, and cool-headedness, got himself chosen territorial governor of the Galilee district. It was perhaps the most strategic district, since Rome's counterattack was expected to be launched there.

Historian Solomon Grayzel calls the appointment of Josephus the "most serious blunder" of the revolutionary government. Instead of organizing the populace for war, he concentrated on enhancing his personal authority. Instead of training an army, he prepared an alibi to prove to the onrushing Romans that he was never really their enemy.

Following some feeble attempts at open-field battle against Vespasian's army, Josephus withdrew into Jotapta and fortified the town for the expected siege. It took forty-seven days for the Romans to penetrate the defenses, but while his companions were dying at the battlement, Josephus was plotting an escape. Wise to his deceit, his junior officers came close to murdering him. But he quickly suggested a "suicide pact"—each member of the remaining group would, in turn, kill the next one. When the "pact" was down to two, Josephus persuaded the other man to live, and they surrendered to Vespasian.

It was first reported in Jerusalem that Josephus had fallen in the takeover. Grief and mourning filled every household; "all alike wept for Josephus . . . for thirty days." But when it was announced that the commander was alive and—worse yet—being treated by the Romans with undue cordiality, "the demonstrations of wrath . . . were as loud as the former expressions of affection. . . . Some abused him as a coward, others as a traitor, and throughout the city there was general indignation, and curses were heaped upon his devoted head."

Josephus was treated kindly because he made a startling prophecy: "Vespasian will one day become Emperor." This seemed far-fetched when uttered, for the Julian line still occupied the throne, and no Emperor had ever been selected outside the capital city. Less than a year later, however, Nero's suicide ended the Julian dynasty of Caesars. Two years later Vespasian's troops declared him Emperor.

The flattering prediction and its fulfillment earned Josephus a place of privilege among the Romans. When the general was crowned, Josephus took the name Flavius, the family name of Vespasian, and returned to Jerusalem with the Emperor's son to witness the destruction of the Holy City in A.D. 70. Josephus claimed to believe that the devastation was preordained by God and that God had granted him the power to foresee the results of the war. His belief was true: Jerusalem's doom had already been pronounced by Christ (Matt. 24:2, Mark 13:2, Luke 19:41-44). His countrymen, though, hated Josephus bitterly for his activities.

Declining the gift of a tract of land near Jerusalem, he went to Rome, received citizenship, and was commissioned to write a history of the Jews. Thus, three famous historians were simultaneously at work in the capital: Josephus, writing about the Jews; Tacitus, the budding Roman annalist; and Luke, who chronicled the events of the early Church.

Josephus's first work was *The Wars of the Jews.* Written originally in Aramaic, later in Greek, *The Wars* was decidedly pro-Roman.

The historian contended, though, that his purpose "was not so much to extol the Romans as to console those whom they have vanquished and to deter others who may be tempted to revolt."

Fifteen years later, in A.D. 93, Josephus published *The Antiquities of the Jews.* Whereas his first work aroused the hostilities of his people, *Antiquities* was designed to exalt the Jews before the Graeco-Roman world.

All of this is interesting, perhaps, but it is but background to the core significance of this Jew's writings. "Josephus," H. St. John Thackeray once commented, "has always found more friends among Christians than among his own countrymen." Why? There are three reasons: his references to John the Baptist, to James (the brother of Christ), and to the Lord Jesus.

Josephus could not have avoided hearing of the growing band of first-century Christians. He may not have heard much truth about them on his first trip to Rome in A.D. 64, for that was the year Nero burned the city and blamed it on the believers, but by the time he released *Antiquities* in A.D. 93, the four Gospels, Acts, and Paul's letters were certainly in circulation. "Mere curiosity would lead Josephus to make inquiries concerning this sect which was already gaining adherents in the upper circles."

So, from the knowledge he must have acquired, Josephus first described the imprisonment and murder of John the Baptist by Herod Antipas the tetrarch.

> For Herod had slain John (surnamed the Baptist)—a good man who bade the Jews to cultivate virtue by justice towards each other and piety toward God, and (so) to come to baptism; for immersion, he said, would only appear acceptable to God if practiced not as an expiation for specific offenses, but for the purification of the body, when the soul had already been thoroughly cleansed by righteousness. Now when men flocked to him—for they were highly elated at listening to his words—Herod feared that the powerful influence which he exercised over men's minds might lead to some form of revolt, for they seemed ready to do anything on his advice. To forestall and kill him seemed far better than a belated repentance when plunged in the turmoil of an insurrection. And so, through Herod's suspicions, John was sent as a prisoner to the fortress of Machaerus and there put to death.

The tetrarch's adultery with his sister-in-law is also mentioned, but not as the direct cause of John's death. Josephus's passage is not inconsistent with Matthew 14:1-12, and certainly not contradictory; rather, it supplements the Gospel narrative.

The death of James is likewise treated sympathetically. Annas, the newly appointed high priest and the son of Annas who was responsible for Jesus' death, decided to kill the head of the Jerusalem church at a time when King Agrippa II was away and the new Judean governor, Albinus, had not yet arrived.

> The younger Annas . . . was a rash and extraordinarily daring man, a follower of the sect of the Sadducees, who, as we have already stated, are more ruthless than all Jews in judicial cases. Annas, then, such being his nature, thinking that he had a favorable opportunity, . . . summoned the court of the Sanhedrin, brought before it the brother of Jesus who was called Christ (James was his name) and certain others, and, after accusing them of transgressing the law, delivered them up to be stoned.

The passage about John and James leads the reader of Josephus to assume that more is forthcoming about "Jesus who was called Christ." The expectant reader is rewarded with but a single, concise, yet declaration-filled paragraph in the 18th chapter of *Antiquities.* "Seldom can ten lines have caused such controversy as these." observed Thackeray. The passage is known as the *testimonium Flavianum,* and reads thus:

> Now about this time arises Jesus, a wise man, if indeed he should be called a man. For he was a doer of marvellous deeds, a teacher of men who receive the truth with pleasure; and he won over to himself many Jews and many also of the Greek (nation). He was the Christ. And when, on the indictment of the principal men among us, Pilate had sentenced him to the cross, those who had loved him at the first did not cease; for he appeared to them on the third day alive again, the divine prophets having (fore) told these and ten thousand other wonderful things concerning him. And even now the tribe of Christians, named after him, is not extinct.

For a dozen centuries, the *testimonium Flavianum* was accepted without question. Christians revered this secular verification of their creed and some even included it in the canon of Scripture. A few hailed Josephus as a convert, while others regarded him as another Balaam (Numbers 22-25)—an inspired albeit unwilling, witness to truths which did not reflect his personal convictions.

When so-called higher criticism was the vogue in the nineteenth century, however, Josephus was cut up as mercilessly as was the Bible itself by modernistic theologians. The whole passage, they scoffed, was inserted by Christian "editors" long after Josephus died. In the twentieth century, the pendulum has returned, and reputable scholars have pronounced the passage authentic.

One of the modernistic complaints was that the paragraph seems to break the narrative, that its style differs from surrounding passages. But Josephus was a "patchwork writer." The paragraph on Christ could well have been an afterthought or a thorny subject which was earlier passed over.

More than likely, the ten lines we possess today are an abridgement of the original. Josephus was not a Christian, and his draft may have been longer and included some antagonistic phrasing—a Christian could have edited out the offensive words. Even so, some of the extant phrases have non-Christian coloring. "He was the Christ" is not a profession of faith but rather a form of identification in the manner of "David . . . was the father of Solomon." A Christian would have written "He *is* the Christ" instead.

"Ten thousand other wonderful things" is somewhat of a snide exaggeration on Josephus's part. And "tribe" is likewise disparaging—not a term a Christian author would readily employ.

Josephus died sometime after A.D. 100; the date is not known. He was esteemed in the early centuries of Christianity as one whose work deserves high respect for its research and integrity. Church historian Eusebius spoke of him as "worthy of all credit," and some treatises honored him as "the lover of truth."

Josephus's works are certainly not crucial to Christianity. Our faith does not hinge on the outcome of the argument over whether or not he wrote the *testimonium Flavianum*. We stand only on the inspired, infallible Word of God. Nevertheless, Josephus makes fascinating reading—both because of who he was and what he wrote about.

Suggestions for Further Reading

The most published English translation of Josephus is that of William Whiston (1667-1752) and is available from several publishers. Other translations, on the whole superior to Whiston's, are also available.

F.J. Foakes Jackson. *Josephus and the Jews.* 1930; reprint Grand Rapids: Baker, 1977. (A good work, but theologically liberal.)

G.A. Williamson. *The World of Josephus.* Boston: Little, Brown, and Company, 1964. (Williams has also translated a highly readable version of *The Wars of the Jews.*)

The Easter Date

by Raymond St. John

Some historians tend to dismiss many of the controversies of the early Church's history as "much ado about nothing." No controversy would seem to bear out that claim better than the long and bitter wrangle over the date of the celebration of Easter. This article demonstrates, however, that the issues underlying such controversies are not always trivial.

Unless you have a calendar handy, you probably cannot give the date on which Easter falls this year. The date shifts abruptly from year to year with little apparent logic to the casual observer. Our unusual method of dating this celebration traces back to a centuries-old church council decision. At the Council of Nicaea (A.D. 325), the nondoctrinal but divisive problem of when to celebrate Christ's resurrection was resolved for both the eastern and western branches of the Christian church.

Christians of Jewish descent, living mainly in Asia Minor, based their commemoration of the resurrection on the Jewish Passover date, which always fell on the 14th of Nisan (the Jewish month corresponding to the second half of April). To these Christians Christ had seemingly authorized this date by His own celebration of the Passover with His disciples just prior to His arrest and death as the paschal Lamb. Essentially, these Christians were commemorating the Passover but with Christian significance. With the date of the Passover remaining constantly the 14th of Nisan, just as our Christmas is constantly December 25, these Quarto-decimans (from *quarta decima,* Latin for 14) honored Christ's resurrection three days later, no matter what the day.

Gentile Christians, following the practice of the increasingly influential church at Rome, celebrated Christ's death and His resurrection on the Friday and Sunday immediately after the March full moon, the days that the events had actually taken place. Thus, while Easter for them always fell on Sunday, the date itself varied from year to year.

What created tension within the early Church, then, was the spectacle of one group's sorrowing because of Christ's death while the other was joyfully celebrating the resurrection.

About the middle of the second century, Polycarp and Anicetus, bishops respectively of Smyrna and Rome, made amiable attempts to standardize the date. But since neither side would budge, each claiming historical precedent for its method of dating, the issue remained unresolved. Toward the end of the century, though, the controversy became more heated. Victor, bishop of Rome and not noted for his tact, flexed his ecclesiastical muscles by declaring that the practice of following the Jewish calendar was heretical and anyone who differed from the Roman practice was in danger of excommunication. Only the peacemaking skill of Gallic bishop Irenaeus prevented open rupture within the church.

In the next century the Roman method of dating Easter became so widespread that when the matter was officially settled in the fourth century at the Council of Nicaea, the Roman practice became the standard. The council, in establishing the rule that governs our date today, proclaimed that Easter should be commemorated on the first Sunday after the first full moon succeeding the vernal equinox (the time in March when the sun creates equal-length days and nights around the world) and always after the Jewish Passover. This meant that Easter could come on any date from March 22 to April 25. If the full moon occurs on a Sunday, the council said, the next Sunday is Easter. After this Nicene decision the Quartodecimans were considered heretics and at the Synod of Antioch (A.D. 341) were excommunicated.

Although the paschal debates have been fallaciously likened to the notorious medieval disputes about how many angels could crowd onto the point of a pin, the ramifications are significant. At the center of the dispute was a difference of emphasis. Should Christ's death be the key in determining the date, as the Quarto-decimans were doing by their stress upon the Passover? Or should Christ's resurrection, which we commemorate weekly by meeting for worship on Sundays, dominate?

Also crucial was the question of whether Jewish or Christian influence should be predominant in the Church. How could the Christian Church, asked many, base the commemoration of its most important event on the calendar of the nation that had rejected the Saviour? The conciliar resolution in favor of the western practice shows the fortunate triumph of the Christian influence.

Although far removed today from this early Church dispute, we can joyfully enter into the celebration of Easter with the same spirit and certainty. Called by the ancients "the Day alone Great," this oldest of church festivals reminds us that Christ, in rising from the dead, has anticipated every Christian's resurrection, an event whose date is yet to be revealed.

Suggestions for Further Reading

Philip Schaff. *History of the Christian Church.* Vol. 2. 1910; reprint Grand Rapids: Eerdmans, 1981. (Pages 209-20.)

The Triumph of Truth

by Edward M. Panosian

The Christian Church is painfully familiar with opposition from the world. The Apostle Paul wrote, "Yea, and all that will live godly in Christ Jesus shall suffer persecution" (II Tim. 3:12). Of the numerous oppressions of the saints recorded in church history, none has garnered as much attention as those of the early Christians by the Roman Empire. The following article discusses several important questions concerning these early persecutions, in particular why Rome persecuted Christians. Rather than content himself with simply recounting facts, however, the author stresses the great lesson of these persecutions: God's providence assures the ultimate triumph of His truth.

The providence of our great and gracious God is seen nowhere more evidently in history than in His concern and care for the early Christians as He permitted their testings at the hand of heathen Rome. In Philip Schaff's memorable phrase, all the efforts "of wild beasts and beastly men" were unable to accomplish Rome's intent of stamping out the gospel in its temporal infancy. The Christian Church, because it is Christ's workmanship, triumphed and endured, whereas the Roman Empire was destroyed. Again God's Word—that no weapon formed against God's people shall prosper (Isa. 54:17)—was vindicated.

Why did Rome persecute the infant Christian Church? It was because Christians reflected the light of Him who is the Light of the world and owned Him as Lord. For them it was *Christus Dominus,* "Christ is Lord"; Rome demanded *Caesar Dominus,* "Caesar is Lord."

To a noble, patriotic, heathen Roman, Christianity was a cancer in the body of the empire; it had to be destroyed if the body were to live. There were many reasons behind this necessity. For one, Christianity was too exclusive. Rome was polytheistic, believing in many gods, and was, therefore, necessarily tolerant of all gods and religions. However, Rome could not tolerate the exclusiveness of the gospel of Jesus Christ. Christians, believing and preaching that "there is none other name under heaven given among men, whereby we must be saved" (Acts 4:12), became the objects of the wrath of men.

For these reasons too the Church would not worship the emperor. Although the emperor was not considered a deity (at least while he lived), his office was elevated to a place of divine prominence. He was assumed to possess a kind of aura of divinity; he was the Augustus, far more than man only, ruling by the gods and for them. So, practical worship must be accorded the image of the emperor. This no true believer could do without violating his conscience, for he had been taught in the commandments, "Thou shalt have no other gods before me. Thou shalt not make unto thee any graven image. . . . Thou shalt not bow down thyself to them, nor serve them." (Exod. 20:3-5).

Christians were also too "missionary" for the Romans. They were not content to "live and let live." Instead they labored to spread to all men the knowledge of His salvation, to "publish glad tidings." This led to confrontation; men to whom the gospel was presented resisted and were offended by it.

The lives of believers were an offense to Rome. The morality and virtue of the Christian stood in sharp contrast to heathen immorality. While Rome acknowledged honor, loyalty, duty, and courage, she also practiced homosexuality and abortion. Fathers possessed mastery over the lives of children (even to abandonment of the unwanted), divorce was easy, and life was cheap. Prostitution for "proper" people was respectable. Christian writers of the second and third centuries emphasized the superiority of the morality of the Christians over that of the heathen. When light exposes the deeds of darkness, darkness seeks to extinguish the light. So Rome attacked the Church.

Christians seemed unpatriotic. The Romans thought that failure to acknowledge the gods of Rome would evoke the displeasure of those gods and that Rome's decline would follow unless her people demonstrated their zeal to the gods by eliminating these "atheists" from their midst.

This seeming lack of care for the state was reflected also by the Christian's general hesitation to participate in civil government, not because it was evil, but because doing so required virtual acknowledgement of the gods of Rome; for the oaths of office demanded emperor-worship.

In another incredible paradox, Christians were charged with the grossest and most base immoralities. Because Christians met in secret, their worship was described by their enemies only by out-of-context hearsay. Since in the commemoration of the Lord's Supper they partook of bread and juice as symbols of Christ's body and blood, they were considered cannibals by their contemporary enemies. Since they were heard to "greet one another with a holy kiss" and often addressed one another as brother or sister, they were charged with sexual impurities, even incest! Inflamed by their corrupt hearts and conscious of what moral licentiousness went on in their own temples under the guise of worship, the heathen were quick to accuse the righteous of the very unrighteousness of which they were themselves guilty.

Thus persecution came. At first Nero, and soon other emperors of the first and second centuries, began to employ physical torture and the threat of death to persuade Christians to renounce their faith. These tortures displayed wonderful variety in their ingenuity. Crucifixion, assaults of beast in the arenas, boiling in oil, roasting over grids, forced gladiatorial contest, dragging, burning—these were among means employed in the martyrdom of Christians.

More remarkable than the cruelty and inhumanity of their enemies were the believers' constancy and poise in the midst of this persecution. More often than not, the fear and horror of physical pain were replaced by a peace and expectation of divine deliverance through—not always from—suffering. Their composure and singing reflected a joy that was of another world. Nothing confounded the efforts of the Romans so much as this. What should have caused both men and maidens to cower was met with a courage that nature could not explain. It is true that more of the heathen were won to Christ by the deaths of some Christians than by the lives of many others.

The Church grew, rather than shrank, under persecution. It grew in numbers as the gospel spread, and it grew in purity and in power. A testimony that literally hazarded life made for genuine dedication to the Word and will of God. When a man knows he may breakfast on earth and take supper in heaven, temptations must lose much of their power. And when persecution causes Christianity to grow, the opposite of their tormentors' intent, the zeal of the persecutors must eventually wane.

Before it waned, however, that zeal increased. In the middle of the third century, to celebrate the millennial anniversary of the traditional founding of the city of Rome, the Emperor Decius decreed the first empire-wide persecution of Christians. For the first time, throughout the whole rim of the Mediterranean, all Christians were to be put to death. The decree was made in A.D. 250; Decius was dead in 251, and with him died his decree. The desired end was not achieved. God's providence arranged it.

A final fierce onslaught was begun by the Emperor Diocletian (285-304). Every effort was made to wipe out Christianity. Decrees were made demanding the surrender of holy writings, the deaths of pastors and preachers, and finally the deaths of lay Christians as well. But the triumph of the Christian faith had been guaranteed by a higher decree. The Lord Jesus Christ Himself had promised that the gates of hell would not prevail against His Church.

A decade later the Emperor Constantine, for whatever motives, decreed the toleration of Christianity. By three-quarters of a century more, the Emperor Theodosius made Christianity the official religion of the Roman Empire. The empire that had lifted its hand against the people of God had ceased to prosper. By the end of the fifth century it had fallen to barbarians. God had so ordered it, and again the weapon formed against God's purpose and people did not prosper.

Many thousands of believers were called to suffer much for His name at the hands of the heathen, but in the end God's Word was vindicated, and God's truth triumphed.

Suggestions for Further Reading

John Foxe's *Acts and Monuments* (usually known in abridged versions as *Foxe's Book of Martyrs*) is a thorough if somewhat graphic collection of martyr stories. Most abridgements contain accounts from the Ancient Church and the Reformation.

James and Marti Hefley. *By Their Blood: Christian Martyrs of the Twentieth Century.* Milford, Mich.: Mott Media, 1979.

Lessons from the Catacombs

by David O. Beale

The catacombs enjoy an aura of romance, mystery, and intrigue. Actually, part of this interest results from misconceptions—for example, that Christians lived in the catacombs during times of persecution. As this article indicates, however, the catacombs retain value for what they really contain: the earliest examples of Christian art and the knowledge that art gives us of early Christian life.

A "symbol" is an outward sign of a concept or idea. Our Lord himself often used symbols to instruct his disciples, not only in the mysteries of the Kingdom, but even in practical Christian living. For example, the fowls of the air, the lilies of the field, the candle, the wind, salt, and the fishnet provided just a few of the object lessons or symbols which our Lord employed in His teaching.

The earliest Christians used symbolism quite freely, even on their household utensils, according to Clement of Alexandria. The ancient catacombs, however, preserve the oldest extant examples of Christian art. Throughout these underground burial chambers of ancient Rome, such primitive symbols as the fish, the ship, the anchor, the lamb, the Good Shepherd, the dove, and the lyre reflect a "blessed hope" which no power on earth could take away from those persecuted believers of the first three Christian centuries.

These Christians utilized pictorial teaching both to instruct believers and earnest inquirers and to baffle scoffers. Thus, a picture of the Good Shepherd with his musical lyre was a sermon to illiterate peasants, while the fish sign was a secret symbol unknown by persecuting pagans. Up to Constantine's time, Christians often disguised even the sign of the cross. Most symbols, however, were simple object lessons to point men to God's truth, and the earliest symbols reflect a wide range of Bible doctrine.

God the Father

The Jews' repugnance to any use of "images" accounts for the strong feeling among early Hebrew Christians against making "pictures" of God. This by no means, however, prevented pious Hebrew Christians from using various symbols, such as an eye, a hand, or an arm to illustrate Jehovah's omniscience and omnipotence. Even in the Old Testament, the rainbow symbolizes God's faithfulness, and the tabernacle with all of its furnishings constitutes practically a whole course in theology.

In a tomb dated about A.D. 359 a "hand of God" represents the earliest known Christian symbol of the Father's perfections. Suggestive of His creative power, possession, and protection, the hand soon became the most commonly used symbol of the Father. Often it appears emerging from the clouds; sometimes a man's figure appears sheltered in the hand, signifying God's protection of the faithful. This picture reminded persecuted believers of such passages as Psalm 139:10, "Thy right hand shall hold me"; Isaiah 49:2, "In the shadow of his hand hath he hid me"; and Isaiah 49:16, "Behold, I have graven thee upon the palms of my hands."

God the Son

The Fish: The Greek word for *fish,* transliterated ICHTHUS, forms an acrostic; I = Iesous (Jesus); CH = CHristos (Christ); TH = THeou (God's); U = Uios (Son); and S = Soter (Saviour). Among persecuted believers the sign of the fish constituted both a confessional statement of faith and a secret symbol which would attract no notice from the outside world. The sign appears on catacomb walls, signet rings, lamps, and other objects. Archaeologists have even discovered ornamental glass fishes hidden in the catacombs. Occasionally, the fish represents the believer caught by the hook of the gospel, but most often it signifies Christ. The symbol appears frequently in Christian literature of the ancient Church, including works by Tertullian of Carthage, Clement of Alexandria, Jerome, Ambrose, and Augustine of Hippo.

The Lamb: The lamb symbol emphasizes Christ's vicarious atonement (Isa. 53:7). John the Baptist cried, "Behold the Lamb of God, which taketh away the sin of the world" (John 1:29). Depicting his deity, a nimbus often encircles the lamb's head in the ancient Christian art of the catacombs.

The Good Shepherd: A favorite portrait of Christ in primitive Christian art was the Good Shepherd caring for his sheep and guiding them even through the valley of the shadow of death. The Shepherd is usually carrying a lamb in his arms, signifying his love and protection in the hour of persecution. In catacomb art this picture illustrated the earliest "funeral-text" of Christianity. For example, in John 10 Christ is the Good Shepherd of Isaiah 40:11; in Hebrews 13:20 He is the Great Shepherd of Psalm 23; and in I Peter 5:4 He is the Chief Shepherd of Ezekiel 34.

God the Holy Spirit

The Dove: In the catacombs, the most familiar symbol of the Holy Spirit is the white dove, often with a three-rayed nimbus— symbolic of a member of the Trinity. The dove illustrated purity and appears in Genesis 8:8-12 and Matthew 10:16.

The Menorah: The seven-branch lamp stand, or Menorah, is Jewish in origin. Early Christians often used it to symbolize the gifts of the Holy Spirit mentioned in Isaiah 11:2.

The Church

The Ship or Ark: One of the earliest and most often-used symbols for the Church is the ship or ark sailing in troubled waters (of persecution) and displaying a cross-shaped mast. Many believe that the word *nave,* which designates the central aisle of a church, comes from the Greek word for *ship,* transliterated *NAUS,* which comes from *NAO* (or *NEO*) which means "to swim or float." The symbolism recalls the story of Christ's calming the stormy Sea of Galilee and causing Peter to walk on the water. The ancient work called *The Constitutions of the Holy Apostles,* which was not written by the apostles but which does date back to the fourth century, contains a long passage which likens the Church to a ship. Here the pastor (or bishop) is the steersman, the deacons are the seamen, and the congregation represent the passengers (2. 7. 57-59). Other ancient writers, including Clement of Alexandria and Tertullian of Carthage, discuss this popular symbol.

The Vine and Branches: The Old Testament often depicts God's chosen people as a vine or vineyard (Isa. 5:1-7; Jer. 2:21). Romans 11:16-25 describes Israel as branches broken off from the olive tree and the Church as branches grafted into the tree. In John 15:1-6 our Lord is the true vine and his followers are the branches, symbolizing the vital doctrine of the believer's union with Christ. Such imagery provided a beautiful and especially meaningful object lesson for God's people during times of persecution.

Is Catacomb Symbolism Pagan in its Origin?

Although most of the symbols appeared in ancient pagan worship, there is no reason to conclude that dedicated, persecuted Christians simply imitated heathen symbolism. Actually, heathen religious worship was a perversion of God's original revelation of truth (Rom. 1:18-32). The passage says that "when they knew God, they glorified him not as God . . . but became vain in their imaginations . . . and changed the glory of the uncorruptible God into an image made like to corruptible man, and to birds, and fourfooted beasts, and creeping things. Wherefore God also gave them up. . . . who changed the truth of God into a lie." The fact that something good has been abused does not mean that Christians cannot use it properly. Even the brazen serpent was abused and corrupted by idolatrous worship (II Kings 18:4).

The early Church rightly attempted to *restore* truth which existed in corrupted form in pagan legend, folklore, and mythology. It is true that Romanism is only another form of paganism, but there was no "Roman Catholic church" during the first four Christian centuries. The catacomb art of this period is distinctively Christian; it represents a Scriptural effort to restore truth that had been corrupted from its rightful use.

The Christian Church in history has often utilized even "pagan symbolism" to refocus attention on God's absolute truth. For example, the phoenix of catacomb art speaks of Christ's resurrection (from the pagan legend that the bird always rose from its own ashes); the peacock of Augustine's day symbolized immortality (from the pagan belief that its flesh was incorruptible); and even the female pelican on the title page of the venerable King James Version of 1611 depicts Christ's vicarious atonement (from the heathen tradition that whenever a serpent bit her young, the pelican tore open her breast to revive them with her own blood). So paganism, as a perversion and corruption of God's original revelation, actually became in a sense a harbinger of the rediscovery of certain aspects of that truth.

Any use of symbolism today should be with moderation and with the specific purpose of teaching truth. Without that purpose, symbolism degenerates into modern fad and even back into paganism.

Suggestions for Further Reading

Walter Oetting. *The Church of the Catacombs.* St. Louis: Concordia, 1964. (Despite the title, the book discusses the early Church in general.)

J. Stevenson. *The Catacombs: Rediscovered Monuments of Early Christiantiy.* London: Thames and Hudson, 1978.

Augustine: The Restless Heart Satisfied

by Mark Sidwell

Augustine was the greatest of the Western Church Fathers and possibly the greatest of all the Fathers. His brilliant mind and numerous writings shaped the history of the Church for hundreds of years. As this article demonstrates, however, Augustine was not an "ivory-tower scholar." His faith was shaped by real-life struggles with which many saints today can identify.

Restlessness, conflict, and unfulfilled desire characterized the early life of Aurelius Augustine. Even the circumstances of his birth in A.D. 354 in Tagaste, North Africa, bred conflict. His father, a pagan named Patricius, desired wealth and prominence for his son. His mother, a Christian named Monica, longed for her son's salvation. Augustine's father encouraged his son to enjoy himself—usually in sin. His mother wept as she watched her son wander further from her faith. She talked to her pastor constantly about her son, often with tears. The pastor eventually told her, "Go, . . . it cannot be that the son of these tears will perish."

As a boy Augustine found his unregenerate heart leading him along his father's path. He recalled years later how one night he and some friends had sneaked into a neighbor's orchard and carried off a large haul of pears—which they immediately fed to the pigs. What bothered Augustine as he looked back on the event was not simply the theft; he grieved at the sheer pleasure and delight that he had taken in stealing and wanton vandalism. He knew firsthand the nature of the depraved heart of man.

Augustine's restlessness extended as he matured to include a burning desire for knowledge. He rejected Christianity, which he considered intellectually beneath him, and began to dabble in pagan philosophy. He decided to become a teacher of rhetoric and went to Carthage to study. "To Carthage I came," he wrote later, "where a cauldron of unholy loves bubbled up all around me." The unholy loves were not only sexual passion but also philosophical seductions. When he returned to Tagaste after finishing his studies, Augustine was both a philosopher and a moral reprobate.

Augustine left Tagaste for Carthage again, this time in order to practice his profession. True advancement, however, could come only in Rome, the capital of the Empire. So in 383, after assuring his mother that he would not leave her, he secretly sailed to Rome. The city, however, did not prove to be the ideal that he had hoped for. Augustine found it difficult to attract students, and those he attracted did not always pay for their rhetoric lessons. He also fell physically ill and was beginning to find less spiritual comfort in his philosophical speculations. Looking back on this situation years later, Augustine told God in his *Confessions,* "Inside me your good was working on me to make me restless until you should become clear and certain to my inward sight."

After an unhappy year in Rome, Augustine seized the chance to become a professor of rhetoric in Milan. There, God gathered several influences to bring him to Christ. First, Monica followed her son to the city, and her prayers and pleas began to move him. He also began to attend church. Ironically, he went at first only as a teacher of rhetoric in order to study the rich speaking style of Bishop Ambrose. "I was led to him unknowingly by God," Augustine wrote, "that I might knowingly be led to God by him."

The Holy Spirit began to grip Augustine's heart as the young man heard Ambrose and as he read the Scripture for himself. The pull of the flesh still tugged at him, though. At one point Augustine actually prayed, "Grant me chastity and continence—but not yet." He became sick with conviction and a sense of unworthiness. While seated in a friend's garden under a fig tree, Augustine began to pour out his heart to God. "But Thou, O Lord, how long? . . . How long, how long? Tomorrow, and tomorrow? Why not now? Why is there not this hour an end to my uncleanness?"

After praying and weeping even more, Augustine heard a child from a neighboring house chant in sing-song fashion, "Take up and read. Take up and read." It was only a child's rhyme, but Augustine took it as a command of God. He picked up the copy of the Scriptures lying beside him, opened it, and read, "Not in rioting and drunkenness, not in chambering and wantonness, not in strife and envying. But put ye on the Lord Jesus Christ, and make not provision for the flesh, to fulfil the lusts thereof" (Rom. 13:13-14). Augustine put the book down. "No further would I read, nor did I need; for instantly, as the sentence ended—by a light, as it were, of security infused into my heart—all the gloom of doubt vanished away."

At the age of thirty-one, Augustine found his life completely changed. He quit teaching and went into seclusion with several friends to study the Bible and pray. The year after his conversion, Augustine was baptized by Ambrose. Accompanied by his mother, with whom for the first time he was sharing Christian fellowship, Augustine prepared to return to Africa. At the port of Ostia, however, Monica fell deathly ill. Before she died, her son asked her whether she dreaded dying so far from home. Monica replied, "Nothing is far to God; nor need I fear lest He should be ignorant at the end of the world of the place whence He is to raise me up."

Back in North Africa, Augustine was ordained in the city of Hippo. His deep learning, fervent piety, and practical sermons won the admiration of the citizens of that city, and in 396 they made him bishop. Augustine had a pastor's love for his people as well as a pastor's concern. Once, when he learned that his people planned a wild festival to "honor" a saint, the bishop spoke out boldly against the affair. First, he preached a sermon on the text "Give not that which is holy unto the dogs" (Matt. 7:6). When that failed, he preached another fiery sermon, this time on the text "Nevertheless, if thou warn the wicked of his way to turn from it; if he do not turn from his way, he shall die in his iniquity; but thou hast delivered thy soul" (Ezek. 33:9). He added to this second sermon the warning that he would resign and leave if they proceeded with the festival. The people relented.

Augustine is remembered today for his writings and the numerous controversies in which he participated. His autobiography, *The Confessions,* has already been alluded to. Likewise his writings in defense of the doctrine of the Trinity are considered some of the finest to emerge from the Western Church. Two controversies and the writings that emerged from them represent, perhaps, his greatest contribution: the Pelagian controversy and the circumstances surrounding the writing of *The City of God.*

The Pelagian controversy began when a British monk, named Pelagius, and his followers began to teach that man was born as sinless as Adam was at his creation. Man, the Pelagians argued, has the complete ability to keep God's law and be saved. Although man can draw on the power of the Holy Spirit, he does not need Him. To Augustine, such doctrines were abominations. He believed that salvation is all of God's grace. Man, because of the depravity inherited from Adam as well as his own sins, is helpless and totally dependent on God to save him. "Give what Thou commandest," Augustine prayed, "and command what Thou wilt." In many ways, Augustine reflected the errors of his time. He put too much stress on the visible, institutional church, for example, and many see traces of the doctrine of purgatory in his writings. On the doctrines of sin and grace, however, Augustine stands as the greatest testimony to the Biblical teaching among the Church Fathers.

In 410, the barbarian leader Alaric and his Goths sacked Rome. The event shocked the ancient world. Jerome wrote, "My voice is choked, and sobs prevent my words as I dictate. The city is taken which took the whole world." Since the Roman Empire had become nominally Christian, pagans blamed the disaster on Christianity. The pagan gods, they said, were exacting revenge for Roman unfaithfulness.

Augustine refuted the pagan charge in the longest and greatest of his works, *The City of God.* He began by pointing out that even under paganism Rome had experienced attacks as bad as and even worse than that of Alaric. Augustine did not stop there, however; he went on to enunciate the first Christian philosophy of history. History, he said, does not consist of the building or preservation of earthly empires such as Rome's. History is God's building His "city," that is, His Church. Human kingdoms will rise and fall, but God's kingdom will stand and ultimately triumph. God sovereignly moves history to fulfill His purpose, and whatever happens in history, the Christian knows that his Father is in control.

The City of God took thirteen years to write. By the time he had finished, Augustine was nearing the end of his life, and barbarians known as Vandals were overrunning northern Africa. When Augustine lay dying in 430, the city of Hippo was surrounded by the Vandals. Ironically, the man who could find no peace in his early life now felt a sense of God's peace while the world around him seemed to be falling into chaos. Circumstances no longer ruled Augustine's life. As he had written years earlier, "Thou movest us to delight in praising Thee; for Thou hast formed us for Thyself, and our hearts are restless till they find rest in Thee." On August 28, 430, Augustine's restless heart found eternal rest with his God.

Suggestions for Further Reading

Augustine. *The Confessions.* (Several editions are available.)

Frederic Farrar. *Lives of the Fathers.* Vol. 2. London: Adam and Charles Black, 1907. (Pages 403-614; a highly readable account, but the liberal Farrar is overly critical of Augustine's theology.)

Christa Habegger. *Saints and Non-Saints.* Greenville, S.C.: Unusual Publications, 1987. (Pages 41-56.)

Michael Marshall. *The Restless Heart: The Life and Influence of St. Augustine.* Grand Rapids: Eerdmans, 1987.

John Chrysostom:
Prince of the Ancient Preachers

by Craig Jennings

*Whereas Augustine was the pre-eminent theologian of the
ancient Church, John Chrysostom was its pre-eminent pastor.
Despite his voluminous and often-quoted writings, Chrysostom
remains more a man concerned with the duties of the ministry.
His glorious oratory showed that he was the consummate
preacher, but Chrysostom added to that a warm compassion
for his flock and a fearless denunciation of sin—whether
committed by the lowly or the mighty. The life of John
Chrysostom is a stirring example of courageous adherence to
God's commands despite personal cost.*

John Chrysostom, the prince of ancient preachers and Bible
commentators, is the most frequently quoted, praised, and read
of all the writers in the ancient Church. His numerous sermons,
which actually constitute commentaries on a number of Bible
books, were taken down in shorthand by eager listeners and have
been preserved through the centuries. These sermons, which give
a clear insight into Chrysostom's theology and character, disclose
a man of personal integrity and courage, a man who stood as
a shining light in the midst of spiritual declension. Because of
his uncompromising stand, Chrysostom often endured both political and religious persecution. His unshakable faith in time of trial
is a valuable lesson for us today.

John was born about A.D. 345 in Antioch of Syria, the place
in which the disciples were first called Christians. His father, a
pagan army officer, died while John was an infant, and his devout
Christian mother, Anthusa, reared him. In spite of his mother's
teaching, John was not yet converted at the age of twenty. At
that time he became the pupil of the famed rhetorician and scholar,
Libanius. He soon began to practice law successfully, and his
brilliant achievements in that field opened the way for a political

career. However, the worldliness and corruption which permeated society and government disturbed him; so he left his career and earnestly began to study the Scriptures. He was soon converted and later baptized at the age of twenty-three.

Years of preparation for service now lay ahead. For four or five years John remained in Antioch living in quiet seclusion at his mother's house and continuing his study of the Scriptures. He grew rapidly as a Christian, and the bishop of Antioch, recognizing John's leadership potential, gave him the responsibility of publicly reading the Scripture during the worship services. When his mother died, John left the city and went into the mountains, where he studied alone for another six years. Finally, in poor health, he returned to Antioch where he became a deacon and then a minister. His stirring eloquence in preaching earned him the name *Chrysostom,* meaning "golden-mouthed."

For twelve years John preached to a wordly, self-satisfied group of church members who enjoyed his brilliant preaching but for the most part ignored his message. One day, in exasperation, John told his congregation:

> If therefore you would not have us wearisome or annoying, practice as we preach, exhibit in your actions the subject of our discourses. For we shall never cease discoursing upon these things till your conduct is agreeable to them. And this we do more especially from our concern and affection for you. For the trumpeter must sound his trumpet, though no one should go out to war; he must fulfill his part.

John preached every Sunday, and at certain times of the year he sometimes preached five times a week. Each sermon urged Christians to live godly lives, and when the occasion demanded, it contained an attack on public vice in the city. It was during these years in Antioch that John wrote and preached the majority of his sermons.

His ministry in Antioch came to an abrupt end in A.D. 398 when, against his own wishes, the emperor Arcadius compelled him to become the patriarch (chief bishop) in the capital city of Constantinople. Following his installation into office, John energetically began to correct various abuses in the church, and as he did so the favor of the emperor, nobility, and clergy waned rapidly.

The empress Eudoxia, furious over John's attack on sin and vice in the palace, determined to get rid of him. Her opportunity came when (at the request of the churches in Ephesus) John went to Ephesus to investigate the conduct of several bishops whom he subsequently deposed. While he was absent for several months, the empress, many of the licentious women in the palace, and even some of the clergy began to plot his overthrow. On his return Chrysostom preached on the story of Elijah and Jezebel with obvious application to the empress. In response, a wrathful Eudoxia quickly put her prearranged plan into motion by organizing a church council led by Theophilus, the unscrupulous and treacherous bishop of Alexandria. Thirty-six bishops soon gathered in the city of Constantinople and began their proceedings.

The council met secretly in a suburb of the capital and drew up twenty-nine charges against Chrysostom. The false accusations included everything from immorality to high treason, and John, when summoned to appear before the assembled bishops and answer the charges against him, refused to attend. The council then deposed him with the concurrence of the emperor, and Chrysostom was sent into exile.

In response the people of the city angrily marched on the palace and demanded that the emperor restore their beloved bishop. He refused. The next night, however, an earthquake shook Constantinople, and a frightened Eudoxia persuaded her husband to recall her hated rival. John returned triumphantly to his former position and continued his work just as before. He later wrote:

> When I was driven from the city, I felt no anxiety, but said to myself: If the empress wishes to banish me, let her do so; "the earth is the Lord's." If she wants to have me sawn asunder, I have Isaiah for an example. If she wants me to be drowned in the ocean, I think of Jonah. If I am to be thrown into the fire, the three men in the furnace suffered the same. If cast before wild beasts, I remember Daniel in the lion's den. If she wants me to be stoned, I have before me Stephen, the first martyr. If she demands my head, let her do so; John the Baptist shines before me. . . . Paul reminds me, "If I still please men, I would not be the servant of Christ."

For two months following John's return, empress and preacher seemed to be reconciled. However, the peace was soon shattered when Chrysostom launched yet another attack on the empress. Eudoxia, as vain and haughty as ever, had ordered a silver statue of herself to be erected upon a stone column in the square in front of Chrysostom's church. At the dedication of the statue to which the people were to pay honor, wild festivities disturbed services going on in the church. Chrysostom ascended his pulpit and with his usual mixture of brilliant oratory and sharp criticism alluded to the empress in these words: "Again Herodias is raging, again she is dancing, again she demands the head of John on a platter."

In spite of threats and opposition, John continued preaching and carrying out his duties for several more months until Easter eve when imperial guards broke into his church, violently disrupted a baptismal service, and put John under house arrest. Finally, on June 5, 404, with the legal maneuvering completed, John was officially deposed for the final time. Before he left the city, he gathered some of his faithful friends around him for prayer and then left by ship for Asia Minor.

Even in exile John continued his ministry through letter writing. Hundreds of letters which left the small village of Cucusus brought advice and encouragement to Christian friends throughout the empire. Eudoxia, angry that the hated Chrysostom should still be able to exercise his influence in favor of righteousness, ordered him to be moved farther from the capital into the Caucasus Mountains on the east coast of the Black Sea. The old bishop, already sick and feeble, never finished his journey but died on September 14, 407, at the age of sixty-two near the village of Comana (Tokat) in what is modern Turkey. His last words, "Glory be to God for all things, Amen," eloquently sum up a life of dedication and submission to the will of God.

Throughout his life John Chrysostom was a man who studied, preached, and defended the Word of God. He constantly exposed sin and would not alter his preaching to please either the wealthy or the powerful. Historians remember Chrysostom as a great orator (and he certainly was one of the best), but the flawless, polished delivery of a sermon was not his ultimate concern. "I take no account of style or delivery," he said; "yea let a man's diction be poor and his composition simple and unadorned, but let him not be unskilled in the knowledge and accurate statement of doctrine."

Suggestions for Further Reading

Frederic Farrar. *Lives of the Fathers.* Vol. 2. London: Adam and Charles Black, 1907. (Pages 615-706.)

Christa Habegger. *Saints and Non-Saints.* Greenville, S.C.: Unusual Publications, 1987. (Pages 27-39.)

The Medieval Church
(590 to 1517)

The Middle Ages are commonly called "the dark ages," and that designation seems no more appropriate to the Christian than when considering the state of medieval religion. The light of the gospel would seem to have been all but extinguished during that era. In reality, God always preserves at least a remnant of His people in all ages.

Some Christians find that remnant only in the various groups that separated from the Roman church in the Middle Ages. There is some truth to this claim. Many members of these small sects were probably true Christians. The Waldensians of northern Italy, for example, rejected many of the false teachings of Rome and traveled about southern Europe preaching and distributing the Bible. Many of these groups, however, held to some false teachings worse than those of Rome. Also, there were few of these groups, and in some periods in medieval history no record exists of *any* groups separate from the Roman church.

Most of the true Christians in the Middle Ages were probably members of what we now call the Roman Catholic church. Such an assertion understandably troubles some believers. We should keep in mind that much of the false doctrine of Roman Catholicism grew over a period of centuries. Some superstitions did not become official dogma until late in the Middle Ages or even long afterwards. (For example, the bodily assumption of the virgin Mary into heaven was not declared a Catholic dogma until 1950.) Also, the medieval church tolerated many viewpoints; so men could hold to true doctrine without conflict with Rome.

In all ages, salvation has come by the Word of God (Rom. 10:17). Some churchmen added error to Scripture over the centuries, but the gospel still reached people's hearts. Even though few people had copies of the Scripture in the Middle Ages, they still might have heard the Word of God. Some men learned Latin and read the Bible in the official Latin translation, the Vulgate. Others received the Word of God from traveling monks or priests who understood Latin. By the grace of God some people in the Roman church came to a true understanding of salvation. The modern Christian must learn to appreciate the testimony of such men and admire the manner in which they rose above their times. At the same time, the Christian must always reject the errors that such men held.

Dissent from error and adherence to truth were always present in the medieval period, both outside and inside the institutional church. As the Middle Ages drew to a close, the leaders of the Roman church became more corrupt and the church's doctrine became more false. As the corruption increased, dissent grew louder and more vigorous. Some men spoke out boldly against the abuses of the medieval church. In the fourteenth century, John Wycliffe of England denounced the corruption of the pope and proclaimed that the Bible should be the true standard of faith and practice. Shortly thereafter, John Huss of Bohemia also condemned the increasing decadence within the Roman church. The work of men such as Wycliffe and Huss foreshadowed the great moving of the Spirit of God in the 1500s which we know as the Reformation.

We do not excuse the ignorance of those people who were saved but stayed in the Roman church. However, we rejoice that God has preserved a remnant in all ages, including the Middle Ages. These medieval Christians used the knowledge that they had to serve and glorify God to the best of their ability.

Patrick of Ireland

by Christa G. Habegger

Foolish medieval legends encrust and obscure some of the noblest figures of the Christian Church. With no one is this more apparent than with St. Patrick of Ireland. Some people recall only the legends about Patrick, such as his supposed cleansing of the Emerald Isle of snakes. In Irish folklore Patrick emerges as a cross between Santa Claus and a leprechaun. This almost trivial reputation obscures the real story of one of the most self-sacrificing, most determined missionaries that the Church has ever known. In contrast to the usual order of things, the real story of Patrick is far more interesting than the legend.

I am greatly a debtor to God, who has bestowed his grace so largely upon me, that multitudes were born again to God through me. The Irish, who had never had the knowledge of God and worshipped only idols and unclean things, have lately become the people of the Lord, and are called sons of God.

This simple testimony by Patrick, the "Apostle of Ireland," differs greatly from the popular conception of "Saint Patrick," whose memory is celebrated by "the wearing of the green" on March 17 every year. Legend and folklore would have us believe that Patrick was a venerable Roman Catholic saint, that he was responsible for driving the snakes out of Ireland, and that he was a white-bearded, miracle-working, spell-casting magician. In short, the myths surrounding Patrick are as rich and varied as lively Irish imaginations can paint them.

The real Patrick was certainly a saint, in the sense that all believers in Jesus Christ are saints. He was not in any way connected with the papacy in Rome. He probably would not take credit for ridding Ireland of any snakes, unless one were referring to "the Devil, whom the Bible denounces as the old serpent" (Raymond Cox, "Was St. Patrick a Protestant?" *Christian Life,* March 1969,

p. 25). And the only miracles with which Patrick may be positively associated are the miracles of new birth and changed lives which were evident in the lives of literally thousands of his converts in fifth-century Ireland.

Patrick is best introduced to us through his own writings, two of which exist as our only legitimate record of his life and ministry. At the time of his death, his exploits were already becoming fictionalized. During the Middle Ages, Catholic "biographies" based on the St. Patrick legends abounded, and these are wholly unreliable. Their authors operated on the assumption that any religious occurrence in recent history was rooted in Roman Catholicism. According to DeVinné in *History of the Irish Primitive Church,* "Many, not well read in church history, imagine that the present Roman Catholic Church dates much farther back than it really does. The claim of that church to universal jurisdiction was not made till the seventh century, or one hundred and fifty years after the commencement of the Irish Church" (p. 61). He goes on to say, "The Irish Church, for a period of at least five hundred years after its commencement, was independent of the Bishops of Rome, and free from the peculiarities of Romanism." Those interested today in learning more of the first missionary to Ireland study Patrick's own writings, his *Confession* and his *Letter to Coroticus.*

The *Confession,* written near the end of his life, "is properly a written acknowledgment of the special providences of God, which he had experienced in connection with the establishment of Christianity in Ireland" (Daniel DeVinné *History of the Irish Primitive Church,* p. 205). It is not intended to be an autobiography, although it provided many autobiographical details. A "confessor" in Patrick's day was one who had risked his life by openly following the Lord Jesus. The *Letter to Coroticus* provides insight into Patrick's character and missionary zeal.

Patrick begins his *Confession* with "I, Patrick, a sinner, the rudest and the least of all the faithfull, and the most inconsiderable among many," and goes on to a brief description of his parentage. His father was Calpornius, a deacon, and his grandfather, Potitus, a presbyter. Patrick reveals the church offices without acknowledging any consciousness whatsoever of the Romanist doctrine of clerical celibacy, a point which Roman Catholic biographers are careful to ignore. The author gives as his place of birth Banavem of Tabernia, which cannot be positively identified geographically today, but which was undeniably somewhere in Roman Britain. His father, in addition to holding the office of deacon, was a decurion, or a magistrate of nobility.

Patrick's birth date is another matter of conjecture. Authorities agree that he was born around 389. During this era, Britons considered themselves solidly under Roman rule, but in actuality, Rome was steadily decreasing her control over the territory. Wars against invaders on the continent claimed all of the Roman military forces which had previously maintained order and provided protection for British-Roman citizens. Thus Britain, and in particular the coastal sections of the island, was left defenseless against bands of Irish raiders who swept in from the sea to pillage farms, slaughter townspeople, and carry away slaves.

Banavem was the unfortunate scene of one such raid. Patrick tells us that he was sixteen when he and a great many others were taken captive to Ireland. This calamity he refers to in the *Confession* as "our deservings; for we had gone away from God and had not kept his commandments, and were not obedient to our pastors, who admonished us of our salvation."

As a slave, Patrick was put to work tending sheep for his Irish master. Through these circumstances, Patrick testifies, "the Lord opened to me a sense of my unbelief, that I might . . . be converted with all my heart unto the Lord my God, who had looked upon my humility, and had compassion on my youth and ignorance." Following his conversion, Patrick became a man of prayer. "More and more," he says "the love and fear of God burned, and my faith increased and my spirit was enlarged, so that I said a hundred prayers in a day, and nearly as many at night . . . for then I felt that the spirit was fervent within me."

After six years in captivity Patrick obtained his freedom and was finally able to return to his country and his parents' home. "My parents," he says, "entreated me, that after so many years of tribulation through which I had passed, that I never again would go away from them."

However, God called Patrick to return voluntarily to the people who had held him captive a short time before. He saw in a "vision of the night . . . a man coming, as if out of Ireland, with a very great number of letters, and gave one of them to me. . . . When I had read the principal of the letter, I thought that at that very moment I heard the voice who lived near the woods of Flocut, which is near the Western Sea. And thus they cried out, as with one voice: 'We entreat you, holy youth, that you come here and walk among us.'"

Patrick commenced his work in Ireland when he was about forty-three. Ireland, in the middle of the fifth century, was almost wholly unevangelized. There is some evidence of a few scattered Christian communities prior to the time of Patrick's arrival, but no lasting work had been established. The Romans, with their state religion, had never invaded Irish territory. The Irish were organized by tribes, each having its own chieftain or king, and pagan Druidism was uncontested as the religious practice of the day.

No one can state confidently how many years passed before Patrick answered the call to missionary service in Ireland, whether he went under auspices of any local assembly or how he passed the interval of several years between his return from captivity and going back to Ireland. We may assume that during that interval he prepared himself for his future ministry by extensive study of the Word of God and by some sort of church association, for his *Confession* reveals him to have been a deacon and later a bishop.

Roman Catholic authors speculate that Patrick spent these years studying in a monastery in Gaul and that he was ordained for his mission to Ireland by Pope Celestine. But there is no reference at all in Patrick's writings of his having been a monk or of his having received a commission from the papal authority. Moreover, it is clear that Patrick received no formal ecclesiastical training. He laments his "rusticity" repeatedly, grieves that he had not availed himself of a better education in his youth, and demonstrates in his writings that his knowledge of Latin was only rudimentary. Scholars point out that the simplicity and straightforward style of Patrick's writings distinguish them from the works of any other early Church personality, most of whom had had formal training in rhetoric and ecclesiastical Latin. Patrick's *Confession* and *Letter* reveal that the source of his learning was the Word of God. His narrative is so interwoven with quotations from Scripture that one cannot escape the conclusion that he had absorbed great portions of the Bible.

Although Patrick does not enlighten the modern reader with regard to his official church connections, he repeatedly expresses his confidence that his commission to evangelize Ireland came from God Himself. "God directing me," he says in section XV of the *Confession,* "I agreed or consented with no one in coming to Ireland." In fact, his going to Ireland was opposed, not only by his family, but by churchmen who apparently doubted that his training was adequate for the job and by one unnamed man who brought up some sin committed by Patrick as an uncoverted youth as an obstacle to his ministry. Patrick testifies that he remained unmoved in his determination to follow God's call to Ireland. "Therefore," he concludes after narrating the account of the opposition he faced, "I give thanks unto him, who has comforted me on all occasions, so that nothing has hindered me from the accomplishment of that which I had laid down to do, and also of my work, which I had learned of Christ. But rather on account of it, I have felt myself strengthened not a little, and my faith has been proved before God and man."

Details of Patrick's long ministry among the Irish are missing from his *Confession,* but he does provide for us the general outline of his work. We know, first of all, that he was motivated by a sincere love for the souls of men. More than once he refers to "a care and a great anxiety for the salvation of others" and to himself as a fisher of men. "It very much becomes us," he states, "to stretch our nets, that we may take for God a copious and crowded multitude; that wherever the clergy are they may baptize and exhort the needy and willing people."

Patrick does not present himself as a flawless, selfless missionary. He alludes to some of the same problems that any Christian servant in an isolated field faces. He speaks of yearning to see his brethren at home but tells of his refusal to succumb to homesickness in order that he should not "lose the labor which he had begun." He says he had long ago decided that "if I went [to Ireland], I should be with them the residue of my life."

He refers also to his constant battle against the weaknesses of his flesh: "I do not confide in myself as long as I am in this body. . . . The flesh is inimical and always draws to death." But he can add triumphantly at the end of his life, "I am not ashamed in his sight, because I lie not; from the time I knew him, from my youth, the love of God, and his fear, have increased in me, until now, by the help of God I have kept the faith."

Patrick's *Confession* refers to his personal chastity and also to vows that several of his converts took to remain unmarried. This vow is a peculiarity of his ministry and apparently not of his alone. The "monks and virgins of Christ" to which Patrick refers in the *Confession* "were neither monks nor nuns, in our present meaning of the word. . . . There were Ascetics in almost every country, one class of whom abstained from all pleasant food, and the other from marriage; but still they lived in society as other Christians. Ascetism [*sic*] sprang from the Essenes or the Gnostics in the first century. Many of the best Christian fathers partially imbibed some of their notions, and it has always, more or less, troubled the Christian churches; but it was not then peculiar to the Roman, or to any particular church" (DeVinné, p. 222).

Although Patrick saw much fruit for his labors among the Irish— he refers to the "thousands" whom he baptized—his ministry was not without opposition. Once, he records, "minor kings . . . even desired to kill me, but the time had not come; everything which they found with us they seized at once, and bound myself with fetter [sic]; but on the fourteenth day the Lord delivered me out of their power, and whatsoever was ours, was returned to us."

The *Letter to Coroticus* speaks of intense persecution of both Patrick and many other believers. The *Letter* is addressed to Coroticus, a British chieftain, whose soldiers had attacked a large assembly of newly-baptized believers, killing some and abducting others to sell into slavery. Patrick is strong in his denunciation of the outrage committed against God's people. He holds the chieftain responsible for the crimes his men perpetrated by telling him, "Not only they that do evil are worthy to be condemned, but they also that consent to them."

Although Patrick preaches a powerful sermon of judgment to Coroticus and his men, the tone of his letter is one of compassion and concern for his flock. When he introduces himself to Coroticus, he says that he writes, not because he wished "to utter anything so hard and harsh; but I am forced by the zeal for God; and the truth of Christ has wrung it from me, out of love for my neighbors and sons for whom I gave up my country."

History dates Patrick's death on March 17 sometime between 461 and 493. He is said to be buried at Downpatrick in Northern Ireland. His influence has certainly been felt throughout the centuries following his death, although that influence has not always been consistent with historical fact. Patrick, always humble and eager to acknowledge the power of God working through him, concluded his *Confession* with these words: "The gift of God is to be most assuredly credited for what has been done."

Suggestions for Further Reading

The Works of St. Patrick. Westminster, Md.: Newman Press, 1953.
Christa Habegger. *Saints and Non-Saints*. Greenville, S.C.: Unusual Publications, 1987. (Pages 57-66.)

Bernard of Clairvaux

by Mark Sidwell

As mentioned in the introduction to this section (pp. 73-74), believers are often troubled by the mixture of good and bad qualities in the leading Christians of the Middle Ages. Some avoid the problem by focusing on more consistently evangelical believers, such as Patrick or John Wycliffe. A full appreciation of the period, however, demands the study of those "ambiguous" figures who combined evangelical fervor with medieval superstition. No better example can be found than Bernard of Clairvaux, who characterized many of the errors of his age but rose above his contemporaries in his humility and his love for Christ.

Bernard of Clairvaux was born in 1090 in Fontaines, France, into a noble family. His mother, a pious woman, powerfully affected his religious development, although she died when he was only fourteen years old. Concern for the salvation of his soul and an eagerness to please God led Bernard to join a monastery, the Cistercian house at Citeaux, at the age of twenty-one.

Bernard's choice of a monastic life may puzzle the modern believer. Monasticism is based on a misunderstanding of several Bible passages (e.g., Matt. 19:21; 22:30; Luke 20:35; Rev. 14:4) and the equally mistaken notion that bodily discipline results in spiritual holiness. Christian monasticism had arisen first in Egypt in the fourth century and by Bernard's time monastic orders and their individual houses stretched across Europe. Normally, the more earnest a man was in seeking salvation, the more likely he was to become a monk. Ironically, as a result of this tendency, the people most concerned with righteousness and holy living were set apart and shut away from the rest of mankind. Also, the rituals and practices imposed on the monks burdened them instead of freeing them from their burden of sin. Monasticism often clouded the way of salvation altogether.

Bernard's medieval understanding of the nature of salvation, what we might call his *mis*understanding, is revealed by his motive in joining the small but rigorous Cistercian order. "I was conscious," he said, "that my weak character needed strong medicine." He became a zealous monk—so zealous, in fact, that his bishop began to fear for Bernard's health because of the young monk's sparse diet and lack of rest. Indeed, Bernard fell so ill from his monastic activities that the leaders of the Cistercians ordered him to live under the bishop's care for a year in order to restore his health. In later years, Bernard regretted the excessive zeal of his youth, and he often counseled younger monks below him to temper their zeal in physical discipline.

Bernard also showed zeal as a recruiter. He managed to persuade his brothers and his cousins to join him in a monastic life. Bernard's sister refused to enter a convent, however, and he held it against her. When she came to visit him on one occasion, Bernard refused to see her. Stung by his action, his sister sent a message to him: "If my brother despises my body, let not the servant of God despise my soul." Bernard then came to her, but only to admonish her again to renounce the secular life. Eventually, Bernard's sister and her husband agreed to separate and join different houses. Such was the medieval idea of piety.

In addition to zeal, however, Bernard also displayed gentleness, compassion, and concern for others. Contemporary accounts describe Bernard as having eyes like those of a dove, apparently a reference to his gentle appearance. Recognizing Bernard's abilities, the leaders of the Cistercians asked him to leave Citeaux and found a new Cistercian house with himself as leader. Bernard and a select few chose a spot in northeastern France with the unappealing name "Wormwood." Bernard changed its name to *Clairvaux* ("clear view"), and he became known as "Bernard of Clairvaux."

The monastery was a humble one. It resembled more than anything else an oversize log cabin. The building was made of hewn logs and had a simple dirt floor. The monks slept in the attic on beds of straw and dry leaves with logs serving as pillows. The day began at 2:00 A.M. and consisted of a succession of services; periods of silent prayer, study, and meditation; plain meals; and several hours of work in the fields. Bedtime came anywhere from 6:00 to 8:00 P.M., depending on the season.

Bernard's role as head of Clairvaux was perhaps most comparable to that of a pastor. He was responsible for running the monastery, overseeing all the work, preaching constantly, and counseling the other monks. He also spent time writing to other monasteries about both major and petty problems as well as writing to various high church officials. Bernard's personal wisdom and sense of fairness made him a popular choice to settle disputes, and his fame grew enormously.

That a man could rise to prominence in Europe almost solely on the basis of his reputation for piety says something about the character of the age. That it was Bernard who rose to prominence says something about the character of the man. Many political and religious factions vied for his blessing, hoping to win support for their cause by virtue of association with his popularity and sterling character. For example, when two popes were elected in 1130 (both illegally), Bernard's siding with Innocent II (whom Bernard considered the more virtuous) lent great weight to Innocent's cause and probably enabled to him to win the dispute.

Bernard usually showed great discernment in choosing the causes he supported, and he tried to maintain a balance even after he committed to one side. One possible exception was the Second Crusade. When the Christian city of Edessa in Palestine fell to the Muslims in 1144, the pope called for a crusade to save the Holy Land from the "infidel Turks." Bernard became enraptured with the glory and scope of this holy cause, and he lent his eloquent voice to help raise funds and levies of men. So great was the eagerness and enthusiasm that he spread that the crusade would have been hard-pressed to live up to expectations. As it was, the Second Crusade was a dismal failure. The Europeans quarreled so much among themselves that they never had a chance to defeat the Muslims. Afterwards Bernard wrote, "The judgments of the Lord are just, but this one is an abyss so deep that I dare to pronounce him blessed who is not scandalized by it."

Bernard is better remembered today for his writing than for his monasticism or crusading. It is not his formal writing that is well-known, although he compiled a notable commentary (or rather a series of sermons) on the Song of Solomon. Instead, Bernard's hymns are most familiar to modern Christians. Three famous hymns are traditionally associated with Bernard. (Definite authorship has never been proved or disproved.) Two are hymns of joy, peace, and love that center on the person of Jesus Christ: "Jesus, Thou Joy of Loving Hearts" and his even more famous "Jesus, the Very Thought of Thee."

> Jesus, the very thought of Thee
> With sweetness fills my breast;
> But sweeter far Thy face to see,
> And in Thy presence rest.

Bernard's greatest hymn derives from a seven-part poem he wrote about the body of Christ on the cross. The last part, on the head of Christ, has become one of the most famous Easter hymns, "O Sacred Head, Now Wounded."

> O sacred Head, now wounded,
> With grief and shame weighed down;
> Now scornfully surrounded
> With thorns, Thine only crown;
> O sacred Head, what glory,
> What bliss till now was thine!
> Yet, though despised and gory,
> I joy to call Thee mine.

Doctrinally, Bernard did not differ significantly from most theologians of his age, although he did deny the immaculate conception of Mary and pled for a more generous treatment of the Jews. Bernard also did not hold a high view of papal infallibility; at least, he did not hesitate to scold the pope on occasion. For example, he wrote to one pope who had overruled some reforms by a group of bishops,

> What they ordain aright you annul, what they justly abolish, that you re-establish. All the worthless contentious fellows, whether from the people or the clergy, run off to you, and return boasting that they have found protection when they ought to have found retribution.

To another pope, who had demoted a worthy bishop, he wrote,

> God forgive you, what have you done? You have put a modest man to shame; you have humiliated before the whole Church a man whom the whole Church praises.

In general, Bernard's appeal to modern Christians lies in his stress on humility and love. These were the pre-eminent Christian virtues to Bernard, and he believed that their cultivation brings the believer closer to God. Most observers agree that both qualities were clearly present in Bernard's life. Unlike most great men of history, Bernard was genuinely humble. For example, he wrote to one admirer, "That other people should believe me to be better than I know myself to be, is an indication more of human stupidity than of any virtues in myself." As for Bernard's love, Martin Luther—no admirer of monks or medieval theologians—wrote, "Bernard loved Jesus as much as any one can."

Bernard apparently placed a greater value on trust in Christ than most medieval churchmen. Bernard particularly stressed Christ's mercy in the face of human weakness. He said in one sermon,

Christ is called not only righteous, but righteousness itself, our justifying righteousness. Thou art mighty in justifying as Thou art rich in pardoning. Let the soul, penitent for its sins, hungering and thirsting after righteousness, believe on Him who justifies the ungodly through faith, and it shall have peace with God.

Perhaps Martin Luther explained the reason for such lasting and widespread admiration of Bernard when he said, "Bernard is superior to all the doctors in his sermons, even to Augustine himself, because he preaches Christ most excellently." Bernard himself probably would have blushed at the compliment.

Suggestions for Further Reading

Christa Habegger. *Saints and Non-Saints.* Greenville, S.C.: Unusual Publications, 1987. (Pages 67-81.)

Philip Schaff. *History of the Christian Church.* Vol. 5. 1910; reprint Grand Rapids: Eerdmans, 1981. (Pages 342-57.)

Wycliffe and Huss:
Forerunners of the Reformation

by Craig Jennings

No movement of history ever emerges full-grown like Athena from the head of Zeus. Every current of history has its source, and the Reformation is no exception to this rule. The origins of the Reformation lie in the Middle Ages and the era's social, political, cultural, and especially religious milieu. Just as John the Baptist served as a forerunner to the Lord Jesus Christ, so courageous saints of the late Middle Ages paved the way for Luther, Calvin, Knox, and the others who led the Reformation in Europe. The two most important of these leaders were Englishman John Wycliffe and Bohemian John Huss.

Two ignoble events of the early 1400s marked the repudiation of two noble men. In 1415, at the insistence of the Council of Constance, John Huss of Bohemia was burned at the stake. In 1429, as a result of a decree by the same council, the body of John Wycliffe of England was dug up and burned; his ashes were then scattered on a nearby river. What should have been a shameful end for both men, however, eventually became a badge of honor. Rejection by a corrupt church only served to vindicate two men who loved truth more than they loved life.

John Wycliffe

The fourteenth century was an age of turmoil and change in England. John Wycliffe, a man of controversy and herald of reform, lived during this tumultuous period and did much to prepare the way for the great Reformation of the sixteenth century. This "morning star of the Reformation," as he has been called, criticized both in speech and writing the spiritual corruption of his age and urged Christians to follow Scripture rather than the church. "Wycliffe's contribution," as one of his biographers has said, "was to pinpoint the issues on which the later Reformers could spend their theological insight and reforming zeal."

John Wycliffe was born in Yorkshire sometime between 1320 and 1330. About 1345 he entered Oxford and by 1361 was master at Balliol College. Wycliffe's education was not complete, however, for he soon began studying for a degree in theology which he earned in 1369. By 1372, when he received his doctor of divinity degree, Wycliffe had already begun to doubt certain Roman Catholic teachings. Throughout the rest of his life, which he spent at Oxford and in his parish at Lutterworth, Wycliffe was regularly denounced by the church hierarchy. He not only saw his teaching condemned but also faced trial on several occasions. Wycliffe never wavered in his faith, in spite of fierce opposition from his enemies. He died a natural death December 31, 1384.

The hatred and opposition which Wycliffe frequently faced resulted from his direct attacks upon Roman error. The special object of Wycliffe's attacks was the Roman clergy, and primarily the pope. Wycliffe ridiculed the papal title "most holy father" and characterized the pope as "Christ's enemy . . . poison under color of holiness," "anti-Christian and a devil," and "falsehood itself."

Since the Bible is inerrant and inspired, he argued that it must be the final authority, for "to ignore the Scriptures is to ignore Christ." In fact, Wycliffe even had the audacity (in the eyes of his contemporaries) to make the radical assertion that "God's law" must be higher than church pronouncements. He was convinced that "faith depends on the Scriptures" and that "every Christian ought to study this book because it is the whole truth." Consequently, Wycliffe undertook the task of translating the Scriptures. He knew no Hebrew and Greek, but with the Latin Vulgate and the help of friends he produced the first complete translation of the Bible into English. In order to more effectively spread the Word of God, Wycliffe also sent out itinerant evangelists whom he called "poor priests."

In essence, Wycliffe struck at the root of medieval Romanism by advocating a return to Scripture. He clearly perceived that theological error and heresy inevitably result when speculation and human authority replace Scriptural teaching. The Bible to him was not an object of idle curiosity but the very power and Word of God. He taught that no man can be an effective pastor unless he first understand and then apply the Bible to his personal life. A minister, said Wycliffe, "should live holily, in prayer, in desires and thought, in godly conversation and honest teaching, having

God's commandments and his Gospel ever on his lips . . . and so open his acts that he may be a true book to all sinful and wicked men to serve God. For the example of a good life stirreth men more than true preaching with only the naked word."

Wycliffe's powerful life and testimony remained such a rebuke to a wordly church that in 1413, twenty-nine years after his death, the Roman church ordered his books burned. Two years later at the Council of Constance (which burned Huss) the bishops ordered Wycliffe's bones to be dug up and burned and passed a resolution in which "the holy synod declares said John Wycliffe to have been a notorious heretic, and excommunicates him and condemns his memory as one who died an obstinate heretic." Finally in 1429 at the command of Pope Martin V, the English church carried out the orders of the council. Wycliffe's bones were exhumed from the Lutterworth church yard, burned, and the remaining ashes were cast into the Swift River which flowed nearby.

John Huss

Bohemian priest John Huss was born about 1369 in a small village seventy-five miles outside of Prague. John lived at home until his late teens when he went off to the University of Prague. Since his parents were poor and could not provide a university education for their son, John worked his way through the university by singing and working in the church. Through his diligent efforts he earned three degrees: a bachelor of arts in 1393, a bachelor of theology in 1394, and a master of arts in 1396. In 1400 Huss was ordained a priest, and soon afterwards he was given an important faculty position at the university and was appointed preacher at the Bethlehem Church in Prague. Through the writings of John Wycliffe, and his personal study of the Scriptures, John Huss began to denounce the corruption and error he saw about him. Large crowds gathered whenever he preached, and they listened intently as he courageously censured the worldliness and immorality of the clergy.

In both his writings and his preaching, Huss taught that the church is not a visible organization composed of bishops and cardinals but that the true church is made up of all those redeemed by Christ. No pope is infallible, he declared, and the final standard of doctrine must be found in the Scriptures. Such preaching created so much tumult in the city that the government forced him to withdraw into exile in 1412. Huss's enemies were not satisfied, however, and sought to silence this fearless preacher permanently. Their opportunity came in the year 1414.

In that year the Roman church ordered Huss to appear before a church council in the city of Constance, Germany, to explain his teachings. The emperor Sigismund promised Huss his protection both to and from the city. When Huss arrived he rented a few rooms from a widow who ran a bakery. He expected to present his views before the council. However, a few weeks following his arrival, he was imprisoned on the false charge that he had tried to escape from the city.

Finally, seven months later, the council summoned John Huss and had him brought to the cathedral where they were meeting. After a long delay, he was made to enter, charged with heresy, and asked to recant. Huss tried to defend himself by appealing to the authority of Scripture, but every explanation was shouted down by the bigoted prelates. The council declared him to be an obstinate heretic and ordered his immediate execution. There were no dissenting votes. They removed his priestly robes and upon his head they placed a tall paper hat covered with painted devils and the word *heresiarch* ("leader of heresy"). As the council committed his soul to the Devil, he quickly replied, "And I commit it to my most gracious Lord Jesus Christ. The crown my Savior wore on His most sacred head was heavy and irksome. The one I wear is easy and light. He wore a crown of thorns even to the most awful death, and I will wear this much lighter one humbly for the sake of His name and the truth."

As the council continued its business, a military contingent led Huss out of the city to the place of execution. When he arrived at the stake, he knelt down with tears in his eyes and prayed. His hands were quickly tied behind him, and a rusty chain put about his neck held him to the stake. The executioners heaped wood and straw up to his chin and poured pitch over the entire pile. At this last moment, the church offered Huss one final chance to recant and live, but Huss replied, "I shall die with joy today in the faith of the Gospel which I have preached." Huss died that day singing the hymn "Christ, thou Son of the living God, have mercy on me."

The council declared that the execution was most pleasing to God, and many expressed the hope that with the death of Huss his followers would all eventually return to the church. Although several hundred years of war and persecution did severely diminish the number of Hussites and although the original movement faded away, the Roman church could not burn that which really mattered—Huss's example. His courage and fidelity to the Scripture remain a shining light in a dark age.

Heritage

Despite their inglorious fates, Wycliffe and Huss were by no means failures. The heritage of their work endures. English historian Thomas Fuller, realizing this truth, wrote of Wycliffe,

> They burnt his bones to ashes and cast them into Swift, a neighboring brook running hard by. Thus this brook hath conveyed his ashes into Avon, Avon into Severn, Severn into the narrow seas, they into the main ocean. And thus the ashes of Wycliffe are the emblem of his doctrine, which now is dispersed the world over.

Suggestions for Further Reading

Victor Budgen. *On Fire for God.* Welwyn, England: Evangelical Press, 1983. (Despite the unintentionally humorous title, this is a fine work.)

G.H.W. Parker. *The Morning Star: Wycliffe and the Dawn of the Reformation.* Grand Rapids: Eerdmans, 1965. (Actually covers entire era of Wycliffe and Huss.)

Douglas Wood. *Evangelical Doctor.* Welwyn, England: Evangelical Press, 1984. (On Wycliffe.)

Savonarola:
Preacher of Righteousness

by Edward M. Panosian

Girolamo Savonarola differed from other "pre-reformers" such as Wycliffe and Huss in that he offered no great doctrinal protest against the Roman church. In fact, some Catholic historians consider the Italian monk a precursor of the "Counter Reformation," the Catholic reaction to the Protestant Reformation in the sixteenth century. Savonarola's opposition to the pope, however, his strict demands for moral purity, and his insistence on personal liberty under the kingship of Christ make him inimical to Roman Catholicism. Even if he did not fully understand the implications of his position, Savonarola prepared the way for the great moral reform that accompanied the doctrinal reform of the Reformation. "What do I preach, then with all my strength and the power of my voice," Savonarola asked, "but repentance of sin and the mending of our ways, for the sake of our Lord Jesus Christ?"

The story of the Reformation begins not with the reformers themselves but with their forerunners—men who prepared the way for the great changes to come. Prominent in the record of these pre-reformers is the story of Girolamo Savonarola, the Dominican friar who endeavored to make Jesus Christ the King of Florence.

While never formally a Protestant (he lived a generation before the term was used), Savonarola was vigorous in his protest against corrupt churchmen. He was known as a powerful preacher of righteousness; for when he called for regeneration, the people responded with religious enthusiasm.

His story is really the story of how the Roman church treats one of her own who will not submit to the authority of a corrupt, renegade, lecherous pope. Savonarola insisted ultimately on the authority of Scripture. He called for a church council, as in ancient times, to settle matters of ecclesiastical dispute, and he rejected papal authority when the pope commanded anything contrary to Scripture. He is acknowledged by Romanist historians to have rejected no dogma of the Roman church; yet he was charged as a heretic and hanged, his body burned May 23, 1498, though heretic he was not.

The story of this "reformer before Reformation" is also an illustration of how fickle is popular favor. When he was at his height of popularity in Florence, crowds of ten and twelve thousand thronged the cathedral to hear him; they hung on his words; they were driven to fever pitch by his warnings and appeals. None so dominated the city's masses as did Savonarola.

Almost overnight the tide turned. Those who had hailed him yesterday railed at him today. Denied the spectacle of vindication they had been led to expect, they grew wrathful and became a menacing mob. Crowds gathered for his execution; many flung insults who, in recent days, had heaped praise. The parallel with the "Hosanna" of Palm Sunday's triumphal entry and the "Let him be crucified" in a few short days is difficult to ignore.

Savonarola's eventual involvement in political affairs and his identification with one of the volatile parties of Florence can serve as another caution. It was more than participation; it became direction and leadership, to the extent that primary calling became indistinguishable from secondary responsibilities and interest. His efforts to establish a practical theocracy—a state ruled by God under the precepts of the Decalogue—could not succeed without a regenerated citizenry. The people wanted the benefits and blessings of an orderly society, civic and social virtue, and prosperity, without the cost of personal discipleship. One may at least wonder whether more permanent good may have been achieved for Italy in his day if he had spent less energy seeking a righteous city on earth and more energy seeking to make men righteous citizens of heaven.

Yet we err if we judge the fifteenth-century servant of God, who sealed his conviction with his blood, from the more illuminated (but not always more consecrated) position of the twentieth century. While it may be often true that "hindsight makes wise men of us all," we should respect the achievement and the memory of this aggressive spokesman for God. While we may regret that he did not go further to effect the break with Rome that seems to us so clearly to have been required, we should rather be grateful that he went as far as he did toward paving the way for that break. He helped expose the rottenness of the papacy. When the wickedness of the papal throne condemned the righteous monk, when error called truth error, it was not to be long before thoughtful men would demand a reversal of that reversal.

With such observations in mind, let us now see some of the highlights of this unusual life. Girolamo (Jerome) Savonarola, the third in a family of seven children, was born in Ferrara in northern Italy, September 21, 1452, about the time of the introduction of movable-type printing into western Europe. His paternal grandfather was a famous and pious physician; so the grandson, bookish but brooding, began the study of medicine. But, disappointed in love, despairing of joy, disturbed by the worldliness and wickedness he saw around him, he fled at the age of twenty-three to Bologna, taking no leave of loved ones.

At Bologna he entered the cloister of the Dominican order, the Order of Preachers, brothers of St. Dominic. Two days after assuming the black habit of the order which had been charged with preaching against heresy in the Middle Ages, he wrote to his father explaining his sudden departure. This portion is revealing:

> I could not endure any longer the wickedness of the blinded peoples of Italy. Virtue I saw despised everywhere and vices exalted and held in honor. With great warmth of heart, I made daily a short prayer to God that He might release me from the vale of tears. "Make known to me the way," I cried, "the way in which I should walk, for I lift up my soul unto Thee," and God in His infinite mercy showed me the way, unworthy as I am of such distinguishing grace. . . . The reasons which drove me to become religious are these: the miserable condition of the world and the evils of which men are guilty, such as rape, immorality, robbery, pride, idolatry, cursing, all in such grave measure that it may be said that no one can be found who has any regard for what is good. Each day, therefore, weeping, I often repeated the line of Virgil's *Aeneid:* "Alas, flee these cruel lands, flee this avaricious shore."

Here he studied the Scriptures and the writings of Thomas Aquinas and Augustine, gave himself to prayer and fasting, and meditated on the wickedness of the world contrasted with the demands of a holy and righteous God. He committed whole portions of Scripture to memory and became a tutor and teacher of monastic novices, instructing them in Hebrew and Greek. These were six years of undistinguished preparation for coming days of unsought fame.

Soon the young monk was sent to his home town, but made little impression there. He long remembered a cutting remark he heard after his preaching in Ferrara: "The brothers must be in great need of workers." When threat of war forced the dispersal of the Dominicans there, he was relieved to be sent to Florence.

Florence was to be the city linked to his name through the centuries after his death; yet only the last seventeen of his almost forty-six years were spent there, and only the last seven of those seventeen were years of his fame. Florence was the city of the Renaissance arts *par excellence;* every art flourished there. The city was under the sway of the Medici family, merchants and bankers of Italy known throughout Europe, patrons of art and literature. While they held no office in the city's government, they controlled its policies by their influence and beneficence.

Cosimo de Medici, major founder of the family's Renaissance position, had commissioned Michelozzi, the architect, to build for his family a "modest" palace. Cosimo was so pleased with the result, and so embarrassed that he lived in a beautiful residence while the Dominican monks of his city lived in such contrast, that he commissioned the same architect to rebuild St. Mark's (San Marco), their cloister, at Medici expense. Each of the cells were subsequently decorated with a scene of Christ's dying on the cross, painted by Fra Angelico.

To St. Mark's came Savonarola in 1481. His first preaching at San Lorenzo, the Medici's parish church, met with no success. Hardly twenty-five hearers listened to him. So he discarded philosophy and scholastic learning and mere literary form and preached the Bible. He applied its principles to everyday life. His audiences grew. His superiors sent him on preaching missions to neighboring cities. It was by the "foolishness of preaching" that he communicated the urgency of his message.

This preaching was composed of Scripture, mysticism, dramatic "flashes of lightning and reverberations of thunder," attacks upon corrupt and insincere clergy, and prophetic insight (an acute political and religious intuition)—enhanced in the view of the people when some bold forecasts came true. But behind these elements was the man himself. He was variously described as of an "impressive, eager countenance, deep-set flashing eye, massive jaw, full lips, with hands and fingers fine, white, lithe, flexible, muscular, firm," and "of middle height, dark complexion, lustrous eyes dark gray in color, thick lips and aquiline nose."

In 1489 and 1490 he began the years of his establishment in Florence. People thronged to hear him. His name was on the city's lips. About 1491 he was made prior of his convent and proceeded to require of its inmates a stricter life, effecting a wholesome internal reform.

Two great controversies shaped the last seven or eight years of his life. One was with Lorenzo de Medici—the Magnificent—who represented to him the world; the other was with Alexander VI—the Borgia pope—who represented the Devil. And there were plenty of dissolute young nobility to represent the flesh.

Lorenzo sought to win over to himself the popular friar by blandishments and praise. For the Medici even to take notice of the monk was condescension. But the temporal power and the luxuriant culture of the fine banker and patron were alien to the monk's independence; he remained unmoved. Rebuffed and offended, Lorenzo was yet honest enough, when he sensed that his own soul was soon to take its journey of accounting, to call for Savonarola, with whom he had never before spoken face to face. Although reminded that his own regular confessor was nearby, Lorenzo replied, "I know of no honest friar save this one."

The prior of St. Mark's, coming to his bedside, declared three conditions on which he would give the Magnificent his final blessing: first, that he declare a strong faith in God's mercy; second, that he return any ill-gotten gains; and third, that he restore to the people of Florence their liberties. To the first, Lorenzo readily gave consent and to the second, he gave haltingly. But to the third, he made no reply, turned away, and in a few hours was dead. It was 1492.

The death of Lorenzo brought his ill-favored son, Piero, to the leadership of the family. This fact contributed to Savonarola's fortunes. Piero was weak and insolent and lacked the charm and diplomacy of his late father, vacillating in decisions and alienating friends. In 1494 there came into Italy the scourge of the north, King Charles VIII of France. Conquering and pillaging, his presence seemed to lend substance to the Dominican friar's claim that Florence was about to be chastised by God for her sins. He had declared that this chastisement would come speedily and that the city would be restored.

Piero surrendered too much of wealth and land to the French invader in his interest of peace. The price was too great for the Florentines to approve. Their antagonism to this weak son of so magnificent a father had already grown. They would tolerate no more and expelled the Medici from their midst in a bloodless revolt. Savonarola now ascended to the moral leadership of the city. He was approaching the height of his influence. He interceded with the French invader, gained a lessening of the terms of peace, encouraged the king to be on his way, and warned him against going back on his word. Savonarola now found himself the leader of the city, responsible for building up what had been torn down.

Having been a Florentine for more than a decade, and having the public ear, the reformer was the logical leader. He possessed qualities needful in such a crisis: farsightedness, levelheadedness, honesty, conviction, common sense, and "a disinterested zeal for principle." He played the largest role in framing the republican government, modeled after Venice, in which various city councils were to do the actual ruling. He took no office himself, but made Jesus Christ, God Himself, King of Florence. He pleaded for moral regeneration and the removal of public and private vices. He called upon the people of all classes to repent and do works of righteousness, generosity, and social reformation. A transformation, soon found to be only temporary, followed.

The second controversy of his last years was Savonarola's conflict with Pope Alexander VI. Words are somehow inadequate to convey fully the baseness of this character—this occupant of the falsely-supposed throne of Peter. There is perhaps no better description of this pope than the words of the commission he appointed to examine and bring charges against Savonarola. Their words describing the monk are utterly false; the same words, if applied to Alexander, would have been singularly appropriate: "that iniquitous monster, call him man or friar we cannot, a mass of the most abominable wickedness."

The catalog of Alexander's sin is full. Within its pages are found bribery, lewdness, incontinence, fornication, lechery, nepotism, simony, debauchery, inordinate ambition, perfidy, gross obscenity, blasphemy, robbery, concubinage, and murder. He shrank from no evil to achieve his ends. He held nothing sacred, although he occupied the "most sacred seat." Surely the pontificate of Alexander VI alone is one of the clearest arguments against the divine origin of the papal institution. As another has asked, "Would God commit His church for twelve years to such a monster?"

With such a man, the preacher of righteousness was now in contest. Enemies of Savonarola reported to the pope the tenor of the friar's sermons attacking and condemning unholy priests. The pope invited him to Rome for discussion; the friar demurred, protesting his need to direct affairs in his own city. Late in 1495 he was forbidden by the pope to preach; for five months he obeyed. But early in the next year he was called by the city fathers to preach the Lenten sermons. In them he lashed out once more against the sins of the pope.

Alexander next offered him a cardinal's hat in return for his silence. Savonarola not only rejected the bribe but proclaimed his own preference, not for a cardinal's red hat, but for a hat reddened with blood. In the carnival season of 1497, popular frenzy of religious devotion was at such a pitch that, at Savonarola's invitation, the people fed a huge bonfire in the city square with "vanities": lewd books, obscene pictures, carnival costumes, playing cards, dice, games of chance, various trinkets, false hair, and objects of vain luxury. The huge mound was described as 60 feet high and 240 feet in circumference at its base. The burning was to the accompaniment of religious songs.

Next came excommunication of the friar in May of 1497. The council vouched for his good conduct and wrote Rome in his defense, while he retired briefly to employ his pen instead of his pulpit voice. In December he resumed preaching, with no less colorful vigor and denunciation than before. The pope threatened interdict (the suspension of the regular sacraments for the faithful), an ecclesiastical weapon to force the city leaders to bend to papal will. The city would be banned; none could trade with her; no tithe tax could be collected by the city. This touched near; it affected Florence's purse. Consternation and frustration followed. Then came the relaxing of popular support. Having moved from doubt to fanaticism, Florence was moving from fanaticism back to doubt. Never had she become truly devout.

Letters were intercepted, written by Savonarola to heads of states of Europe, calling for a convening of a general council to settle affairs of the church. This clearly aimed at a power above the head of the pope. It became more fuel for flames soon to be kindled.

The last incredible straw was a Franciscan challenge to the preacher to prove his innocence and divine commission by submitting to the medieval test of ordeal, trial by fire. A path of burning embers was prepared. A champion had to pass over the path without being burned. Controversy and dispute over procedure delayed the spectacle for which the people had gathered with intense emotion. During the delay, a sudden rainstorm extinguished the embers. The expected was denied; the people were angered and stormed St. Mark's. Savonarola was arrested, tried, and condemned along with two other monks. In his cell, between periods of torture, the preacher composed meditations on the penitential Psalms, in which his evangelical understanding is left without doubt.

Papal commissioners had been sent to Florence charged with seeing to his death. The sentence for Savonarola and the two monks was death by hanging, followed by the burning of their bodies. At the hour of execution, the bishop pronounced, "We separate thee from the church militant and the church triumphant."

Girolamo Savonarola, preacher of righteousness, replied, "Not from the church triumphant; that is not thine to do." Their souls were dispatched, Savonarola's last, on May 23, 1498.

The papal triumph was apparent, but in the providence of God, it was brief. Already born, indeed in his mid-teens by that year, was one, farther to the north, who would be used of God to break the monopoly of Rome. The time was not yet ripe, the cup of iniquity was not yet full, but they were soon to be. Martin Luther, empowered by the Spirit of God, would defy pope and prelate and live to die a natural death, twenty-five years after doing so.

In the city of Worms, Germany, today, the city in which that dramatic defiance was spoken before an imperial assembly, is a quiet memory of Savonarola. Two blocks from the main business street, in an open grassy square, is an imposing Reformation monument, composed of over a dozen statues in bronze, well-discolored by oxidation and the passage of time. Each of the figures played a part in the movement which culminated in that April in Worms, in 1521. At the feet of Luther, supporting and contributing, with Wycliffe and Huss as fellow pre-reformers, is Girolamo Savonarola, preacher of righteousness.

In Florence today there is no such statue. There is only a bronze plaque set in the pavement of the public square, marking the place of his burning. As another has written: "You may silence a prophet in death, but you cannot stifle the truth, or stay the day; it is of God, and must prevail."

Suggestions for Further Reading

William H. Crawford. *Girolamo Savonarola: A Prophet of Righteousness.* Cincinnati: Jennings and Graham, 1907.

Roberto Ridolfi. *The Life of Girolamo Savonarola.* New York: Alfred A. Knopf, 1952.

Philip Schaff. *History of the Christian Church.* Vol. 6. 1910; reprint Grand Rapids: Eerdmans, 1981. (Pages 684-715.)

The Modern Church
(1517 to the Present)

The era known as "modern" church history covers fewer than five hundred years, about a fourth of the total history of the Church. A reader will find it not at all uncommon, however, for a textbook of church history to devote half of its pages to events occurring since 1517. This emphasis results not only from the greater wealth of materials available for the study of the modern era but also from the greater diversity of men, events, and movements that fill modern church history. The modern period is, in some ways, a "busy" era.

Modern church history begins with the Reformation (1517-1648), an era which itself begins with Martin Luther's nailing of his 95 Theses on the door of the church at Wittenberg, Germany. Luther's simple act set in motion a movement that permanently changed the political, social, and religious face of Europe and—eventually—the world. The doctrinal essence of the Reformation is summarized in three principles: the absolute authority of the Bible, justification by faith alone, and the universal priesthood of believers. From these principles came not only modern religious institutions but also the modern ideas of freedom, the equality of man, and many other blessings that we associate with political and religious liberty. These religious principles and the movements they launched resulted in violent clashes. The end of the last and greatest of these "wars of religion," the Thirty Years' War (1618-1648), also marks the end of the Reformation era.

The second segment of modern church history may be called "the Church in the Age of Reason" (1648-1815). This was in some ways a period of infidelity characterized by a decline in morals, an emphasis on human reason, rationalistic attacks on the Scripture by Deists and other philosophers of the Enlightenment, and an apparent deadening of religious interest. In this light, the excesses of the French Revolution and the Napoleonic era (1789-1815) seem only the natural consequence of such human folly. Yet the era also saw some of the most glorious examples of Christian art and some of the most sweeping religious revivals in church history. Along with the names of Louis XIV, Frederick the Great, John Locke, Voltaire, Napoleon, and the other great men of the era, one must include John and Charles Wesley, George Whitefield, Jonathan Edwards, and others who affected not only the Church but also the course of world history.

Church historian Kenneth Scott Latourette gave the title "the Great Century" to the period stretching from 1815 to 1914. The century was indeed a great era in church history, perhaps the greatest since the first century. During the nineteenth century, revivals of unprecedented length and extent transformed cities and nations. Courageous missionaries carried the gospel to lands such as Asia, Africa, and Latin America which lacked the knowledge of God's saving grace. Some of the Church's greatest orthodox theologians and ministers took up the pen or stepped into the pulpit to defend the Christian faith, to confute its critics, and to edify believers. The Great Century was an optimistic era—but that optimism was shattered and the era ended by the horrors of the First World War.

"The Church in the Twentieth Century" is an apt but elastic title. How one views this century in general determines how one views the Church's history during the same period. Many stress the declension of the age and quote with foreboding Paul's admonition to Timothy: "In the last days perilous times shall come" (II Tim. 3:1). For these, the century is a period of decline against which a remnant of believers struggle. Others, although agreeing that spiritual conditions are bad, reject what they consider a fatalistic view. They believe that Christians need to humble themselves before God and serve Him and then watch Him transform the era as He has transformed previous eras. Whatever one's view, the twentieth century nonetheless has had its share of memorable men and events that have contributed richly to the Church's heritage.

Luther

by Edward M. Panosian

Martin Luther has been called, along with the Apostle Paul and Augustine, one of the three greatest theologians of the Christian church. Luther, however, never meant to be a great theologian. He certainly never meant to shake the foundations of Europe as he did. Martin Luther was originally concerned only with the salvation of his soul. As a result of his inward struggle and the study of God's Word which that struggle spurred, Luther discovered and embraced the doctrines of the Reformation, particularly that of justification by faith alone. These doctrines were not formed in the dry contemplation of the scholar (although Luther was unquestionably a scholar) but in the forge of human experience. Luther, therefore, was not simply the instigator of the Reformation; he was in many ways an embodiment of it.

He was a German peasant born near the end of the fifteenth century. He was to be used of God to lead an unintended revolution away from the ecclesiastical system of the late Middle Ages. He was to be attacked by his enemies for having gone too far and by his friends for not having gone far enough. And he was to pioneer the Reformation of the sixteenth century, which was to become the pioneer modern movement toward the diversity of Christian denominations owning the absolute authority of the Old and the New Testament Scriptures, toward political liberty, and toward the social, economic, and intellectual enfranchisement of the common man.

In some respects, Martin Luther was like the Apostle Peter. He was often blunt and bombastic, speaking first and considering afterward. But like the Apostle, also, he was graciously empowered to stand on a "day of Pentecost" and proclaim the authority of God's Word, to the confusion of earthly powers, to the convicting and converting of those who would become God's.

That day for Luther was in April 1521. Assembled in the city of Worms for the meeting of the imperial assembly (the *diet*) were representatives of all levels of the German "church and state." Presiding was the newly elected, twenty-one-year-old emperor, Charles V. After long preliminaries on the second day of questioning, having acknowledged the writings displayed on a table as his own and having been instructed by his accusers to retract their contents, Luther replied in words which have been variously translated: "Unless I am refuted and convicted by testimonies of the Scriptures or by clear arguments (since I believe neither the pope nor the councils alone; it being evident that they have often erred and contradicted themselves), I am conquered by the Holy Scriptures quoted by me, and my conscience is bound in the Word of God: I cannot and will not recant anything, since it is unsafe and dangerous to do any thing against the conscience."

Expecting full well to be burned at the stake as the Bohemian John Huss had been a century earlier and having been warned before by his friends and reminded of the impotence of the "letter of safe-conduct" should the emperor who had granted it choose to ignore it, the German had nonetheless asserted, with a boldness born of absolute confidence in the living God, his irrevocable stand upon the written Word of that omnipotent God.

Who was this man, this reformer? Born in 1483, reared in Saxony in a typically pious home of the times, trained in the grammar schools of the Brethren of Common Life, and having received a liberal arts education at the famed University of Erfurt, Martin Luther was confronted with the need to find answers to fundamental questions: How can I have peace of heart? How can I be saved from my sin? What shall I do with my life? His search for the answers to these questions became the preparation of the spark which was to ignite a conflagration felt throughout the Christian world—and beyond.

From law to grace—the schoolmaster to Christ—was his experience, in several ways. He first prepared to study law, but finding it no comfort for his need, Luther forsook the potentially lucrative vocation for a supposedly higher calling, the service of the Church of Rome, the only way he knew to Christ. Here again the law, the keeping of vows, the ritual of ceremony and sacrament, of duties and hours, of confession and self-humiliation, brought comfort for only fleeting moments.

Then a monastic superior, Johann Staupitz (while Luther was a monk in the Augustinian cloister at Erfurt), suggested that he simply believe the Word of God. Luther was thus cast upon the Bible, the message of God's love and redeeming grace, and he forsook the law of meritorious works.

Having been driven to the Bible, the reformer-to-be began to make it his daily meat. He was soon appointed, again by Staupitz's suggestion, to the faculty of a newly established university, a project of the Elector Frederick of Saxony, at the town of Wittenberg, which—both town and university—Luther was to write indelibly on the pages of sixteenth-century history. It was here that he soon came to study and lecture on books of the Bible, going back to the Greek texts of the New Testament and the Hebrew of the Old Testament, taking their meaning literally and historically.

There is a powerful lesson here: while the young teacher was about his assigned business, God gave him illumination of truth which was to shatter the exclusive monopoly of the ecclesiastical structure of Rome. He was not off on a tangent; he was doing what his hands found to do as unto the Lord, and God saw to it that that work was God's. He was used of God to do a great work when, in his faithfulness in daily duties, he least expected greatness.

It was the events of the second decade of the 1500s which catapulted the Wittenberg professor to prominence. The broad papal dispensation of certificates of indulgence in the German states became the occasion for conflict. Indulgences were presumed cancellations of some of the purgatorial sufferings of the soul after death of the body, according to medieval Romanist teaching (unchanged even today). While never technically "sold," they were nevertheless being practically exchanged for money "gifts" for the building of a new cathedral in honor of Peter in Rome. So effective was the streamlined "sales pitch" of some peddlers such as Tetzel that the average man came to understand indulgences as virtual "licenses" to sin. This traffic in souls so incensed the spiritually liberated Luther that he responded dramatically with an action which has been commemorated for more than four and half centuries since as Reformation Day.

On October 31, 1517, the eve of All Saint's Day on which the Duke's incredible (but popularly credulous) collection of sacred relics was annually displayed for the benefit of the faithful, Luther posted 95 Theses questioning the whole Romish doctrine of indulgences. Although immediately ignored by Rome, the theses, translated and distributed throughout the Germanies through the medium of the recently developed movable-type printing, soon caused a decline in indulgence revenues. Then, her most responsive nerve having been touched, Rome responded.

Pope Leo X, Medici son of the Renaissance, lover of the arts— "who would have been an excellent pope if only he were also religious"—alternately threatened, counseled, commanded, and cajoled the author of the theses. The pope demanded retraction and silence; the professor promised neither. Instead, Luther wrote more elaborately on the un-Scriptural nature of Rome's teaching and practice. He rejected the assumption that only the Roman church can properly interpret the Scriptures; he rejected most of the seven sacraments as special means of receiving Christ's grace; and he rejected the exclusive authority of the pope to convene potentially reformatory church councils.

A debate with the pope's champion, Johann Eck, at the Univeristy of Leipzig in 1519, in which Eck informed Luther that Huss had been burned by an earlier church council for holding views on Biblical authority very similar to his own, destroyed Luther's remaining hope for reformation through a church council. He was driven to absolute dependence on the absolute authority of the written Word of God.

Three fundamental doctrinal truths, upon which all Christian believers are agreed, emerge from the work and emphases of this German: the absolute authority of the Old and New Testaments, justification by faith only, and the universal priesthood of believers.

The last of those three is illustrated by the paragraph quoted earlier from the speech at Worms. It became a veritable declaration of ecclesiastical independence from priestly tradition at the same time that it was a declaration of voluntary bondage to Jesus Christ and His Word. This was the Reformation rediscovery of the gospel.

After the Diet of Worms, Luther's great work was to "make Paul [and the Evangelists and Peter and the others] speak German" to the Germans. His translation of the New Testament into the vernacular of his people was to set the literary language of Germany. A few years later he married a former nun and with her established the modern married minister's home, reviving and ennobling the married state of the Christian clergy as a "school" for the counseling of married saints. (For more on Luther's marriage, see pages 18-19.)

Some twenty years later, the pioneer work having been done and the work of organizing and consolidating having been undertaken by more fitted hands, the father of the German Reformation died and was received into glory. Far from flawless, a man of like passions with all men, he was a man God used for His own good purpose. He was an imperfect saint, but he was perfected with the saints in the paths of God's choosing. And that phrase "Here I stand" in the conclusion of his words at Worms may well echo in our ears as we, too, in this day, stand poised to do battles on the authority of—and with the sword of the Spirit, which is—the Word of God.

Suggestion for Further Reading

Roland Bainton. *Here I Stand: A Life of Martin Luther.* 1950; reprint New York: New American Library. (Probably the standard modern biography.)

J.H. Merle D'Aubigné. *The Life and Times of Martin Luther.* Chicago: Moody, 1955. (Abridged from the author's full-length history of the Reformation.)

John Calvin: The Theologian

by Mark Sidwell

Historians sometimes argue who was the greater—Luther or Calvin? The question, however, is unnecessary since, in the providence of God, both men played an invaluable role in the spread of the Reformation. Luther was the pioneer who set forth the great doctrines of the Reformation. Calvin's role was that of theologian; he was the pre-eminent exegete and systematizer of the doctrines of Protestantism.

"Calvin has, I believe, caused untold millions of souls to be damned," an unthinking television evangelist once said. Unfortunately, he is typical of many who in their ignorance condemn John Calvin. Critics accuse Calvin of being cold, cruel, and dictatorial. Some Christians mistakenly identify his name as the label for an almost fatalistic view of predestination and consider him an enemy of Christian evangelism. The *real* John Calvin, however, was a great and godly man who labored until death for the defense and furtherance of the Christian faith.

Calvin was born in Noyon, France, in 1509. We know surprisingly little of his personal life, for Calvin rarely wrote of his private affairs. Of his conversion, for example, Calvin wrote only that God saved him "by a sudden conversion," probably sometime in the early 1530s in Paris. When French authorities began to arrest Protestants in 1533, Calvin had to flee. According to one story, Calvin escaped the authorities by tying his bedclothes together and using them to climb down from the window of his room.

For three years after fleeing, Calvin traveled as an evangelist in France, Italy, and Germany. During one trip in 1536, Calvin needed to go from France to Germany. Due to a war between France and the Holy Roman Empire, Calvin had to detour through Geneva, Switzerland. That detour became one of the most important events in Christian history.

Geneva had embraced the Reformation just months before Calvin visited. The city had expelled its Roman Catholic bishop, rejected its Italian Catholic overlord, and allied with the other Protestants in Switzerland. The leader of the reform party was Guillaume Farel, a tall, red-headed, fiery preacher of the gospel. On learning that Calvin was in the city, Farel rushed to Calvin's inn to urge him to stay in Geneva and help in the work there. Calvin declined, saying that he wished for a place of solitude where he might pursue his studies in peace. At this Farel thundered, "You are following only your own wishes, and I declare that if you do not assist us in this work of the Lord, the Lord will punish you for seeking your own interest rather than his." The astonished Calvin relented, feeling that God was commanding him through Farel to stay.

Not all went well after Calvin came to Geneva, however. The people of the city were delighted to be free from their Roman Catholic bishop and priests, but many preferred to be free from the reformers as well. Furthermore, the ruling councils of Geneva were jealous of their power; they did not intend to let the ministers have too much control over the church. When Calvin, Farel, and the others refused to give communion to unruly church members, the councils fired the ministers and exiled them from Geneva.

So in 1538, Calvin found himself again a wanderer. He settled in Strasbourg (then part of Germany), where he became the pastor of a church of more than five hundred French refugees. Calvin enjoyed his time in Strasbourg. He preached to his people and visited them in their homes, and he spent quiet moments in study and writing. In this more relaxed atmosphere, Calvin also turned his thoughts to marriage.

In 1540, Calvin married a young widow in his church, Idelette de Bure. Their married life lasted a little less than nine years, both suffered from poor health, and Calvin often had to be away from home. Nevertheless, they developed a deep affection for one another. Calvin called Idelette "the excellent companion of my life." The Calvins had three children, but two died as infants and the third was stillborn.

In 1541, Geneva recalled Calvin, Farel, and the other expelled ministers. Infighting among political factions had grown so fierce and the church was falling into such decay that the citizens of Geneva thought that only the brilliant and disciplined Calvin could help them. Calvin would have preferred to remain in Strasbourg, but he believed God was calling him to return to the work in Geneva.

Conditions were still far from perfect for the French pastor. One party in particular, known as the Libertines, hated Calvin, the Church, and anything else that smacked of morality. Some Libertines named their dogs "Calvin." Others fired guns outside the church during services. On one occasion Calvin was on his way to a meeting of Geneva's Council of Two Hundred. In the hall outside of the meeting room, Calvin met a crowd of Libertines who brandished weapons and shouted threats at him. Calvin gestured to his chest and said, "If you want blood, there are still a few drops here; strike, then!" His action cowed the mob, and Calvin proceeded to meet with the Council.

Strangely, many people have the idea that Calvin was somehow the "dictator" of Geneva, imperiously enforcing his will on an oppressed populace. In reality, Calvin was not even a citizen of Geneva until five years before his death. He never held political office, and even his position in the church was not completely secure. The rulers of Geneva could dismiss him at any time, as they had done in 1538. Calvin's only "power" was the force of his personality, his character, and his preaching of the gospel. The only dominion that John Calvin exercised over Geneva was moral persuasion.

John Calvin's greatest contribution to the Christian Church was his writing. Lutheran writer Philip Melanchthon called Calvin simply "the Theologian." To Calvin goes the credit for organizing and expositing the great doctrines of the Reformation. Although Calvin wrote numerous books, tracts, and treatises, two of his endeavors stand out for special note. First are Calvin's commentaries on the Scripture. He wrote commentaries on every book of the New Testament except II John, III John, and Revelation and on most of the books of the Old Testament. Unlike earlier medieval commentators, Calvin rejected wild, allegorical "interpretations" of the Bible. He sought always to lay the plain meaning of the text before his readers. Many Bible scholars, students, and pastors still use his commentaries with profit today.

Calvin's other great literary work was his *Institutes of the Christian Religion,* a systematic treatment of Protestant theology. His first version of the *Institutes,* published in 1536, was a short handbook of one hundred pages. Through the years, Calvin expanded his work until the final edition (1559) was more than five times the length of the original. The term "systematic theology" may put off some Christians, who associate that phrase with dull books filled with pedantic logic and dreary argument. Calvin's book, however, is enlivened by the fact that he sought always to appeal to the text of the living Word of God as his proof. Indeed, one may argue that Calvin's *Institutes* was just as much an exercise in Biblical exegesis as his commentaries.

The key to Calvin's theology is the doctrine of the sovereignty of God. Many falsely assume that Calvin seized this single idea and then built his system of thought upon it. Rather, Calvin found this theme throughout the Bible and, as a result, stressed that theme throughout his work. Some of the modern criticism of Calvin results from a misunderstanding of his emphasis on predestination, the sovereignty of God as it applies to salvation. Calvin's critics argue that evangelism is useless if those who are to be saved *will* be saved, regardless of man's actions. In his own day, Calvin scoffed at this misrepresentation of his theology. He said, "For as we do not know who belongs to the number of the predestined or who does not belong, we ought to be so minded as to wish that all men be saved. So shall it come about that we try to make everyone we meet a sharer in our peace."

Words, of course, are always the easiest answer to criticism. The ministry of Geneva, however, also vindicated Calvin's theology. From that city, hundreds of missionaries, evangelists, and pastors traveled to all corners of the continent preaching the gospel. Their efforts, sometimes sealed with a martyr's blood but always crowned with success, thrilled Calvin. In later years, as he thought on these brave preachers and their many converts, Calvin wrote, "God had given me a son. God has taken my little boy. . . . But I have myriads of sons throughout the Christian world."

Living conditions steadily improved in Geneva during Calvin's time there. Calvin successfully urged the ruling councils to clean the city's streets and regulate the food markets for the sake of health. The French reformer drew a detailed plan for producing silk and other cloth in Geneva. This new industry proved so successful that it remained the backbone of Geneva's economy well into the nineteenth century.

Material prosperity was not the greatest blessing to come to Geneva, though. The preaching of the gospel and the flocking of Protestant refugees to Geneva gave it a pious character unlike any other city in Europe. When Scottish reformer John Knox visited Geneva, he called the city "the most perfect school of Christ that ever was in the earth since the days of the Apostles."

Calvin's health was never good. He suffered from asthma, indigestion, severe headaches, arthritis, kidney stones, tuberculosis, and more. The combination of his poor health and the long hours he worked as a pastor, teacher, and writer undermined Calvin's strength. He died in 1564, not quite fifty-five years of age. Yet, even on his deathbed, Calvin would not curtail his labors. When his friends urged him not to tax his strength with further writing and study, Calvin answered, "What! Would you have the Lord find me idle when He comes?"

In retrospect, Calvin's description of Moses in his commentary on Exodus makes an apt eulogy for the great reformer himself:

Moses' outstanding ability and heroic mind are evident in that he submitted to so many annoyances, endured so many troubles, and, unbeaten by weariness, every day undertook new labors. The greatness of his spirit can never be praised enough. He spent himself freely for a depraved and perverse people; and he did not desist from his purpose although he saw no gratitude for his kindness. . . . Surely, he possessed many virtues, worthy of the highest praise.

Suggestions for Further Reading

John Calvin. *Calvin: Commentaries.* Trans. and ed. Joseph Haroutunian. Philadelphia: Westminster, 1958. (This work contains Calvin's brief autobiography [pp. 51-57], and the selections from the commentaries succinctly introduce Calvin's theology. The editor's introduction, however, is liberal in its interpretation of Calvin.)

Philip Schaff. *History of the Christian Church.* Vol. 8. 1910; reprint Grand Rapids: Eerdmans, 1981. (Pages 255-844.)

Thea B. Van Halsema. *This Was John Calvin.* 1959; reprint Grand Rapids: Baker Book House, 1981. (A young people's biography of better-than-average quality.)

John Knox: The Thundering Scot

by Edward M. Panosian

If any single word best summarizes the role of John Knox in the Reformation, it is prophet. *Unlike Luther and Calvin, Knox did not make an original theological contribution to the Reformation. Rather, like an Old Testament prophet, John Knox thundered out the message of God's Word and called on all men, high and low, to submit themselves to its precepts. Under Knox's preaching and leadership, Scotland became— like Calvin's Geneva—a visible example of the blessings and ennobling effects of the Biblical faith on a society. In giving Scotland the truth, Knox not only brought the knowledge of saving faith to Scotland but also led that nation from the Middle Ages into the modern world.*

A post card pictures a simple stone set in the ground of a square in Edinburgh, Scotland, commemorating the traditional spot of an uncertain grave. Inscribed on the stone is only "I.K. 1572" (for Ionnes [John] Knox). I found the post card between the pages of one of the well-used books in the library of Dr. Charles D. Brokenshire, a saintly scholar and revered teacher. On the opposite side of the card he had written to a nephew this message: "Scotland has erected no monument on the grave of John Knox, for Scotland is his monument. He was courageous and true. Dear nephew, may you be such a man." The truth of that message has been remembered profitably by one for whom it was never intended.

The Eve of the Reformation

"Scotland is his monument." That noble testimony is understood best after viewing that kingdom on the eve of the sixteenth-century Reformation. The country was weak; the soil was poor; commerce and learning were backward. Border warfare occurred regularly and full-scale war with England recurrently. Feudal disorganization and blood feuds made peace uncommon. The Roman Catholic church owned half of the country's wealth. That wealth was enjoyed by the higher clergy and by some favored nobles, while the lower clergy and the people paid the tithes. No country in Europe had greater religious corruption. The clergy were ignorant, incompetent, and uncouth. Parsons and monks were often hated by the laity. Superstition and ignorance were only slightly abated by the filtering northward of Renaissance humanism and Lollardy (followers of John Wycliffe's teachings). The condition of the land has been described as "medieval semibarbarism."

The Reformation that followed is a remarkable witness to the truth that when the Word of God is given free course in a land, that land enjoys the blessings of liberty, education, prosperity, and progress. Scotland was translated into modern civilization by Bible preaching, particularly that of three courageous men. Two of these, Patrick Hamilton and George Wishart, are little known today; the third is John Knox. Yet in God's providence, Hamilton and Wishart, both burned at the stake, kindled in the heart of Knox the flame that was to burn until his heart ceased its labor. Knox is best remembered, but heaven honors all three.

An Uncertain Birth Date

Because history does not herald the birth of the son of a respectable Scottish peasant, historians do not agree on the exact birth date of John Knox. Traditionally 1505 is suggested; 1514 may be more correct. But so strong an impress did he make that there is no doubt that the Scot of the Scots left his earthly toil on the 23rd of November, 1572. Perhaps the most familiar epitaph for this man, whom Samuel Johnson called one of the "ruffians of the reformation" and whom a modern biographer has called "the thundering Scot," are the words spoken by the Regent Morton at Knox's grave side: "Here lies one who neither flattered nor feared any flesh."

Knox was never far removed from his people, except against his will. We know little about his life before 1540 except that he had had a university education (probably at St. Andrews) and had been ordained a priest. Priesthood was not in his day and land the result of a conscious calling to parish ministry; it was rather the normal route to government service. Almost all men who were not merchants or farmers became priests—"the learned."

The young Knox had known of the burning of the Scottish nobleman, Patrick Hamilton, in 1528. Hamilton, who had studied in Paris and learned the teaching of Luther at Marburg, had returned as a teacher to St. Andrews University. As a preacher of the new Reformation views and doctrines, he offended the Archbishop, was tried for having taught "theological views deemed heretical," admitted them to be Biblical, and was condemned to the stake.

In the wintry wind of that February day, the difficulty of lighting the fire and the need to relight it several times prolonged the agony of Hamilton's death over six hours. Men later said that the smoke of his burning infected all on whom it blew. While men asked, "Wherefore was Patrick Hamilton burnt?" (as Knox later wrote), more young Scots visited Germany and Switzerland where the Reformation was underway. More Lutheran books and more English New Testaments and Bibles (Tyndale's and Coverdale's) were bought and sold, in spite of repeated injunctions against them.

Retreat for Preparation

Under the preaching of George Wishart, Knox was enlisted in the cause of the gospel in which he was to spend his life. Wishart was a gentle preacher and teacher of the reformed faith. "Suspected of heresy because he read the Greek New Testament with his students," he had fled his native Scotland, studied in England at Cambridge, in Switzerland under the influence of Zwingli, and in Germany. He returned to effect reform—of church and state—at home.

John Knox's first entrance on the stage of church history is as Wishart's literal bodyguard, carrying a sword because of an assassination attempt by a priest upon the preacher. Having preached the evangelical doctrine throughout Scotland, doctrine which according to his trial included salvation by faith, the Scriptures as the only test of truth, the denial of purgatory and confession to a priest, and the rejection of the Roman Catholic mass as blasphemous idolatry, Wishart was arrested by Cardinal Beaton (hated nephew of the archbishop who had burned Hamilton), tried, and burned on the eighteenth anniversary of Hamilton's death (1546). Knox was eager to accompany his noble friend, but the elder Wishart refused saying, "One is sufficient for one sacrifice."

Within a few weeks, Scottish nobles murdered the cardinal and, as refugees, took possession of Beaton's seaside castle of St. Andrews. Knox was invited to be their chaplain and continued to tutor his young students. In this strange parish Knox first preached. So vehement was his excoriation of the lives of his rebel "parishioners" and of the teachings and doctrines of the Roman church that after his first sermon his hearers declared: "Others snipped at the branches of popery; but he strikes at the roots, to destroy the whole." Now the Protestant rebels against an ecclesiastical government awaited help from England. But French ships arrived instead. French troops captured the castle and its defenders, and Knox began nineteen months as a French galley slave, under flogging and cursing learning to be an apostle of liberty to his people.

One incident during those months reveals something of the latent fire in the Scottish preacher, even while in chains. A picture of the virgin Mary was brought aboard, while the galley was in port, to be kissed by the slaves. When Knox refused, the picture was thrust into his face. Outraged, he flung the "accursed idol" into the river, saying, "Let our Lady learn to swim."

After his release, Knox went to England for five years. Now ruled (1549) by the Protestant Edward VI, England welcomed John Knox. He preached in a settled parish, learned much about reforming work, and became a royal chaplain. With the accession of the bloody queen Mary Tudor, Knox became a Marian exile to avoid becoming a Marian martyr and labored and learned at Frankfurt and in Calvin's Geneva. Those were retreats for preparation before advances for battle. In a letter to a friend, Knox wrote a sterling tribute to the moral quality of life in Geneva, calling it "the most perfect school of Christ that ever was in the earth since the days of the Apostles. In other places I confess Christ to be truly preached; but manners and religion to be so seriously reformed, I have not yet seen in any other place besides."

Back in Scotland for several months, his preaching further strengthened the Protestant cause. As a result, many of the Scottish nobility banded together into a covenant in which they renounced "the congregation of Satan, with all the superstitious abomination and idolatry thereof" and affirmed the establishment of "the most blessed word of God and his congregation" and the defense of "the whole congregation of Christ, and every member thereof." These "Lords of the Congregation" became the political backbone of the remaking of a nation.

The Greatest Conflict

After a return to Geneva and more labor there, Knox finally ended the thirteen years of wandering exile. He was to leave the soil of Scotland no more. During 1560 and 1561, the Scottish Parliament accepted the reformed confession of faith drawn up by Knox and others. The time of conflict seemed to be past; the time of building and organization seemed to have come.

But a last great conflict was yet to be fought; this time it was to be with words. Those words, weapons at whose use the thundering Scot was most adept, were with the young queen Mary, widowed in France at eighteen, whose mother was regent in her behalf over Scotland until her death in 1560. Mary, Queen of Scots, a Romanist, was strangely out of place in that northern country, having lived her life in France. She came to rule a country which had become reformed in her absence and had to face the man who was more the leader of her people than was the queen.

John Knox, in his *History of the Reformation in Scotland,* preserves the record of a total of five "conversations" with the queen. Mary erred in almost every calculation. She attempted to argue with one who was a master of disputation. She attempted to restore the Roman mass (in her private chapel) which Parliament had outlawed. She flattered and tried to win Knox with tears and pleadings. She openly lived a life of paramours and suspected adulteries. She married her second husband's presumed murderer. Her actions but paved the way to her own deposition. Knox had preached that one mass was more terrible to him than the landings of ten thousand armed invaders. From his pulpit at St. Giles, the cathedral church of Edinburgh, just up the street from the queen's Holyrood Palace, he thundered against the restoration of the church of Rome which the Lords of the Congregation, following his example, had termed the "Synagogue of Satan."

Five years after her landing in Edinburgh, Mary, Queen of Scots, her armies bested, her domestic enemies far more in number than her friends, abdicated the throne and fled to England, leaving her infant son as monarch of Scotland.

A Steadfast Warrior

There were more years of building to come. Only five of these were to be allotted to John Knox, but there were others to continue the work, as there had been Hamilton and Wishart to begin it. The organization of church and state, the development of an educational system, the discipline of morals—all in an age before separation of church and state was believed either wise or possible—was carried on by Andrew Melville and others. But the one who made the building of that Scotland possible was the compelling, magnetic, stern, dauntless, harsh, intolerant, vehement, indomitable, "stedfast, unmoveable," warrior who had been "always abounding in the work of the Lord" and whose "labour [was] not in vain" (I Cor. 15:58).

Having inducted his successor to St. Giles pulpit in November 1572, barely more than two months after the infamous massacre of (eventually) fifty thousand Protestants had begun in France on St. Bartholomew's Day by unreformed Romanism, the preacher returned to his bedroom, from which he was to enter his eternal home two weeks later. During that fortnight of leave-taking of friends, of colleagues, of life itself, he asked that two Scripture passages be read: his beloved seventeenth chapter of John, "the place where I cast my first anchor," and the ninth psalm, a singularly fitting testimony of his age and a sobering word to our own.

The last four verses state, *The wicked shall be turned into hell, and all the nations that forget God. For the needy shall not always be forgotten: the expectation of the poor shall not perish for ever. Arise, O Lord; let not man prevail: let the heathen be judged in thy sight. Put them in fear, O Lord: that the nations may know themselves to be but men.*

Suggestions for Further Reading

John Knox. *The History of the Reformation in Scotland.* Ed. C.J. Guthrie. 1898; reprint Edinburgh: Banner of Truth Trust, 1982. (An abridged version of Knox's work which is both interesting and enlightening.)

Geddes MacGregor. *The Thundering Scot.* Philadelphia: Westminster Press, 1957.

W. Stanford Reid. *Trumpeter of God.* New York: Charles Scribner's Sons, 1974.

Oliver Cromwell: The Lord Protector

by Mark Sidwell

Politics and religion were inextricably mixed during the Reformation. The career of Oliver Cromwell is an illustration of the problems that Christians faced in that era. Cromwell's Christian virtues—bravery, discipline, and single-mindedness— made him an outstanding military leader. When he became the ruler of England, however, Cromwell found that the art of statecraft was more complicated and more difficult than that of warfare. One writer noted that historians often view Cromwell as "a man who whilst completely victorious was nevertheless unsuccessful." Even so, Cromwell's rule marked the height of Puritan power in England, and he gave the nation a precedent for one of its most precious liberties—religious freedom.

Seventeenth-century England was a troubled place. Faction fought against faction for control of the nation. Sometimes brother fought against brother as families divided over the questions that tore the nation apart. God's people in particular suffered under the changing fortunes of political alliances. Into this situation came a man by the name of Oliver Cromwell—one who was both a leader of men and a servant of Christ.

Oliver Cromwell was born in England in 1599. Although his family was not wealthy, young Oliver grew up in comfortable surroundings. His parents (especially his mother) were sober, pious Christians who did their best to teach him the Word of God. As a young man, Cromwell was friendly but unambitious and scarcely seemed destined for greatness. The turning point in his life, however, came sometime during the 1620s when he was converted. Cromwell later wrote to one of his cousins,

> Blessed be His Name for shining upon so dark a heart as mine! You know what my manner of life hath been. Oh, I

have lived in and loved darkness and hated the light. . . . I hated godliness, yet God had mercy on me. O the riches of His mercy!

During the seventeenth century, England faced many religious and political problems. In the 1500s the nation had embraced Protestantism, but the Anglican church kept many outward ceremonies that seemed almost Roman Catholic to some Christians. This dismay with an "incomplete" Reformation led to the rise of the Puritan party. The Puritans, as their name implies, wanted to "purify" the Church of England from "popish" elements such as the elaborate vestments worn by many of its clergymen. King Charles I (1625-1649), however, wanted to restore closer ties with Rome. Furthermore, the king resented any attempts to reduce his authority to rule. Violence seemed almost certain to erupt.

The Puritans in Parliament tried to curb the king's power and protect the traditional rights of Englishman. In exasperation with the stubborn Parliament, Charles dissolved it and ruled for ten years by his own decree. Charles's bungling, however, sparked a war with Scotland in 1640, and the king was forced to recall Parliament to raise money to fight the war. Instead of granting Charles additional funds, the Puritans began to press for religious and political reforms.

Dismayed at the character of this new Parliament, Charles dissolved it and called a new one. When the second one proved just as stubborn as the first, the king tried to arrest the Puritan leaders. They escaped, however, and war broke out between the king and Parliament.

At first, the Royalists (Charles's forces) seemed to have the advantage. Parliament had few trained officers, and the enlisted men performed poorly in the opening battles of the war. Cromwell, who was a cavalry officer in Parliament's army, called the soldiers "old decayed serving-men." Therefore, Cromwell decided to train his own troops. Proclaiming that "a few honest men are better than numbers," he drilled his men so that they would not panic and flee in battle. In addition, Cromwell made a special effort to provide good spiritual leadership for his soldiers. Under his guidance, hymn singing and Bible reading became as much a part of military discipline as marching. Cromwell wrote proudly, "I have a lovely company . . . they are honest, sober Christians: they expect to be used as men!"

Cromwell's troops soon proved themselves in battle where their steadfastness, hardiness, and bravery earned them the name "Ironsides." At the Battle of Marston Moor (1644) a charge by

Cromwell's cavalry shattered the enemy line. "God made them as stubble to our swords," Cromwell wrote triumphantly. Parliament was so impressed with his success that the entire army adopted his training methods, and Cromwell was appointed second in command over all the Parliamentary forces.

In the year following Marston Moor, the Royalist and Parliamentary forces squared off again, this time at Naseby. At first the battle went badly for Parliament, but at the crucial point, Cromwell's cavalry regiment turned the tide and routed the enemy. Cromwell wrote afterward,

> I can say this of Naseby, that when I saw the enemy draw up and march in gallant order towards us . . . I could not . . . but smile out to God in praises, in assurance of victory, because God would, by things that are not, bring to naught things that are. Of which I had great assurance; and God did it.

Naseby spelled the end for the Royalists. Charles's armies scattered, and the king himself was captured. However, Charles, unhumbled by his defeat, plotted to overthrow the power of Parliament. Angered at the treachery of their own monarch, Cromwell and the members of Parliament tried Charles for treason, found him guilty, and beheaded him on January 30, 1649.

Parliament had won the war, but it proved unable to win the peace. With the king dead, England had to decide who would rule. Theoretically, Parliament was now the supreme governing power. In reality, however, the army became the main power. Cromwell, now commander-in-chief of the army, found himself on the horns of a dilemma. On the one hand, he had just fought in a war to protect traditional English liberties. On the other hand, Parliament was proving increasingly inept at governing the nation. Finally, in 1653 Cromwell and the army forcibly disbanded Parliament. Cromwell became the ruler of England and took the title "Lord Protector."

Cromwell was uncomfortable in his new position. His desire for legitimacy, for example, led him to recall Parliament several times. Each time, however, Parliament proved as troublesome to him as it had to Charles, and the Lord Protector dissolved it.

One of the worst trouble-spots for Cromwell was Ireland. The Irish did not like English rule, and their Catholicism made them even more resentful of the Puritan Cromwell. When Ireland rebelled, Cromwell moved with a vengeance to crush it. Early in the campaign, the English army stormed the cities of Drogheda and Wexford, killing most of the inhabitants. Cromwell defended these actions, claiming that his sternness helped save many lives by bringing an early end to the fighting. Even so, the Irish massacres are the most condemned single event of Cromwell's reign.

Cromwell's rule was not entirely bad, by any means. His unimpeachable personal honesty made him a just and fair ruler. Perhaps his greatest accomplishment was granting the freedom of religion to the English people—although King Charles II revoked this tolerant policy after Cromwell's death. He died in 1658 of complications from an illness contracted during the Irish campaign. On his deathbed Cromwell prayed,

> Lord, though I am a miserable and wretched creature, I am in covenant with Thee through grace. And I may, I will come to Thee for Thy people. Thou hast made me, though very unworthy, a mean instrument to do them some good, and Thee service; and many of them have set too high a value upon me. . . . Teach those who look too much to Thy instruments, to depend more upon Thyself.

Suggestions for Further Reading

Antonia Fraser. *Cromwell: The Lord Protector.* New York: Alfred A. Knopf, 1973.

J.H. Merle D'Aubigné. *The Protector: A Vindication.* Reprint Harrisonburg, Va.: Sprinkle Publications, 1983.

John Bunyan: Pilgrim

by Jeri Massi

Puritanism is undeniably the most influential and important movement to emerge from the English Reformation. In this biography of John Bunyan, the author calls Bunyan's Pilgrim's Progress *"a Puritan epic." In his life as well as in his literary masterpiece, Bunyan captured the essence of the Puritan spirit. The journey of Pilgrim to the Celestial City is more than a sanctified fairy tale or an interesting allegory of seventeenth-century theology. It is the embodiment of the Puritan view of man's salvation from sin. Both Bunyan's life and* Pilgrim's Progress *express the nature and depth of Puritan devotion.*

As I walked through the wilderness of this world, I lighted on a certain place where was a den, and laid me down in that place to sleep: and as I slept I dreamed a dream. I dreamed; and behold, I saw a man clothed with rags, standing in a certain place, with his face from his own house, a book in his hand, and a great burden upon his back. . . .

Thus with a few words, the Bedford tinker drew the reader from his own world and into the world of that most-loved epic of the English language. Life was a long journey, sins and vices were physical, apparent enemies. Help came from unexpected sources. And every struggle was aimed at reaching that far-off Celestial City.

Born to a peasant family in 1628, John Bunyan was mostly self-educated. Although his parents had sent him to school for a few years as a boy, the two schools around Bedford and its small neighbor, Elstow, were remarkable only for the drunkenness and negligence of their masters. Young John Bunyan probably spent most of his time avoiding the notice of his teacher and daydreaming about the bright and—to him—happy world outside the schoolroom door.

121

As a young man, he became his father's apprentice at the forge, and he seems to have preferred this work to sitting still all day. His father was a "brazier" of "whitesmith," a mender of pots and pans and other household utensils. He worked from a shed at the back of his house and also made rounds in his own village of Elstow and to nearby Bedford. Young John was to follow in his footsteps.

As a teen-age boy growing up in seventeenth-century England, John Bunyan was uninterested in the political affairs of his day. Charles I sat on the throne, a monarch unpopular with the growing Puritan party that was coming to control Parliament. Charles had flirted with Roman Catholicism—a mistake in a land preyed upon by its larger Roman Catholic neighbors, Spain and France—and resisted all attempts to limit his rule by law. He believed in the divine right of kings and did not want Parliament interfering with his plans.

Trouble and unrest stirred throughout England, and in 1641 a magnificent procession of nobles and citizens rode on horseback through the county of Bedfordshire towards London to present a petition to the Parliament. John no doubt witnessed the parade of horsemen and was probably impressed by them. But otherwise his interests were taken up in his work and in his play. By then he was a strong, likable lad, a ringleader of the youth, a jolly storyteller, a good athlete, and probably an accomplished drinker at the alehouse.

Vices he had in plenty, swearing blasphemously by God's name, cursing, lying, and playing sports on Sundays at the village green. Yet it is not to be supposed he was a heartless rogue. In 1644 a mysterious illness raced though his village, taking his mother and, one month later, his sister Margaret. John was grief-stricken at this double loss. When his father remarried only a month later, young John was hurt and angered at what he considered his father's indecent haste. War had begun between Parliament and the King, and John rashly left home to join the army. He enlisted on the side of Parliament, lying about his age in order to be accepted.

For three years John was marched to and fro, saw some action, heard much Puritan preaching, and at last returned to Elstow in 1647. Apparently, war had not made many dark impressions on his happy nature. He had matured in his service, but he was just as willing to resume his role as ringleader and athlete, without gloomy reflections on what he had seen.

In the next year he married and for the first time took a serious consideration of his life. He decided that it was time to reform his ways, and so he became—at least outwardly—religious. His wife was a devout woman, and she encouraged him to live a godly life, to pay attention to the Bible, and to listen to the Sunday service instead of sleeping through it.

The next year, 1650, John and his wife had their first child— Mary. She was born blind. Bunyan has not recorded how this affected his attitude toward God, but it is clear from his writings that he dearly loved this oldest daughter and yearned to protect her.

Not long after, as Bunyan was in Bedford making his rounds, he heard several women talk about their religion as they sat in the warm sunshine. He drew near to talk with them, but found himself out of his depth. They spoke of a new birth, of regeneration, of putting off the old man and putting on the new. Bunyan was struck with the sudden fear that he was not as good as he had thought. Several times while in Bedford he stopped to listen to these old women. He asked them so many questions that they directed him to John Gifford, their pastor.

The first great crisis of Bunyan's life had begun. Gifford helped him with the Scripture and opened to him the passages about salvation. But John Bunyan's sensitive imagination had long been under Satan's dominion. Although his heart longed to be saved, his mind and his fears battled with him. He was often confused about the way of salvation. He would read one verse of Scripture and take it hopelessly out of context until he was convinced that it spoke of his damnation rather than his salvation. He felt that God would not save him. Then he became convinced that God would have saved him but that he had committed the unpardonable sin. Finally, he simply believed that he did not really want to be saved.

The unbelievable tortures of Bunyan's inner life lasted for several years. But at last several promises from God's Word brought him through all his doubts. The text "He hath made peace by the blood of His Cross" did much to give Bunyan hope as did also "Who [Christ] of God is made unto us wisdom, and righteousness, and sanctification, and redemption." When Bunyan at last took his eyes off himself and put them on Christ and Christ's atonement, he had peace. He came to realize that he was in Christ and that God had imputed to him Christ's own righteousness, which he would always wear before God.

Over the next several years, Bunyan's life went through several changes. His first wife died. Suddenly finding himself with several children and no mother for them, he remarried—to one of the women in Gifford's congregation, Elizabeth. Probably he came to understand his own father's "indecent haste." Two years later the crumbling Protectorate ended, and Charles II came to the throne, promising liberty to tender consciences. Like so many promises that Charles II made, that one was soon broken.

Bunyan had served as preacher for the Bedford church and was appointed its pastor. Within a few months, he was arrested as an unlicensed preacher. With only a few short breaks, he spent the next twelve years in the Bedford County Jail. Even after his release in 1672, he was by no means safe. In 1675 the pressures to conform to the Church of England were renewed, and Bunyan was arrested the next year and held in prison for several months. He was released in June of 1677 and resumed his ministry as a preacher and pastor of the Bedford church until his death in 1688.

Bunyan's first imprisonment was a sore trial. He had always been a lover of the fields and forests. A great strapping man, he was more able than most to appreciate the joy of simply being alive. Puritans are often unjustly accused of being gloomy and sour, but nothing could have been further from the truth, especially about John Bunyan. Friendly, gregarious, sensitive, kind, imaginative, he was cast into black depression during much of his early imprisonment.

To help his struggling family, he made shoelaces to sell to the shopkeepers in Bedford. He also took to writing and produced many of his major works while in prison. The best known book from his first imprisonment is *Grace Abounding to the Chief of Sinners,* a narrative of his years of doubt.

Published in 1666, *Grace Abounding* captured the hearts of many readers, Puritan and non-Puritan alike. Here was a man's honest confession: his darkest moments, his brightest hopes, and at last his triumphant peace with God. Still in print, *Grace Abounding* is remarkable for its clear writings and its simple elegance. Many theologians fear that new Christians getting hold of the book might also be led into some of Bunyan's fantastic fears. Certainly, it is a book for mature Christians. Nevertheless, it has helped many a tortured soul find peace at last after continuous doubts and struggles over assurance of salvation.

During the second half of his imprisonment, Bunyan probably began notes on his most famous work, *The Pilgrim's Progress.* Historians and biographers can only guess about exactly when the work was begun, but it seems likely that *Pilgrim's Progress* was in Bunyan's mind long before it went to the publisher. After his release in 1672, John Bunyan had numerous preaching engagements and pastoral duties to attend to, and the book was likely set aside for a while.

Bunyan has often been thought of as a Baptist, but the one and only preaching license he ever obtained classified him as a Congregationalist. The Bedford Church was made up of both Baptist and Congregationalists. Bunyan would call himself nothing other than a Christian, and during his pastorate he would not allow anyone to make water baptism a bar to either church membership or admittance to the Lord's table.

During his pastorate, Bunyan may have worked more on *Pilgrim's Progress,* reading snatches of it to his wife and friends. Imprisoned the second time in 1676, he found the time to complete Part One, and it was sent to the printers shortly after his release.

Although Bunyan's other tracts and books were widely read and he was a well-known preacher, *Pilgrim's Progress* probably surprised its author in its popularlity. It went through eleven editions during his lifetime, or 100,000 copies—in short, it was what we would call a best seller.

With its emphasis on Scripture and the necessity of a holy life, *Pilgrim's Progress* is indeed a Puritan epic, and yet it transcends partisan boundaries. Bunyan's love of life shines through it, from Christian's happy friendship with Faithful and then Hopeful, to the loving home pictured at the Palace Beautiful. These and the many other delights along the road are all portrayed in images that the common Englishman could recognize and understand: quiet streams, pleasant arbors, sincere help and hospitality from kind strangers.

The dangers are also presented in terms easily understood: robbers, highwaymen, beguiling men who speak well but intend evil, cruel judges and fixed juries, and even monsters and giants. Bunyan portrayed Christian as often defeated and yet ever rising again, thus striking a chord of understanding with all Christian readers. Who has not been locked up in Doubting Castle, at least for a little while? And what Christian has never fought with Apollyon and suffered a hard fall from him? The hope of *Pilgrim's Progress,* which is ever set upon that King of the Celestial City, still speaks to readers as it urges them to look to Christ for help. And Christian, despite his many falls, even despite his fear while crossing Jordan at the very end of his journey, comes out the victor in the end.

It would seem from his writings that Bunyan almost expected to be fearful when death took him. Yet, in August of 1688, as he lay at a friend's house dying of pneumonia and fighting for breath, he seemed at peace, and his friends noted that he wanted nothing more than to go and be with Christ at last. He died in peace on August 31.

It would be impossible to evaluate all that John Bunyan accomplished by his life. His preaching touched thousands; his writing, hundreds of thousands. One of the best tributes paid him was by Robert Browning:

> His language was not ours:
>   Tis my belief, God spake;
> No tinker has such powers.

Suggestions for Further Reading

John Bunyan. *Grace Abounding to the Chief of Sinners.* (Bunyan's autobiography is available in several editions.)

Ernest R. Bacon. *Bunyan, Pilgrim and Dreamer.* Grand Rapids: Baker, 1984.

Blessed Is the Nation . . .

by Edward M. Panosian

The political history of Europe from 1500 to 1750 has often been called the era of "power politics." The Machiavellian machinations of the European rulers of that time would seem to be a topic far removed from the history of Christ's Church. "The king's heart," however, "is in the hand of the Lord" (Prov. 21:1). As the following article shows, God in His sovereignty guides the affairs of men for His own purposes, even when man thinks that he is independently pursuing his own course. Whether for blessing upon faithfulness or for judgment upon sin or for some purpose unknown to us until eternity, God directs history. As the first paragraph points out, overemphasizing the important historical concept of "multiple causation in history" can obscure the truth that God uses means to accomplish His ends. The article ultimately argues that God controls history so that nations—like individual men—reap what they sow.

The composer who paraphrased the Scripture to read "If with all your heart ye truly seek Me, ye shall ever surely find Me" may well remind us that the man who has an eye to behold the workings of God in the affairs of men and of nations need not look far for examples. What some call accident or chance or fate or circumstances in history, another sees as the hand of God—in blessing and in judgment. The charges of "over-simplification," or "failure to appreciate the principle of multiple causation in history" betray rather an ignorance of the spiritual principle that God often uses natural means to accomplish His purpose, intervening directly only when those means seem not to suffice.

An interesting—for the believer, a thrilling—case in point is the story of the power struggles in European church history from the sixteenth through the eighteenth centuries. The Protestant Reformation of the sixteenth century drew dividing lines both within and between countries of western Europe. Parts of the Germanies and of the Swiss cantons, parts of the Netherlands, some in France, and officially England and Scotland, among others, embraced the authority of Scripture, the priesthood of all believers, and the doctrine of justification by faith, principles upon which all true Protestant Christians agreed and do agree. Much of the subsequent history of these countries and others was to be written in direct relation to their responses to the religious struggles of the sixteenth century.

Spain is a wonderful illustration. Her king in the second half of the century, Philip II, could see no real difference between his throne, his country, and his Roman religion; what was good for any one of them was good, he assumed, for the other two. He sought to prosper the cause of Romanism against the Reformation, Spain against England and the Dutch, and his absolute crown against liberty for his subjects. Concerned to restore England to the Romanist fold after her partial embrace of Protestantism, Philip married Mary, the elder and Catholic daughter of Henry VIII. Any child born of this marriage would have been heir to the thrones of Spain and England, thus uniting those crowns and accomplishing all three of Philip's goals. In the providence of God, no child was born.

The Spaniard worked obliquely next, using intrigue behind the scenes to unseat the Protestant Elizabeth of England, in favor of her Stuart Catholic cousin, the deposed Mary of Scotland. When this scheme was found out and Mary was executed, Philip decided on direct invasion of the island kingdom, an approach which had not succeeded in the half-millennium since the Norman conquest. This was the ultimate effort.

The grandeur of the plan was not without foundation. Spain possessed enormous wealth, gleaned mostly from her far-flung dominions in the old world and the new. Her army was well-practiced and victorious in over a hundred battles. She was able to amass 130 ships for such an armada as she was preparing in 1558. Yet at the same time folly attended the preparations. Of the 30,000 men on the Spanish ships, three-fourths were soldiers, who were—although the best infantry in Europe—virtually useless for a long-range naval battle. The Spanish seemed to little realize that they must first fight at sea before they could march on London. The ships Spain used were mostly the old galleys, clumsy and poorly maneuverable, intended for close grappling alongside the enemy. For this reason also, the 2,500 guns aboard were small, to be used against the enemy's crews, rather than to sink his ships. And the admiral in chief had never before commanded a ship! Yet with blind zeal, the Holy Crusade went forth to sea.

But God had gone before. Although England's army and navy were unprepared, although her queen did not believe Spain would attack, although Richard Hakluyt in his prose epic on the Armada was to say that England could not without a miracle dare approach the Spanish, yet England won. Had the Canaanite Captain Sisera been a Spaniard, the song of Deborah would have been most appropriate: "the stars in their courses fought against Sisera."

The same wind which at first drove the Spanish toward England's coast kept the English ships in harbor at Plymouth, an advantage the Spanish admiral failed to press. After the English had towed their ships out to open water and sent flaming fireboats against the armada, the Spanish cut their own lines, broke their own formation, and were mercilessly tossed by gales. The English pursued, but the winds pursued more fiercely, driving many of the Spanish against the Scottish and the Irish coasts. Fewer than half of the armada's ships returned home, with hardly a third of its men.

There was no invasion of England. In nine days of guns and gales, England was saved. Spain's decline to a third-rate power, from which she has never recovered, had clearly begun. Men had aimed the guns, but God had directed the gales. As one contemporary account put it: "God blew and they were destroyed." The Dutch struck a commemorative medal of the event with the words "Man proposes; God disposes."

While it is an observation after the fact, it is no less true that the country which had vehemently and mercilessly opposed the return to the Word of God in the Protestant Reformation (how rarely does one see the word *inquisition* without the accompanying word or thought, *Spanish*) was defeated on the anvil of God. The country which had avowed the Word of God, which just thirty years earlier had received the Geneva Bible from the continent, which had affirmed the Reformation of God's Church, was preserved and protected as the source from which were to flow unnumbered blessings to mankind.

This is no idle prose. Consider another continental foe of Tudor England. France in the sixteenth century had been alternately neutral and officially opposed to the Protestant movement of the Huguenots. When, finally, a dynastic struggle closed the century in a civil war won by a nominally Protestant Henry Bourbon, that new king turned his religious coat, reaffirming Romanism, on the sophistry of having to represent the majority of his subjects (strange words in a day of growing absolute monarchy). But a sop was granted his former fellows, the Huguenots. The Edict of Nantes guaranteed religious toleration to the French Calvinists.

Almost a century later, the absolute grand monarch, Louis XIV, revoked the edict in his singular insistence on national conformity to the king's will. So what had been half-hearted toleration of the children of the Reformation matured into a whole-hearted rejection. The only alternatives for the non-Romanist were renunciation or exile, and exile was the reluctant choice for the many. Many historians have said in many similar ways that the exiled Huguenots enriched the countries to which they fled to the same degree that they impoverished the France from which they had come.

This enrichment was far more than economic, although it was economic as well. They had represented a middle class of social and economic life, the class which traditionally seems to cushion the burden of contrast between the privileged and the poor. They were the productive, capitalistic craftsmen and merchants, largely, whose removal left little to bridge between the clerical-noble parasites and the impoverished peasants. They were those who were less easily "tossed to and fro with every wind of doctrine," solid, critical thinkers and forceful, convicted doers. They represented a disciplined, serious, industrious people, self-reliant, but in subjection to God.

When this kind of people, these Huguenots, were forced into exile, that middle class of French society was weakened seriously; the political stability represented by the middle class proved fragile, with only the oppressed many at bottom and the privileged few at the top. This was the situation on the eve of that bloody revolution across the channel from England in 1789. France was to suffer the harvest of philosophic rationalism, naturalism, deism, and practical humanism. She had rejected the reform; she was ripe for the revolt.

And what of England? The seventeenth century, after the Armada, saw there the growth of much of the same "Enlightenment" philosophy, which continued in the eighteenth. But there was a real difference. The crown (except for the later Stuarts) and the state church remained nominally Protestant. The tenor of both Parliament and the populace was compromising and conciliatory. Baptists, Puritans, Separatists of many types had a moderating effect. The growth of Stuart absolutism was checked in a Glorious Revolution and a Bill of Rights in 1689. And in the midst of religious, moral, and political corruption in the eighteenth century, God sent England a revival of true heart response to the presentation of the gospel in word and hymn by John and Charles Wesley. England buried John Wesley in 1791, a nation having been blessed by his ministry since the 1740s and 1750s, while France was preparing to enthrone an actress as the "goddess of reason" in the Cathedral of Notre Dame. More than one historian has suggested that England was saved from the excesses of the Enlightenment by the Methodist revival. Again God had intervened, and again God had used men.

These remarks should suggest neither an Anglophile viewpoint nor an equating of Protestant Christianity with all things good and righteous. There is historically sufficient reason to challenge both positions. Yet over the long view, as results and consequences have been viewed in the perspective of time, those nations which have acknowledged God and His Word, however imperfectly, have been recipients of God's singular blessings and the source of blessings to others. Nor is past blessing for obedience an immunity from future judgment for disobedience. It is a sobering truth that countries once having enjoyed God's remarkable providence—England clearly among them—have seen reversal and declension as they turned from Him in their private and public life.

It is difficult to escape the observation that nineteenth-century England became, with America, the nursery of modern Christian missions to the heathen world. Particularly to Africa and Asia sailed a new kind of armada carrying another kind of soldier, soldiers of the cross of Jesus Christ to invade the kingdoms of spiritual darkness and despair. And they succeeded in doing exploits for God with eternal consequence. In contrast things temporal and transient engaged the French. An attitude of skepticism and excess, concern for style and form, preoccupation with feeling and things frivolous, political instability and radicalism—these were French concerns, the *avant-garde* of the modern.

So nations no less than men reap according to their sowing, both today and tomorrow. And if there are any lessons to be learned from a review of history (and that man is doubly blind who will not see even their outlines), this is surely one: God's revelation teaches that the nation is blessed whose God is the Lord, who acknowledges dependence upon Him and affirms His Word; human history teaches its converse—that nation is judged, is punished, immediately or ultimately or both, whose god the Lord of Scriptures is not, who lends ear to the counsels of prideful men, and who depends on the sufficiency of human wisdom and might.

Suggestions for Further Reading

Garrett Mattingly. *The Armada.* Boston: Houghton Mifflin, 1959. (An award-winning history of the Armada campaign.)

G.A. Rothrock. *The Huguenots: A Biography of a Minority.* Chicago: Nelson-Hall, 1979.

For sources on John Wesley, see page 144.

Johann Sebastian Bach:
A Life of Faith in Music

by Stewart Custer

Johann Sebastian Bach was perhaps the greatest composer in history and certainly one of the greatest of the Baroque era. He lived through the transition from the Age of Reformation to the Age of Reason and in some ways embodied that transition. His music is rich in the disciplined emotion of worship and reaches to glorious heights in the praise of God. Bach also represents the ideal of the Christian artist. Instead of being a great musician who just happened to be a Christian, Bach was a Christian who expressed his faith through and brought his faith to bear on every aspect of work.

The apostle Paul commends the Thessalonian believers for their "work of faith," and that particular phrase characterizes the ministry of Johann Sebastian Bach. His was a work of faith. For many musicians, faith is a facade to be worn for special occasions, but Bach had an "unfeigned faith" that governed his whole life.

The Bach family were devout Lutherans. Bach's great-great-grandfather first came to Eisenach from Hungary, where, as a Lutheran, he had experienced persecution by the Roman Catholics. The Bach family multiplied in Eisenach, generation after generation of skilled musicians, and faithful they were to their faith.

Faith is a gift of God, a token of God's grace. We see God's providential grace in Bach's life even in the death of his parents. When he was nine, he lost his mother. When he was ten, he lost his father. Thus, very early in life he became acquainted with death. His father having been the town musician, he probably would have reared his son in a secular music profession, but instead Bach had to live with an older brother who "happened" to be a church organist. Young Bach learned the organ and studied at school with a godly teacher, from whom he learned what real service for God could be. This young teacher taught Bach both his Bible and his music, and he stirred within Bach the desire to do something in the sanctuary. From his childhood he was devoted to the service of God.

All of Bach's music was written to the glory of God. His music touches the hearts of all who can understand music. Pop musicians, serious musicians, and the laity—all appreciate at least some of Bach's music. The professionals, of course, realize what Bach accomplished. He reached a capstone of music by his work. He was the end of an age, unappreciated by his time—people thought he was out of date. Nowadays, the most modern musician recognizes that Bach is still ahead of us, and there is always more that we can learn from him.

In a sense Bach brought to consummation all the past ages of music and became the fountainhead of all modern music. His achievement is deeply rooted in his faith in God. It has been said that the person who is of faith has an advantage over the unbeliever, even where the gifts are identical, and for Bach, the gifts were certainly unusual. By the age of twenty-three he was reputed to be the greatest organist the world had ever seen. He went on to become unquestionably the greatest composer of organ music that the world has ever seen. And in the hearts of many he remains the greatest musician the world has ever seen. In his own field of church music he has no rivals.

A peerless musician, Bach was also an outstanding Christian. He studied the Bible. He learned Luther's shorter catechism and became a devout, orthodox Lutheran. His worst enemies had to admit that all his life he was an absolutely orthodox believer, a serene, devout, untroubled Christian. And during his life he faced some rather bitter occasions.

Following the death of his wife, he inscribed into his son's music book this chorale of an old Lutheran hymn: "If you but suffer God to guide you and hope in Him through all your ways He'll give you strength whate'er betide you and bear you through the evil days. Trust God and His all-loving hand and build your faith on more than sand."

Bach also had the difficult task of burying ten of his children. He lived seemingly in the midst of death, living as he did in the shadow of the plagues of the Thirty Years' War. Never once did his faith waver. In the face of all sadness and tragedy, his faith was absolutely serene. And one of the little poems he wrote was dedicated to those who sleep in the Lord: "Oh child of man, you die not death, though bone and blood themselves lack breath. You know that your Redeemer lives who wakes you and salvation gives. Lord Jesus Christ, thy word is sure, but make my faith in thee secure. Thine is the kingdom, thine the power, and thine the glory evermore."

Bach's faith was manifested in his music. As he composed, he would inscribe the letters *SDG—soli Deo gloria,* "to God alone the glory"—at the end of the piece. At the beginning of his pieces he often wrote the letters *INJ—in nomine Jesu,* "in the name of Jesus." And on the margins of difficult passages—where he found the harmonization taxing—Bach wrote the letters *JJ,* standing for *Jesu juva* —"Jesus, help me."

When Bach died, his library consisted of eighty-three volumes, every one of them a book on theology. He had Luther's works, Luther's commentary on the Psalms, and a famous work by Stinger on the foundations of the Augsburg Confession. He had a devotional work by Rambach of reflections on the tears of Jesus. He had Spinner's famous book against Roman Catholicism, *Zeal Against Popery.* His life was devoted to music, but above all, it was devoted to his faith. Bach was not a great musician who happened to be a Christian. Bach was instead a devout, born-again Christian living to the glory of God and who also happened to be the world's greatest musician.

Bach taught his students how, in music, to interpret the words of the hymns through the melody. The music was not the most important thing—the message was, and the melody had to teach the message. Bach accomplished this blending of message and music with tremendous insight in the *St. Matthew Passion,* for example. Every time the voice of the Lord Jesus occurs in the *St. Matthew Passion,* it is surrounded by a halo of stringed instruments which provides accompaniment. All through the piece this feature is striking every time the Lord's voice occurs but one—upon the cross when He cries, "My God, my God, why hast thou forsaken me?" The halo is gone. Bach knew exactly how to underscore the drama, the pathos, and the power of the passage he was setting to music.

Bach's theology carried over naturally into his teaching. Bach intended to glorify God in the simplest of musical offerings. He wrote a little organ book to teach others how to play the organ. In the dedication he wrote, "To honor God, the most high, and to train my neighbor too thereby."

Bach was a very humble man. Considering his gifts, it would have been easy to act arrogant and proud, but this he did not do. On one occasion when he played with his usual skill, someone came up to gush over the superb musicianship that he had just manifested. Bach replied humbly that it was nothing; all you had to do was hit the right notes at the right moment and the instrument did all the rest. Any piano and organ student will appreciate that!

Bach's was a life of faith in the face of hardship, of sacrifice, and of bereavement. When he came to his deathbed, his sight had failed him. The doctor had performed operations upon his eyes, hoping to restore the sight. The operations had failed. And now Bach, racked with pain from the failed operations, knew he was at the end of his life. There, too, he had an unerring sense of what was appropriate in music, and as he lay on his deathbed, he dictated to his son-in-law arrangements of the old chorales. One of the last ones that he dictated was this: "Before Thy throne, my God, I stand. All that I am is in Thy hand. Turn to me now Thy approving face, nor from me now withhold Thy grace."

By God's grace, Bach lives a saint, one of the spirits of just men made perfect in the presence of God, the God he served and glorified. Bach's life was a work of faith; his music is an enduring monument; his destiny is before the throne of God. The Master he served no doubt has said, "Well done."

Suggestions for Further Reading

Jan Chiapusso. *Bach's World.* Bloomington: Indiana Univ. Press, 1968.

Russell H. Miles. *Johann Sebastian Bach, An Introduction to His Life and Works.* Englewood Cliffs, N.J.: Prentice-Hall, 1962.

Werner Neumann. *Bach, A Pictorial Biography.* New York: Viking Press, 1961.

Christian Men of Science

by George Mulfinger, Jr.

Because many scientists promote un-Scriptural ideas, some Christians mistakenly believe that all scientists must be atheists— or at least that all "great" scientists must be. To these believers, the "Age of Reason" as it applies to the sciences appears to be little more than the "Age of Infidelity." As the following article demonstrates, however, some men found no difficulty in combining the advances in man's knowledge with a genuine faith in God and His Word. The lives of Johannes Kepler and Robert Boyle prove that a great man of science can also be a great man of faith.

When you hear the word *scientist* what picture immediately comes to mind? Do you visualize a man in a white coat surrounded by test tubes and white mice, trying to prove an evolutionary principle through the discovery of a new biochemical formula? Or maybe you envisage an archaeologist digging for fossil remains to support his hypothesis that the world is billions of years old. At any rate, the picture is seldom one of a dedicated Christian devoting his scientific efforts to the glory of God.

It may surprise you then to learn that many outstanding scientists you have read or heard about were also outstanding Christians. These were men who recognized the supremacy of a personal God in all things and were determined to give Him the glory He is due. They were aware of the limitations of science and consistently interpreted their experimental results in the light of Biblical philosophy.

Johannes Kepler

The first man to demonstrate that the motions of the planets are precise and predicatable, obeying definite rules, was Johannes Kepler (1571-1630). The German astronomer's three famous laws of planetary motion are used extensively today in calculating the orbits of satellites and in mapping routes for space travel. Kepler is also called "the father of modern optics" because of his masterful mathematical analysis of lenses and mirrors.

Kepler was a devout Lutheran who trusted Christ as his Saviour at an early age. Although he was persecuted for his Protestant beliefs, he remained true to the Lord throughout his entire life. Kepler saw himself as an instrument in God's hands for revealing more of the details of His handiwork to men. "Since we astronomers are priests of the highest God in regard to the book of nature," he once wrote, "it befits us to be thoughtful not of the glory of our minds, but rather, above all else, of the glory of God." A devoted family man who sought to give his children a thoroughly Christian upbringing, he wrote Bible study guides to aid their understanding of the Scriptures.

Although Kepler felt certain that he was destined for the Lutheran ministry, an unexpected opportunity arose in 1594 before he was able to complete his final examination at the Theological Faculty of the University of Tübingen. There was an immediate need for a mathematics and astronomy teacher at the Protestant seminary in Graz, and Kepler was recommended because of his extraordinary mathematical ability. After considerable thought and prayer, he finally became convinced that it was the Lord's will for him to accept the position.

Kepler's years at Graz were both challenging and rewarding. It was here that he produced his first serious scientific treatise, *The Mystery of the Universe,* an ambitious geometric description of the solar system. The work closed with a magnificent hymn of praise to the Creator. The treatise was well received, and, as a result of his shrewdness in placing it in the hands of several leading astronomers (including Galileo and Tycho Brahe), Kepler's name became known in the important scientific centers of Europe.

As a result of severe religious persecution, Kepler and his family were forced to flee from Graz in 1600. He joined the staff of Tycho Brahe, imperial mathematician to Rudolph II, emperor of Bohemia, in Prague. Kepler's task was to interpret the massive columns of remarkably accurate data Tycho had assembled during his twenty-year observation of the positions of the planets. Kepler appreciated the unique opportunity that had been afforded him; it was indeed providential that circumstances had brought together these two giants whose abilities complemented each other so perfectly.

Kepler's name has been immortalized by his three famous laws formulated while on Tycho's staff. A prominent crater on the moon has been named for him; monuments and museums have been erected in his honor in his native Germany. Any fame he achieved, however, was simply a by-product of his lifelong endeavor to glorify the name of the heavenly Father. "Let also my name perish," Kepler stated, "if only the name of God the Father . . . is thereby elevated."

Robert Boyle

Although we usually associate the name of Robert Boyle (1627-1691) with Boyle's law, an important concept in physics, this Irishman's major work was in the field of chemistry. Labeled by many scientific historians "the father of chemistry," Boyle guided the great transition from alchemy to true chemistry. Before his time, men spoke of "elixirs" and "essences"; after his work had made its impact on the scientific world, they spoke in terms of "elements" and "compounds." As a result of his contribution, the chemists of the eighteenth century were able to launch out in new directions, unhindered by the errors of previous generations.

Boyle studied the Scriptures in their original languages and was intimately familiar with all of the important theological writings of his day. Having been converted in his early teens, he dedicated his scientific endeavors to be a witness to God's creation and control of the universe. Writing on a variety of scientific and religious subjects, Boyle became a powerful force for reproving evil and combating heresy. His influence was felt even after his death. In his will he provided funds for the "Boyle Lectures"—a series of eight sermons to be delivered each year to demonstrate that Christianity is, in fact, intellectually defensible and far more reasonable than the various philosophies that seek to discredit it.

Boyle was strictly orthodox in his Christian beliefs. He did his utmost to defend and uphold the great doctrines of Scripture in both word and deed. He was intolerant of preachers who spiritualized or allegorized important truths of the Bible rather than accepting them at face value.

Throughout his life Boyle read the Bible each morning, in spite of illness, eye trouble, and other adverse circumstances. As a result of his faithfulness and his clear-cut testimony before his fellow men, he was repeatedly offered the highest positions in the Anglican church. Each time he refused, stating that a layman's testimony for the Christian faith could have even more impact than that of a clergyman.

During the later years Boyle became intensely interested in world-wide evangelism. A man of considerable means, he supported missionary endeavors in Ireland, Scotland, Wales, India, and North

America. In addition, he commissioned translations of the four Gospels and the book of Acts into Turkish, Arabic, and Malayan. He financed a new Irish translation of the entire Bible, and thousands of these Bibles were distributed throughout the British Isles at Boyle's expense.

Conclusion

The list of eminent scientists who dedicated their lives entirely to the Lord goes on and on; yet these two men illustrate the power of God as it can be manifested in lives totally surrendered to His will. These were men who were ever ready to bear testimony of the hope that was within them. Although some of their scientific associates smiled scornfully at their beliefs, none of them could charge that their faith in Christ was the product of an inferior intellect.

Suggestions for Further Reading

Henry M. Morris. *Men of Science, Men of God.* San Diego: Creation-Life Publishers, 1982. (Short biographies of religious scientists; interesting, but "men of God" seems too broadly defined.)

John Hudson Tiner. *Johannes Kepler: Giant of Faith and Science.* Milford, Mich.: Mott Media, 1977. (A young people's biography.)

John Wesley: In Pursuit of Souls

by Edward M. Panosian

No figure dominates the history of eighteenth-century Christianity more than John Wesley. Jonathan Edwards was probably a greater theologian, and George Whitefield was perhaps a greater preacher, but neither affected his time or his posterity as much as Wesley did. His life is best explained as the story of a man gripped with the idea of salvation. After searching for and finding the message of salvation for his own soul, Wesley could not restrain himself from sharing salvation with others.

"He acts as though he were out of breath in the pursuit of souls." These words, perhaps more than any others, describe the man whose indelible impress upon eighteenth-century England has become almost legendary.

John Wesley's life (1703-1791) touched every decade of his century, and his work reflected every area of his country's needs. Concerned for the social, moral, economic, political, and physical problems of his land, he was primarily "in pursuit of souls." He was "the man on horseback," coming to woo eternal souls with the power of the gospel of Jesus Christ.

Preacher, popular theologian, author, organizer, he wore many hats and won many crowns. But those who in his day wore earthly crowns were not more effective in shaping the lives of their nations than Wesley was in shaping his.

From Works to Faith

His life follows a pattern often repeated in the lives of serious and sincere men in the past and in present. Wesley was reared strictly and well in a godly Anglican minister's home in a family which had known nineteen births (eight of whom became infant deaths). Spared marvelously at the age of five when his father's parsonage burned, accustomed by his mother to a rigid personal habit of life, an able student, and an avid reader, swimmer, and rider, he became a priest of the Church of England and a fellow at Oxford University. John Wesley was active and industrious in doing good works, especially with the "Holy Club" at Oxford, which eventually became the foundation of those who were at first dubbed—and later more honorably described—Methodist. Wesley later said of this period: "Doing so much, and living so good a life, I doubted not but I was a good Christian."

In keeping with his eager righteousness-by-works he went with his brother Charles as a missionary to the new American colony of Georgia, under the Society for the Propagation of the Gospel in Foreign Parts. He accomplished little, was frustrated by an unwise affair of heart, and was troubled that his profession of faith had not given him the peace and tranquillity of soul which he had observed in some Moravians he had met. After two years Wesley returned to England.

That contact with the Moravians was the instrument which brought him to peace. Much like Luther, Wesley had tried with "works" to achieve salvation. He had returned from America with the heart's cry, "I went to Georgia to convert the Indians, but oh! who shall convert me?" He received the answer on the 24th of May, 1738, when he attended a meeting of a Moravian Society on Aldersgate in London. John Wesley's lengthy entry—a veritable spiritual autobiography—in his journal for that day concludes with a simple eloquence born of the peace which came to his much-troubled soul:

> In the evening I went very unwillingly to a society in Aldersgate Street, where one was reading Luther's preface to the Epistle to the Romans. About a quarter before nine, while he was describing the change which God works in the heart through faith in Christ, I felt my heart strangely warmed. I felt I did trust in Christ, Christ alone for salvation; and an assurance was given me that He had taken away my sins, even mine, and saved me from the law of sin and death.

The World for His Parish

This assurance was the starting point of Wesley's service to the Lord—an energetic service that continued for more than a half century. He had labored—although impotent of spiritual good— to be saved; now he labored—empowered by the Spirit of God— because he *was* saved. It is estimated that during that half century, he preached about forty thousand sermons and traveled well over two hundred thousand miles, usually on horseback. He averaged nearly five thousand miles a year and fifteen sermons a week. Wesley's fervent and enthusiastic preaching was strangely foreign to the Church of England, of which he was an ordained priest. When the parishes of that cold, formal, liturgical church became closed to the intensely personal, direct, evangelistic, awakening preaching of this diminutive giant, he preached wherever there were people. Wesley declared that the whole world was his parish.

The influence of the field-preaching of his contemporary, George Whitefield, and his burning concern to reach dying souls overcame his native reticence and his reluctance toward "abandoning good order." Whitefield, a fellow member with John of the Holy Club during their Oxford years, was seeing remarkable success preaching to the outcast miners around Bristol—men to whom no one had attempted to proclaim the gospel. Tears flowed down coal-blackened cheeks as hard hearts melted at the hearing of the saving truth and as the blood of Jesus Christ flowed to cover their sins.

The resulting converts—in England, Scotland, Ireland, and Wales—were gathered in "societies" for association. Later the societies were divided into "bands" and those into "classes." The lay leaders of these groups were later, though reluctantly, given permission by Wesley to preach and exhort in the classes. These societies were intended only to be fellowships within the Church of England; it was never Wesley's design to establish anything like a new denomination, a movement he strongly resisted throughout his life. In time, however, the organization grew on both sides of the Atlantic, and Wesley ordained presbyters and other ministers who administered the sacraments. What had begun within the Anglican church, never intending to revolt from it, but expelled by it, became a practically independent body. So it could be said with truth that Wesley died, "leaving behind him nothing but a good library of books, a well-worn clergyman's gown, a much-abused reputation, and the Methodist church."

The Transformation of England

It is difficult to estimate properly the role God used John Wesley to play in eighteenth-century England. His brother Charles, possessed of complementary gifts, left hundreds of hymns firmly impressed upon the hearts and lips of modern Protestants. Of these, perhaps the most widely known are "O for a Thousand Tongues to Sing," "Jesus, Lover of My Soul," "Christ the Lord Is Risen Today," "Love Divine, All Loves Excelling," and the Christmas evangel "Hark, the Herald Angels Sing."

No less significant was the transformation of England—the result of the evangelical revival from the work of Whitefield and the Wesleys. Many have written of the low state of morality and virtue in the island on the eve of the century. Christianity seemed to be waning. Watts said that "religion was dying in the world." Moral, social, and political evils were rampant. Drunkenness, gambling, highway robbery, brutal amusements, slave trading, and gross profanity of speech were common. Ignorant and inert clergy offered little offense against such evils and themselves participated in them. Bishop Butler remarked that it had "come to be taken for granted that Christianity is not so much as a subject of inquiry; but that it is now at length discovered to be fictitious."

Across the English Channel, rationalistic infidelity was infiltrating the lands of the Reformation, and France was being prepared for the bloody consequences of the worship of reason. France had no Wesley; England had nothing like the French Revolution. Under the influence of Methodist preaching, personal and practical piety produced a lessening of crime and a reformation of morals. The prison reforms of John Howard, the antislavery campaign of William Wilberforce, the Sunday school movement of layman Robert Raikes, the growth of the modern missionary movement by the end of the century, the advance of access to education, the introduction of more humane conditions of labor—all of these are among the early blessings that followed "the foolishness of preaching." The *heavenly* trophies of grace, the rebirth of souls, are beyond number.

A little incident, often retold, illustrates just one aspect of this picture of England after Wesley: Hot, tired, thirsty, impatient, the English nobleman asked a peasant: "Why is it that I can't find a place where I can buy a drink of liquor in this wretched village?" The humble peasant respectfully replied: "Well, you see, my lord, about a hundred years ago a man named John Wesley came preaching in these parts."

An Unashamed Testimony

John Wesley possessed a quaintness which reflected his humanity. He wrote much, never seeking a polished style, but emphasizing clarity and conciseness. He even wrote a book on home medicine for his people, and he used much of his income to publish inexpensive editions of good books for them, believing in the value of wide reading.

He married in his late forties but was unfortunate in his choice. The Wesley home of happiest memory was that of his parents, Samuel and Susanna, not that of which John was head. He seems to have been unimaginative concerning the nature of children, recommending soul examination at four in the morning and little play. But even though the doctrinal emphases peculiar to his movement have not been universally acceptable to believing Christians, he still left an unashamed testimony of the grace of God and a heritage born of an unqualified embrace of two fundamental and timeless truths:

> *I the chief of sinners am,*
> *But Jesus died for me.*

Suggestions for Further Reading

John Wesley. *Journals.* (Although Wesley's *Journals* run several volumes, several fine abridgments are available. The *Journals* are the best source on Wesley's life.)

Robert W. Burtner and Robert E. Chiles, eds. *John Wesley's Theology.* Nashville: Abingdon, 1982. (Selections from Wesley's writings that illustrate his theology.)

J.C. Ryle. *Christian Leaders of the 18th Century.* 1885; reprint Edinburgh: Banner of Truth Trust, 1978. (Pages 64-105.)

A. Skevington Wood. *The Burning Heart: John Wesley, Evangelist.* Grand Rapids: Eerdmans, 1967.

George Whitefield: The Awakener

by Edward M. Panosian

"I love those that thunder out the Word," said George Whitefield. "The Christian World is in a dead sleep. Nothing but a loud voice can awaken them out of it." Whitefield was almost certainly the greatest evangelist of the eighteenth century. He preached throughout the British Isles and the British colonies in North America. Although Whitefield's reputation has been overshadowed by Wesley's, his contribution to the revivals of the eighteenth century is almost as great.

He was an evangelist, a "chaplain" of ships crossing the Atlantic, a compassionate friend of orphans and founder of orphanages and schools, a fund raiser for their support, an exhorter of the clergy to godliness, and more. But he is remembered first as a remarkable preacher of the grace of God. George Whitefield was an "awakening preacher," awakening sleeping sinners to their eternal need and alerting slumbering saints to their divine responsibility.

The life of this English evangelist is singularly instructive to Christians. He reflected true Christian graces while enduring the great trials of the faithful believer. He knew both struggles and success, frustration and fruitfulness, weariness and wonderful joy in the gospel ministry. His mission and his motives were often misunderstood, but the results which accompanied his message were evidences of divine anointing—conviction, conversions, and opposition.

Born in an Inn

His contemporary, John Wesley, was born and reared in a minister's home; George Whitefield was born in his parent's tavern, the Bell Inn of Gloucester, England, in December 1714. Although he had ample opportunity to witness the ways of the world in his early years, he seems to have been spared its worst consequences.

The youth showed an interest in words and drama, reciting plays frequently during his grammar school days. He knew the drudgery of menial labor, working in and about the tavern (which in the eighteenth century combined the hotel, the restaurant, and the "club" or "bar" of today). He learned the quality of personal industry which was later to keep him busy preaching an *average* of almost twice a day, *every* day, for thirty years.

At Oxford University Whitefield worked hard, waiting on tables and studying with diligence. But he was also seeking heart peace. The little "Holy Club" of Methodists with its regimen of humanitarian works attracted him. But the student found that good works, while noble in purpose, did not meet his real need. Whitefield then attempted self-denial, hoping to conquer his flesh and become worthy of God's release from his sin and guilt. He abandoned his friends and spent long periods in mystic meditation. During six weeks of 1735, Whitefield denied himself any food but coarse bread and tea and so weakened his body that he required the service of a physician. Still, he found no soul comfort.

After this experience, Whitefield realized that the way of the gospel is not by striving. Now came true conversion. Exhausted with his own ways, at the end of all his human resources, the twenty-year-old threw himself on his bed crying, "I thirst! I thirst!" Submitting to God's saving grace, he found deliverance "from the burden that had so heavily oppressed me."

In his *Journals,* Whitefield wrote about his conversion: "O! with what joy . . . that was full of and big with glory, was my soul filled, when the weight of sin went off, and an abiding sense of the pardoning love of God, and a full assurance of faith, broke in upon my disconsolate soul! Surely it was . . . a day to be had in everlasting remembrance. . . . My joys were like a spring tide, and overflowed the banks!"

The Field Preacher

The bishop who ordained Whitefield at the age of twenty-one as a deacon in the Church of England had previously asserted he would ordain none so young. But this young man was clearly ready. He possessed a noticeable variety of gifts—he had known the meaning of the world and sin, he was accustomed to hard work, he had an eagerness to learn, he attracted children, his imagination was fertile, and his speech was compelling. A squint in one eye added a commanding seriousness to the lithe youth's presence. And he had experienced salvation by grace through faith. Now called of God to preach, he responded with vigor.

His preaching was against sin and for Jesus Christ. He invited men, women, and children to be born again. He exhorted clergy of the Church of England to more pious living. His preaching was his very life; in later years when bothered by heart disease, undiagnosed in those days, he was confident that a "good preaching sweat" was his best remedy.

Whitefield soon became known as a strong, vibrant preacher who stirred up his listeners. People of all ranks in life came to hear this man of God, even as he denounced their sins, for he invited them to the Saviour. Many who came to scoff remained to pray. The preaching of the Word of God turned hecklers into converts and detractors into supporters. But the parish ministers of England, jealous of their "territorial rights" over the villages and countryside which provided their congregations, began to close their church doors to the awakening preacher. So George Whitefield turned from the parish churches to "field preaching." He preached from nearly every kind of pulpit which nature and human ingenuity provided: foundries, mounds, tables, wagons, balconies, boats, wherever his body could be elevated so his voice could be heard.

That voice has been occasion for considerable wonder in the two centuries since it was last heard on earth. When preaching out of doors—which had become for him more the rule than the exception—Whitefield would position himself so that his voice could be carried downwind to reach the greatest number of hearers. That number was often recorded as more than twenty-thousand in the journals of eyewitnesses. They testify also that Whitefield's voice could be heard more than a mile away.

But far more important than his voice's volume and clarity was its moving power. Surely this was the empowering of the Holy Spirit of God moving upon the human instrument. That instrument was beautifully tuned to communicate compelling truth. Whitefield was able to accommodate the flavor and application of his message to the immediate circumstance. He would turn a heckler into an illustration. He would turn a thunderstorm into a vivid picture of the judgment of God. He was able to illustrate his text from life and from experience, both his and his hearers'.

Luke Tyerman, an outstanding biographer of George Whitefield, described the awakening preacher: "Half a dozen men like Whitefield would at any time move a nation, stir its churches, and reform its morals. Whitefield's power was not in his talents, nor even in his oratory, but in his piety. . . . Such men are the gift of God, and are infinitely more valuable than all the gold in the church's coffers."

Across the Atlantic

George Whitefield's preaching ministry took him across the Atlantic for the first time in 1737-1738 as a missionary to the newly established colony of Georgia. John and Charles Wesley had been laboring there, although themselves yet unconverted, to win the heathen, but had returned in defeat. Whitefield preached throughout the area, finding a ready hearing. When he saw the prospect for the orphanage planned by James Oglethorpe, the colony's founder, Whitefield returned to England to raise funds for the project. The orphanage ministry and the schools in connection prospered as a blessing to many. He raised thousands of dollars for their support, never personally profiting financially, but building up such treasure in heaven that it is certain he enjoyed an abundant entrance to that place for which he helped fit so many.

There were seven "missionary journeys" to America in Whitefield's ministry. Each crossing was long and severe, often aggravated by storms or delayed by calms. But each preaching mission in America gave the Awakener notable opportunities. In 1740, in Philadelphia, which then had a population of twelve thousand, one Sunday evening congregation on Society Hill was estimated at fifteen thousand. Then he traveled to New York, preaching at towns along the way. At Neshaminy, Pennsylvania, five thousand heard him; in New Brunswick, New Jersey, "near seven or eight thousand." After similar meetings in New York, he returned to Philadelphia where his farewell service in the City of Brotherly Love was estimated at nearly twenty thousand, perhaps the largest gathering in America to date.

Charleston, South Carolina, also heard him in great numbers that summer before his return to Savannah, Georgia, and the orphanage. That fall, New England received Whitefield. Four days he preached in Rhode Island before coming to Boston, enjoying much spiritual fruit in both places and in the smaller towns farther to the north.

Whitefield then met Jonathan Edwards in Northampton, Massachusetts, an occasion of great joy for both men. In Middletown, Connecticut, he preached to "about four thousand people." He then preached from New England to Georgia, carrying the Awakening revival up and down the colonies, preaching to literally thousands as he moved along. The Great Awakening of 1740 was only a sample of the ministry Whitefield enjoyed in America.

These revivals and Whitefield's constant zeal to proclaim the message always and everywhere drained his bodily energy. In 1770 he preached his last sermon from the stairs of a parsonage in

Newburyport, Massachusetts. He was still staying in the parsonage when at six o'clock on a September Sunday morning he awakened in heaven.

A Lesson in Balance

There is an interesting postscript to the life of George Whitefield that teaches a lesson of spiritual balance among the people of God.

Today we commonly hear the name of Whitefield with that of John Wesley—contemporaries, sometimes co-laborers, sometimes contenders for opposite doctrinal truths, but always mutually respectful of God's respective gifts. Their relationship is an instruction to us. Their largeness of soul taught John Wesley and George Whitefield a toleration of different viewpoints when no disobedience to the clear Word of Scripture was concerned. They learned to subordinate their differences to the performance of their callings without compromise of the truth.

John Wesley and George Whitefield, often with an ocean between them, each believed in different aspects of the "mystery of the ages," divine sovereignty and human responsibility. While both are true, if irreconcilable by finite reason, undue emphasis on either has always divided good men.

In emphasizing man's responsibility, Wesley decided that a man who believes that God foreknows those whom He calls must also believe that it is useless to preach the gospel to all. Whitefield's reply was that since we do not know who are the elect, we are to preach to all. And Whitefield, who believed in election but preached to all, wrongly understood that when Wesley said all men may be saved he meant all *would* be saved. So Whitefield charged Wesley with universalism, and Wesley charged Whitefield with teaching the arbitrary damnation of souls. Each accused the other of the logical conclusion of his position, yet neither actually held those extremes.

Although the relationship between the two men was thus strained, their love and respect for each other was never quenched. It was John Wesley, who was to outlive Whitefield by twenty-one years, who gave him the most generous tribute as he gently chided his friend who asked, "Do you think we shall see Mr. Whitefield in Heaven?" Wesley replied, "No, sir, I fear not. Mr. Whitefield will be so near the Throne and we at such a distance we shall hardly get sight of him."

Suggestions for Further Reading

Arnold Dallimore. *George Whitefield.* 2 vols. Edinburgh: Banner of Truth Trust, 1970, 1980.

"A Wretch Like Me":
The Story of John Newton

by Rebecca Lunceford Foster

The story of John Newton, the author of "Amazing Grace," is indeed a testimony to the power of God's grace. Newton typified the startling conversions that characterized the Evangelical Awakening in England, and it is no surprise that he became one of the leaders of the Evangelical Party within the Church of England. His hymns, that for which we best remember him today, are the expression of that revivalistic piety as much as Bunyan's Pilgrim's Progress *is the expression of Puritanism.*

"I was a wild beast on the coast of Africa; but the Lord caught me and tamed me," wrote John Newton of his dramatic conversion. Indeed, storms at sea, slavery, and romance sound more like the ingredients of an exciting jungle adventure than of training for the ministry, but the life of one of England's great preachers and hymn writers illustrates the truth of the hymn, "God moves in mysterious ways, His wonders to perform."

Young John Newton's early life gave no hint of the wild years that were to follow. In his autobiography, *An Authentic Narrative,* Newton wrote, "The tender mercies of God towards me were manifest in the first moment of my life; I was born as it were in His house and dedicated to Him in my infancy." From his birth in 1725, John's mother, a dedicated Christian, had great hopes for her son's future. She began his education very early, and even—as young mothers often do—discussed her hopes for his marriage. Her dearest friend, Mrs. George Catlett, had a daughter four years younger than John. The two women planned that their children would grow up and delight their mothers by marrying each other. But more important even than John's marriage was his call. Mrs. Newton planned and prayed that her son would enter the ministry.

Mrs. Newton was not to see the results of her planning, and John was deprived of the influence of a godly mother, for she died just before his seventh birthday. John's father, a sea captain, soon remarried, but neither he nor his new wife was concerned with spiritual things—or with John.

The boy went to a boarding school where he forgot most of what he had already learned. It was when he was eleven that he traded in his books for adventure, going to sea with his father.

Troublesome Sailor

In the eighteenth century, the life of a sailor—even under a father's watchful eye—was not designed to train a teen-age boy in the things of the Lord. Newton recalled later,

> In this period my temper and conduct were exceedingly various.
> . . . I took up and laid aside a religious profession three or
> four different times before I was sixteen years of age; but all
> this while my heart was insincere. I often saw the necessity
> of religion, as a means of escaping hell, but I loved sin, and
> was unwilling to forsake it.

To add further confusion to John's spiritual ideas, he discovered the writings of Lord Shaftesbury, an Enlightenment philosopher who emphasized morality but denied the truth of Christianity. Under this influence, the boy whose mother had dedicated him to the ministry became an atheist.

Although one of his mother's dreams now seemed hopeless, the other was about to be granted. In 1743, eighteen-year-old John made an impulsive visit to the George Catlett family, whom he had not seen since his mother's death. His visit was to be a hurried one (by eighteenth-century standards); he could stay only three days because he was scheduled to sail for Jamaica, where he had a job as a plantation manager.

Mary Catlett changed everything. Before the three days were over, John had fallen irrevocably in love with the girl his mother had chosen for him so many years before. He wrote later,

> Almost at the first sight of this girl (for she was then under
> fourteen) I was impressed with an affection for her, which
> never abated or lost its influence a single moment in my heart
> from that hour. In degree, it actually equalled all that the
> writers of romance have imaged; in duration, it was unalterable.

The time for John's departure came all too soon. How could he leave Mary—leave the first real love he had known since his mother died? "I concluded it would be absolutely impossible to live at such a distance as Jamaica, for a term of four or five years, and therefore determined at all events that I would not go," the *Authentic Narrative* says. But making the decision was one thing;

telling his father about it was quite another. John could guess what Captain Newton's reaction to his true reason would be, and none of the lies he dreamed up seemed likely to convince his hardheaded father! He settled for the simplest solution: without a word to Captain Newton, John quietly remained at the Catlett home for an extra three weeks—more than enough time for his ship to sail so far away that there was no hope of his catching it, even if he had tried.

When he finally showed up in London, John was surprised at his father's reaction. True, the older man was angry—but not nearly as angry as his son had feared. Once more, Captain Newton found a job for his unruly son as a sailor on a ship commanded by a friend of the captain. After the voyage, while the ship was in port for a short time, John rode off to see Mary—and stayed several weeks. Once more, young John Newton was out of a job.

This time his father was furious. John was as irresponsible as ever! So angry that he nearly disowned John, Captain Newton flatly refused to find the boy another job. Much to John's dismay, the Royal Navy solved the problem.

In those days, unemployed sailors had to be careful because representatives of the navy, looking for seamen, would forcibly seize them and conscript them into service. John was not careful, and almost before he knew it, he was a member of the Royal Navy.

It was not long before he was in trouble—and for the same old reason. He got permission to go ashore for a day while his ship was in port. As soon as he reached shore, he got a horse and headed for the Catlett home to say good-bye to Mary before he sailed to the West Indies—a venture that took considerably longer than the day's leave he had. That put an end to any hopes John might have had of succeeding in the navy, for the captain was not nearly as tolerant as Captain Newton had been. John made matters worse by deserting the next time he got into port. He was caught and taken back to his ship in irons.

Once the ship was underway for the West Indies, John had no place to go, but that did not keep him out of trouble. He was a constant discipline problem on his ship, so much so that the officers were eager to get rid of him—but not in a way he would enjoy.

It was a common practice for ships—even those of the navy— to exchange sailors with one another. It was unfortunate for John that his captain chose to work out such a deal with the captain of a slave trader bound for Sierra Leone on the west coast of Africa.

John did not realize his misfortune immediately. His first reaction to the transfer, now that he would be away from the naval officers who were acquainted with his father, was to say, "Now I can be as abandoned as I please." But the captain of the slave trader had been told all about John's troublemaking by the navy officers, and Newton's subsequent behavior did nothing to erase that first impression. John's wildness and profanity shocked even the ungodly sailors on the slave ship. His new officers despised him almost as much as John hated them, and both parties were pleased when Newton was discharged in the Plantane Islands off the African coast.

Servant of Slaves

There were a few wealthy Englishmen in that part of Africa, men who made a business of buying slaves from the interior and selling them to the slave-trading ships. One of these men had been to England and had returned to Africa in the ship John had been on. He offered the young man a job as his assistant. Seeing a chance to get rich, John instantly agreed.

For once in his life, John Newton applied himself and worked hard—not out of diligence but from greed, because only hard work could bring success and wealth. But before he could win the approval of his new employer (who had known him on board ship and had seen his life there), two circumstances intervened.

His employer lived with an African woman, known only as P.I., who had great influence in the area. For some reason, which Newton never found out, P.I. hated him from the very beginning and turned the young man's employer against him.

On top of everything else, Newton became seriously ill. His employer, who had made a lengthy business trip, left him in P.I.'s care. She immediately sent him to live and work among the slaves, in spite of his illness. When he became too weak to work, he was forced to depend on her care, and she delighted in mistreating him, occasionally neglecting to feed him at all or generously allowing him to eat her table scraps. John eventually recovered but continued to be a slave for two years. At times, only the thought of Mary kept him from despair.

At last, in desperation, he managed to get a letter to his father. After some time, a British slave ship, the *Greyhound,* arrived. Its captain—a friend of the senior Newton—arranged for John's release. He was to remain on board the *Greyhound* for the remaining year of its voyage and return with it to England.

Storm and Survival

On the way to England, the ship was caught in a tremendous storm. To Newton, manning the pumps, it seemed that they were certain to sink. He later wrote,

I said almost without any meaning, "If this will not do, the Lord have mercy upon us." This (though spoken with little reflection) was the first desire I had breathed for mercy for the space of many years. I was instantly struck by my own words; and . . . it directly occurred, "What mercy can there be for me?"

The *Greyhound* survived the storm, but the thoughts of mercy it had brought did not vanish with the tempest. John considered his life and the advantages he had wasted, and he concluded that his sins were far too great to be forgiven. Nevertheless, he began to read and study the Bible.

He was particularly affected by Luke 11:13—"If ye then, being evil, know how to give good gifts unto your children: how much more shall your heavenly Father give the Holy Spirit to them that ask him?" Newton instantly realized his need. Although he was still plagued with doubts, he continued to study the Bible, hoping to find faith.

Newton's experience proved that "faith cometh by hearing, and hearing by the word of God" (Rom. 10:17), for he said, "Before we arrived in Ireland, I had a satisfactory evidence in my own mind of the truth of the gospel. . . . I stood in need of an Almighty Saviour, and such a one I found described in the New Testament." He accepted that Saviour on board the *Greyhound*.

A New Profession

Although many years later Newton was to condemn the African slave trade, at this point he knew no profession besides sailing and was familiar with only one area of the world outside his homeland—the slave-country of Africa. He became a slave trader.

It had been many years since John had seen Mary, and his new understanding of the evil life he had lived made him hesitant to return. How could he, with his wild past, hope to marry gentle, sweet Mary Catlett? Besides, his father had never approved of John's love for Mary (perhaps because of the trouble it had gotten him into), and for the first time in years, John was eager to please his father, who had greeted him with great kindness and forgiveness. But Captain Newton visited the Catletts himself, and once he had met Mary, he consented to the marriage. John worked up his courage and wrote to Mary. (He could not go to see her; he was about to go to sea, and the days of his missing his ships to visit her were over.) To John's amazement and delight, she agreed to marry him, and in 1750, twenty-one-year-old Mary Catlett became the wife of the man who had loved her for seven years.

Mary Newton loved her husband—but she hated his profession. John himself was becoming more and more revolted at the cruelty of the slave trade and began to pray that God would open another door for him. His prayer was answered in an unexpected way. One day, he suddenly suffered a seizure which left him dizzy and subject to terrible headaches. His doctors were baffled but urged him not to go to sea again. Gladly, John left the slave trade forever, and took a job as a tide surveyor. Almost at once, his symptoms cleared up and he never suffered from them again.

Contented with his new profession, John devoted more time to studying the Scripture. He had—like all English schoolboys in those days—learned Latin during his short time at boarding school. Now he began to study Hebrew and Greek in order to read the Bible with more understanding. After several years, his Christian friends began to urge him to enter the ministry, pointing out that his private studies were excellent preparation. With much careful thought and prayer, John decided that they were right and that the Lord was calling him to preach.

It was several years before the decision could be carried out, however, because the Church of England refused to ordain him. It was bad enough that he did not have a college education without adding the fact that he had had no formal schooling since he was eleven! On top of that, the church felt that he was too sympathetic toward Methodism, which was then developing under the leadership of John and Charles Wesley. At last, however, his mother's second dream came true. He was ordained in 1764 and immediately took a strong evangelical stand within the Anglican church. The Evangelical Party of the Church of England grew up around Newton and others like him, and he is considered to have been the center of a great evangelical awakening among his fellow clergymen.

Preaching at Olney

Thus it was that the "old African blasphemer," as Newton sometimes called himself, came to the church in the little town of Olney, where he stayed for fifteen years. Olney was not an easy parish for the new preacher. The Industrial Revolution was gradually destroying the town's main source of income, handmade lace, since factories in other towns could produce lace more cheaply and in greater amounts. As a result, the crowded population of Olney grew poorer and more desperate. With desperation came starvation and unusually high rates of mental illness and drunkenness. Newton threw himself into the task of bringing spiritual food and as much material help as he could raise from wealthier friends to the needy people of Olney.

Newton's schedule might make even the busiest modern pastor quail. He held at least one and often two services daily. On Sundays, he held three worship services—preaching a different sermon at each—and two prayer meetings, one in the early morning and one after the afternoon service. In addition, he spent many hours visiting the sick and counseling the members of his growing congregation.

Newton was not a great pulpit orator, but his clear, simple sermons reached the hearts of the people, and in spite of opposition from some of the local residents who had been happier when the church was small and ineffective, the church grew steadily.

During this period, Newton began to write hymns, most of which were published in a book, *Olney Hymns,* along with some by his friend, the poet William Cowper. Many of the hymns were, in a sense, sermon outlines. Newton would write the words, and then, in one of his weekday services, preach from them. *Olney Hymns* included many that are still popular today, such as "Glorious Things of Thee Are Spoken," "Oh, for a Closer Walk with God," and the well-loved "Amazing Grace."

Newton's family life was as blessed as his ministry in the quiet country town. Although John and Mary had no children of their own, they took two orphaned nieces into their home and raised them as their daughters. Friends such as Cowper and many others visited often, and Newton carried on voluminous correspondence with friends who lived farther away, writing long letters of encouragement and exhortation.

The Final Years

In 1779, God opened a new door, and the Newtons went to St. Mary Woolnoth Church in London, at a time when John was only the second evangelical preacher in the city. His direct, Biblical preaching changed the hearts of the poorest slum dwellers and the most wealthy, influential citizens alike. All responded to his warmth and fervor. "Written sermons may be excellent in their own kind," he observed, "but a word warm from the preacher's heart is more likely to warm the hearts of the hearers."

His picturesque, pungent comments made conversation with him memorable and instructive. He observed, "A Christian should never plead spirituality for being a sloven; if he be but a shoe-cleaner, he should be the best in the parish." "Worldly men," he declared, "will be true to their principles; and if we were as true to ours, the visits between the two parties would be short and seldom." "When we first enter into the divine life," he warned on another occasion, "we propose to grow rich; God's plan is to make us feel poor."

A long and painful illness—probably cancer—took his beloved Mary in 1790. "The Bank of England is too poor to compensate me for such a loss as mine," he said. "But the Lord, the all-sufficient God, speaks and it is done. Let those who know Him and trust Him be of good courage."

For seventeen more years John Newton labored on in a triumphant ministry that saw thousands of souls saved and great works begun for God. His converts—and his converts' converts—built churches and started mission works (like that of Adoniram Judson in Burma, who was greatly influenced by one of Newton's spiritual children), until the influence of the former slave trader spread as far as he had ventured as a seaman. At last in 1807, after long and faithful service, the "wild beast" went home to the Master who had tamed him.

On a marble tablet at St. Mary Woolnoth Church is carved the epitaph which John Newton wrote himself. It reads:

JOHN NEWTON,
Clerk,
Once an infidel and libertine,
A servant of slaves in Africa: was,
By the rich mercy of our Lord
And Saviour, Jesus Christ,
Preserved, restored, pardoned,
And appointed to preach the Faith
He had long laboured to destroy.

Suggestions for Further Reading

Letters of John Newton. Edinburgh: Banner of Truth Trust, 1960.

Brian Edwards. Through Many Dangers. Welwyn, England: Evangelical Press, 1976.

John Pollock. Amazing Grace. San Francisco: Harper and Row, 1981.

Thomas Chalmers:
Champion of the Poor

by L. Gene Elliott

The nineteenth century brought the Industrial Revolution, and with it came wrenching changes in society. Cultures that had long been predominantly rural and agricultural suddenly became urban and industrial. Although the effects of the Industrial Revolution were more positive than negative, this dramatic transformation was not accomplished without human suffering. Cities—crowded, dirty, bustling places teeming with life—presented a new challenge to society and, in particular, to the Church. Many Christians today associate concern for the poor with the social gospel, the un-Scriptural emphasis on social reform over personal regeneration. Scotsman Thomas Chalmers, however, met the challenge of the cities with Christian solutions that were compassionate as well as orthodox.

Thomas Chalmers was born in Scotland on March 17, 1780, the sixth of fourteen children. His father worked at the trades of "dyer, shipowner, and general merchant," and the family lived comfortably. Reading helped develop young Thomas's mind, and the Bible and *Pilgrim's Progress* influenced him greatly.

He entered United College at St. Andrews at age eleven, the second youngest ever to enroll there. His eloquence and persuasiveness in public speaking led him into the ministry as a licensed preacher at age nineteen. Chalmers' training was unusual; whereas most preachers studied theology and related topics, he studied the liberal arts. He learned to think and analyze. But as yet he lacked the motivation to pursue the duties of the ministry. While preaching at his church, he also lectured on philosophy, chemistry, and mathematics at one of the leading universities.

In 1803 he became a pastor of a church in Kilmany, Scotland. Chalmers did the minimum required by the church and lectured in mathematics at St. Andrews several days a week. A speech he made in the General Assembly of the Church of Scotland drew attention to him, and, as a result, he was requested to write an article on Christianity for the Edinburgh Encyclopedia.

The Lord used this assignment together with several other experiences to bring about Chalmers' salvation. His brother George and sister Barbara, who were both Christians, died suddenly in 1806 and 1808 respectively. Then Thomas contracted a liver ailment, causing him to be bedridden for four months. He was afraid he too was going to die. These events led Chalmers to wrestle with the condition of his soul and to face the need for forgiveness of sin.

In March 1810 he wrote a confession to God which said he had largely wasted his time in intellectual pursuits and had pursued only what interested him at the moment. "My prayer to Heaven is . . . that the labors of my mind may be subservient to the interest of the Gospel." In December 1810, weary of trying to please God by doing things his way, Chalmers surrendered to Christ.

After his salvation, he turned his thoughts to the care of his parish. Acknowledging his own guilt, he awakened sinners to the blessed hope, and there came a revival in his church. The first action Chalmers took after being saved was to visit the sick, dying, and bereaved in his parish. Because he desired to do right, God multiplied the effect of his few words of consolation to levels of great blessing and benefit.

Chalmers more than compensated for the damage done in his unregenerate ministry at Kilmany. During his remaining years there, he gained unsought fame as an eloquent preacher.

When in the pulpit, Chalmers gave a first impression of being ragged and unpolished. There was little to indicate the power of his preaching. But a qualified observer noted,

> I have heard many men deliver sermons far better arranged in point of argument, and have heard very many deliver sermons far more uniform in elegance, both of conception and style; but most unquestionably, I have never heard, either in England or Scotland, or in any other country, a preacher whose eloquence is capable of producing an effect so strong and irresistible as his.

Though he read a manuscript, Chalmers put his whole being into a message. While his eyes and one finger were on the text, the other hand waved in the air. With his voice rising and falling with emotion, he swept the audience along until they breathed only when he did. Sporadically, he ceased speaking and sat down to catch his breath. Individuals in the audience relaxed, coughed, and moved about. Then, as he resumed, absolute quiet reigned.

Others in Scotland began to want his services. Chalmers turned down several offers, but in 1815 he decided the Lord would have him and his family in Tron Parish in Glasgow. It was a difficult change from the tranquil rural life of Kilmany to the confusion of a thriving but dirty industrial city.

The Tron church had well-to-do members, and the Chalmers family lived comfortably. But Chalmers disliked the press of crowds and the constant pressure of entertaining and being entertained. His preaching continued to be extraordinary. Not only did he preach during the services, but he also delivered two series of messages on Thursdays. In one he attempted to bring science into harmony with Christianity by showing the comparative insignificance of the earth against the magnificence of God's whole creation. The other showed businessmen how to live in the spirit of the gospel.

Spurred by a burning desire to help the poor in his parish, he declared war on the welfare system. He believed that it destroyed the poor person's right of independence and hindered the ability of children to assist their parents in old age. Chalmers sought and gained approval of the town council to administer funds for the poor raised by the church (the established Church of Scotland).

"The remedy against extension of pauperism does not lie in the liberalities of the rich; it lies in the hearts and habits of the poor," Chalmers declared. He organized the parish population of over ten thousand into twenty-five districts, each encompassing sixty to one hundred families. An elder and a deacon were assigned to each proportion or district. The elder provided spiritual help, and the deacon (according to the Biblical admonition to serve tables) provided temporal aid.

Each district had at least one Sunday school with forty to fifty teachers. On a given day these teachers were in the parish working with the parishioners' needs, not to coddle the poor, but to make them independent of charity. The object was to eliminate charity by finding work where it was available, to stimulate mutual cooperation among the people, to administer monetary aid where needed (in secret as much as possible), and to edify with the Word of God.

Although liberal writers minimized the success of this plan and relegated it to the category of idealism, the results were evident. The city had been paying £1,400 per year to the poor, and in three years, Chalmers had reduced it to £280 per year. An English poor-law commissioner visited Glasgow in 1833 and observed that "this system has been attended by the most triumphant success." Results included an increase in morality and the care of children and a decrease in drunkenness.

Chalmers exploded the myth of the welfare society in word and deed. He wrote that "it is in the power of charity to corrupt its object." Charity could leave a recipient lazy, dependent, and mean. It would unhinge the basic constitution of society by removing the blessings of an industrious people. The evils of poverty would increase to the point where more charity would be insufficient to meet needs. The country would then move toward a "nauseating spectacle of sloth and beggary and corruption."

In 1823, Chalmers moved to a new position, the chair of moral philosophy at St. Andrews University. For the next five years, he taught Scriptural principles to students, wrote, and continued working with the poor. He taught children from his own district in St. Andrews in a Sunday school in his own home.

The University of Edinburgh elected Chalmers to the chair of theology in 1828 where he remained until 1843. While at Edinburgh, he never lost his vision for the work with the poor. With the help of a publisher friend, he started twenty new churches in Glasgow. This done, he traveled and preached throughout Scotland to help plant two hundred churches and parishes.

The greatest problem Chalmers faced was church polity. The civil courts ruled that the Church of Scotland could install ministers even if they were unacceptable to the local churches. Chalmers believed that the members of a local congregation should have a voice in the selection of a minister. He promoted enactment of the Veto Law, whereby male heads of families had a right to veto after the nomination of a minister by the patrons of a church. He also worked to heal the breach between church and courts.

When all efforts failed to persuade the government to see the church position and when the government prevented the establishment of new parishes and the free choice of ministers, Thomas Chalmers led 470 ministers out of the Church of Scotland and formed the Free Church of Scotland. He then set up a sustentation fund for ministers. Each congregation member contributed one penny a week. This contribution resulted in £150 per minister per year for 500 ministers.

Chalmers, who was by now the principal of Free Church College in Edinburgh, turned his attention once again to the poor. West Port was one of the poorest districts in Edinburgh. He divided its two thousand people into districts and subdistricts, each of which had Christian workers to minister to the needs of the families. A Christian day school opened in 1845 for the children and families who agreed to pay a small tuition charge. A Sunday school was added to the day school, and a building was built to house these and the church. Chalmers left other parishes with a model to be duplicated.

Thomas Chalmers went to be with the Lord during his sleep on Sunday night, May 30, 1847. It was estimated that half of the population of Edinburgh came to the funeral.

Chalmers had grown to be a Christian statesman; yet he also grew in humility and never tired of his responsibilities. Someone once said about him, "Thomas Chalmers was not one man, he was a thousand men."

Suggestions for Further Reading

Stewart J. Brown. *Thomas Chalmers and the Godly Commonwealth in Scotland.* Oxford: Oxford Univ. Press, 1982.

The Réveil: The Second Reformation of Geneva

by Mark Sidwell

The nineteenth century was an era of revivals. The Second Great Awakening (which included the frontier camp meeting revivals) and the Prayer Meeting Revival of the 1850s touched the United States. The British Isles underwent the '59 Revival. Later in the century, evangelists such as Dwight L. Moody led urban revivals all around the world. Less familiar to English-speaking Christians is the réveil *(French for "revival" or "awakening"), a revival among French-speaking Protestants in Switzerland and France which began around 1815 in Geneva, Switzerland. The following is the story of three of the most famous leaders of the* réveil.

Revivals of religion can stir churches, transform regions, and even move nations, but they begin by touching individual lives. The *réveil* in Switzerland and France is no exception. Something of the character of that revival and its effects can be seen in the lives of three men that it touched: César Malan, J. H. Merle D'Aubigné, and Félix Neff.

César Malan

Henri Abraham César Malan was born in Geneva in 1787. As a young man, Malan took an interest in the ministry and entered the theological school of Geneva. The Genevan church, however, had fallen far from the days of Calvin. By the early 1800s, many pastors and most professors were unitarians who denied the deity of Jesus Christ and who rarely used the Bible in their sermons or lessons. Malan recalled later, "Were I to go back to my recollections of academical life and its theological teaching, I should fail to find a single instance in which instruction was given me on the divinity of our Saviour, man's fallen nature, or the doctrine of justification by faith."

The state church ordained Malan in 1810, but he later confessed, "At the time of my ordination at Geneva I was in utter ignorance of the truth as it is in Jesus." On one occasion he spoke in the church of an orthodox pastor. Afterwards the pastor said to Malan, "It appears to me, sir, that you have not yet learnt that, in order to convert others, you must first be converted yourself. Your sermon was not a Christian discourse, and I sincerely hope my people didn't understand it."

This rebuke was one of several factors which caused Malan to pause, reconsider his state, and begin to search the Scripture. Finally, in 1814, he was converted. The young Christian was further encouraged in 1816 by the arrival of Robert Haldane, a Scottish preacher who had come to proclaim the gospel in Geneva. Helped by Haldane's teaching and his own avid study of the Bible, Malan grew bolder in his faith.

On March 15, 1817, Malan mounted Calvin's old pulpit in St. Gervais Church and preached on justification by faith alone. His reception was anything but warm. Some members of the congregation grumbled and shifted in their seats. Others laughed out loud. Malan's parents tried to sneak out of the church quietly, and even his wife shot him reproachful glances. Virtually the only encouragement he received was from Haldane. The Scottish preacher came to Malan's home and said to the younger man, "Thank God, the gospel has again been preached in Geneva."

The leaders of the state church reacted quickly. They forbade Malan from preaching on "controversial" points such as the deity of Christ and justification by faith alone. When Malan refused, they dismissed him from the church. Undaunted, Malan built a little chapel near his home and called it *la chapelle du Temoignaige* ("the chapel of testimony"). There, he preached to all who would hear him.

As others learned of Malan's stand for truth, they invited him to come preach to them. By degrees, he became an evangelist as well as a pastor, and he spoke in Switzerland, the Netherlands, England, Scotland, and Germany. Malan also turned his talents to writing hymns, and he became the greatest hymn writer among French-speaking Protestants. Probably his best-known work to English-speaking Christians is the tune "Hendon," to which Frances Ridley Havergal's "Take My Life, and Let It Be" is usually sung.

Before his death in 1864, Malan's reputation became international. In 1862, Malan was surprised when the queen of the Netherlands came to visit him during her trip to Geneva. More important, his ministry reached thousands of souls whom he had never met. Once, without identifying himself, Malan asked an elderly Christian how he came to the Saviour. The man replied, "Through reading a book written by a Mr. Malan of Geneva."

Jean Henri Merle D'Aubigné

Jean Henri Merle D'Aubigné was born in Geneva in 1794. Like Malan, Merle (as he was called, rather than D'Aubigné) became interested in the ministry and entered the state church's theological school in Geneva. Also like Malan, Merle studied theology while still a stranger to the grace of God. In fact, when the revival began, Merle led a group of students to present a protest against the revivalists and their attacks on the state church's clergy.

God brought Robert Haldane into Merle's life, however. The Scottish preacher held Bible studies with students from the theological school. When they asked questions and presented their arguments, Haldane answered by turning to passages in Scripture and saying, "Look, here it is, written by the finger of God," or "There it stands, written by the finger of God." Merle was particularly taken aback by the unfamiliar doctrine—to him—of total human depravity. After searching through the Bible for himself, Merle said to Haldane, "Now I see that doctrine in the Bible."

"Yes," Haldane replied, "but do you see it in your heart?"

As a result of Haldane's teaching, Merle was converted. After finishing his work in Geneva, Merle went on for further study in Germany. After that, he pastored a French congregation in Hamburg, Germany, and then served a French church in Brussels (then part of the Netherlands). In 1830, Merle returned to Geneva and joined with other revivalists in forming the Evangelical School of Theology. Merle served as Professor of Church History there until his death in 1872.

Merle's greatest fame came not as a teacher, however, but as a historian. During the tricentennial celebration of the Reformation in 1817, Merle began to dream of recording the history of the Reformation in all of its drama and color. After years of study and work, he published two large sets, *The History of the Reformation in the Sixteenth Century* (5 volumes, 1835-1853) and *The History of the Reformation in Europe in the Time of Calvin* (8 volumes, 1863-1878). The works were well read in the French-speaking world, but they became phenomenal best sellers among English-speaking Christians. Merle's fame spread around the world. When Merle visited the Metropolitan Tabernacle during a trip to London in 1862, for example, Pastor Charles Spurgeon shortened his sermon so that Merle might give a few words of greeting.

Faith of Our Fathers: Scenes from Church History

Part of the credit for the success of the works must go to the author's flowing, eloquent style; often, Merle's histories read like a novel. Merle's spiritual sympathy with the Reformation contributed even more. "I write the history of the Reformation," he said, "in its own spirit."

Félix Neff

Félix Neff (1798-1829) was a Genevan soldier who, like many others, originally opposed the revival. He showed his opposition dramatically in 1818, when he was called out to defend one of the "awakened" churches from an angry mob. Despite his purpose for being there, Neff plunged his sword into the wall of the church and declared that he would do the same to anyone who defended the revivalists.

Neff's act may have been simply a reaction to a sense of conviction of sin, for within a month he had been converted and joined the very church whose building he had defaced. Neff resigned from the army and became a minister of the gospel. He served churches briefly in Grenoble and Mens, France. Then in 1823, he went high into the French Alps to minister to the Waldensians.

The Waldensians had arisen during the Middle Ages as a protest against the increasing corruption of the Roman church. Years of persecution and isolation in Catholic France, however, reduced the descendants of the Waldensians to near-barbarism. Neff found a people who recalled little of the gospel of their forefathers. Furthermore, they lived little better than animals in dirty, cold, dark homes. During the seven-month winters, they often lived in stables where they were warmed by the manure piles. Neff described how women often stood behind husbands at meals, waiting for the husbands to throw food over their shoulders that they might eat. "They are degenerated in every sense of the word," wrote Neff.

Neff labored to meet all the needs of his congregations. He taught them how to cultivate potatoes, for example, and found teachers for the children. More important, he preached to them. Neff found that these Waldensians maintained an almost superstitious reverence for the Bible. As Neff preached, they listened. And as they listened, God's Spirit moved and revival came. Neff worked relentlessly and preached in village after village; sometimes he slept only few hours a week. He wrote to a friend,

> I am struck with astonishment at the apparent suddenness of this awakening. I could scarcely believe my senses. Even the rocks, the cascades and the ice seemed inspired with life and offered up to my eye a less dismal and gloomy prospect than

formerly. This wild country has become dear and delightful to me, now that it has become the habitation of Christian brethren.

The strain broke Neff's health, however. After only four years of work in the Alps, Neff returned to Geneva, a dying man. As his health deteriorated, he wrote letters to his congregations in the mountains. In one he said,

> In spirit I often revisit your valleys and long to be able to endure cold and fatigue, to sleep in a stable on a bed of straw, in order to proclaim the Word of God. My words have often wearied you, and my plainness of speech has often offended you, and many of you saw me depart with joy. But were I still amongst you, I should not change my language. Truth is unchangeable. I should still entreat you, in the name of Jesus, to be reconciled to God.

In 1829, Félix Neff died at the age of thirty. His testimony, however, stirred other young men to devote their lives to the ministry of the gospel.

Conclusion

Malan, Merle, and Neff were at the same time beneficiaries and agents of revival. Like Andrew when he met the Christ (John 1:40-41), they could not help sharing the truth that had transformed their lives. All three were giants in what Merle called "the second reformation of Geneva."

Suggestions for Further Reading

James I. Good. *History of the Swiss Reformed Church Since the Reformation.* Philadelphia: Publication and Sunday School Board of the Reformed Church in the United States, 1913. (See pages 353-400 and 461-72.)

Ernest Gordon. *A Book of Protestant Saints.* Chicago: Moody, 1946. (Brief biographies of Malan, pages 189-94, and Neff, pages 199-205.)

E. and L. Harvey and E. Hey. *They Knew Their God: Book 1.* Hampton, Tenn.: Harvey and Tait, 1974. (On Neff, pages 47-56.)

S.M. Houghton. Introduction to *The Reformation in England,* by J.H. Merle D'Aubigné. Edinburgh: Banner of Truth, 1962. (Houghton's sixteen-page introduction is the best English source on Merle's life and work.)

Man of Living Stone

by Donna Hess

Historian K. S. Latourette called the nineteenth century "the Great Century" primarily because of the tremendous expansion in Christian missions in that time. William Carey, the pioneer of modern missions; Adoniram Judson, the father of American foreign missions; Hudson Taylor, the apostle to the Chinese; and many others ministered during that era. David Livingstone is probably the best-known missionary of the era. The impact of his work in Africa and the dramatic events of his life there captured the attention of even the non-Christian public. Because he was an explorer as well as a missionary, Livingstone's story is both the life of a great Christian and the history of an era.

Dr. David Livingstone had been murdered! The news about the popular medical missionary spread quickly. Yet while some newspapers were penning his obituary, others were gleaning information to cast doubt on the report. James Gordon Bennett of *The New York Herald* decided to capitalize on the situation. He sent for his best journalist, Henry Morton Stanley, and ordered him to set sail for Africa, giving him specific instructions: refute the story of Livingstone's murder or bring back the missionary's bones.

Stanley prepared for the journey with little personal interest. He did, however, desire to create a story that would bring him recognition. Consequently, before embarking, he collected all the written information concerning Livingstone he could find. As a reporter, he knew that he must know all he could about the man he sought, even though at the time he failed to understand why one missionary, dead or living, should merit such attention. Thus Stanley began his famous journey, and as he traveled he read; and as he read he grew to understand.

David Livingstone had arrived at Robert Moffat's small South African mission station in 1841. Within the year, however, the two men agreed that the mission did not warrant both their efforts, and Livingstone moved on to extend the mission's influence. He settled about two hundred and fifty miles north in the beautiful but hazardous valley of Mabotsa. It was a fitting first home for the would-be pioneer missionary, for it was here that Livingstone bravely faced the first of many perilous encounters. He recorded the account in his journal:

> The village was much troubled by lions. They even attacked herds in open day. This was so unusual an occurrence that the people thought they were bewitched. [One day] I saw one of the beasts sitting upon a piece of rock. Being about thirty yards off I took aim at his body . . . and fired both barrels into it. The men called out "He is shot, he is shot!" I turned to the people and said, "Stop a little, until I load again." I heard a shout. Starting and looking half round, I saw the lion just in the act of springing upon me . . . ; he caught my shoulder as he sprang, and we both came to the ground below together. Growling horribly loudly in my ear, he shook me as a terrier dog does a rat. Turning to relieve myself of the weight, as he had one paw on the back of my head, I saw his eyes directed at Mebalwe [a native with Livingstone] who was trying to shoot him. His gun missed fire in both barrels; the lion immediately left me, and, attacking Mebalwe, bit his thigh. Another man . . . attempted to spear the lion. . . . He left Mebalwe and caught this man by the shoulder, but at that moment the bullets that he had received took effect, and he fell down dead.

Though Livingstone's life was spared, the bones in his left arm were thoroughly crushed; and the arm, having been improperly set, was maimed for life.

During his time in the valley, Livingstone married Mary Moffat, daughter of Robert Moffat. She, like her father, possessed a heart for Africa, a heart perfectly suited to Livingstone; for Livingstone was not only brave and masculine but also tender, and it was this tenderness that sealed his influence over the Africans. He loved deeply, and as he wrote in his journal, "Here if anywhere, love begets love." Even in the initial years Livingstone revealed himself clearly. He was a fearless man motivated by compassion, determined to achieve his God-given goal—the evangelization of Africa.

It was, however, six years before Livingstone saw fruit for his labor. By this time he had settled in the village of Kolobeng. The head of this village, Chief Sechele, was his first convert and a remarkable man. Livingstone wrote of him, "I was struck by his intelligence, and by the special manner in which we felt drawn to each other. This man has not only embraced Christianity, but expounds its doctrines to his people." It was true that the chief shared Livingstone's burden, but his suggested method for reaching the tribe was somewhat humorous. Concerned, the chief spoke to Livingstone: "Do you imagine that these people will ever believe you by your merely talking to them? I can make them do nothing except by threatening them; if you like, I shall call my head men, and with our rhinocerous-hide whips we shall soon make them believe all together." Of course, Livingstone declined the offer of coercion, but he deeply appreciated the desire it manifested.

For the first nine years of his missionary career Livingstone had settled along the coast ministering to various individual tribes, but by 1850 he felt that God was calling him to the more difficult task of opening up the interior of Africa. Many disagreed, saying that he ought to stay in one place "preaching the simple gospel, and seeing conversions for every sermon." Livingstone's response was, "If I were to follow my own inclinations, they would lead me to settle down quietly." But he was not one to give in to inclinations; thus, Livingstone and his wife set out for the interior.

It was a difficult endeavor. When in 1852 they reached Cape Town, they still had not found a healthful location for a mission settlement in Central Africa. But Livingstone was even more disheartened by the realization that his wife could not endure the arduous search. She had nearly died of fever during their travels. With a heavy heart he sat down to try to chart the future. Mary understood her husband's dilemma. She knew that though it would be hard, they should separate until her husband could find a place for the new mission. On April 23, 1852, Mary set sail for England. Neither of them knew at that time how short their future together would be.

Livingstone renewed his travels alone. En route into the interior he stopped by Robert Moffat's mission. There he met Chief Sechele's wife. She was overwrought from having just escaped from the Boers (South African Dutch inhabitants who opposed the English) who had attacked the village. From the cleft of a rock she had watched them murder many of the tribesmen, burn the village and crops, and carry off the livestock. The reason they gave was that the tribe had become "saucy," allowing an Englishman to dwell with them and then to pass into the interior unmolested. The Boers had left the village with one goal in mind—to find Livingstone and kill him.

Livingstone was outraged, and he immediately expressed his anger to the proper authorities. Once the rage had quieted, however, a great sense of grief came over him. He did not fear for his life—he knew God would protect him as long as He had need of him—

but what of the villagers he had ministered to who had not accepted Christ? He renewed his determination. The Boer attack, instead of thwarting him, made him more convinced—he must enter deeper into Africa with his message.

In 1859, Mrs. Livingstone rejoined her husband and shared with him the joy of seeing a mission established in the interior. In the meantime, Livingstone had sent to England pleading with those at home to send laborers to harvest the new field he was opening. Bishop Mackenzie was the first to arrive in answer to that call, founding the first mission in Central Africa. However, within the year the bishop and several of his co-workers died, the mission all but collapsed, and Livingstone had to begin again.

The failure of the mission was indeed a severe trial, but the event that followed a few weeks later was even more severe. The Livingstones had been reunited less than three months when Mary died. Though David Livingstone had successfully endured many hardships up to this time, her death was a crushing blow. His journal reveals some of his suffering: "Oh my Mary, my Mary; how often we have longed for a quiet home since you and I were cast adrift at Kolobeng. Surely the removal by a kind Father who knoweth our frame means that He rewarded you by taking you to the best home, the eternal one in the heavens. . . . For the first time in my life I feel willing to die." In 1865 Livingstone made his last visit to England; then, returning to Africa, he disappeared into the interior.

When Stanley arrived in Africa in 1871 he was no longer a disinterested reporter in search of a story. His voracious reading had given him insight into this remarkable man, and he moved into Africa with renewed purpose. For five years no one had heard from Livingstone. Was he still alive, plodding across unknown terrains with the same steadfast purpose, or had he died in the wilderness without seeing any of his goals fulfilled?

For nearly a year Stanley and his men searched and found nothing. By the end of October food and water were becoming scarce—so scarce in fact that Stanley carved on a tree "Starving. H.M.S." Within a few days of this incident Stanley's expedition met a native caravan. One of Stanley's servants began conversing with one of the caravan travelers and found that a white man had just entered the Arab settlement of Ujiji.

"A white man?" the servant queried.

"Yes, a white man."

"How was he dressed?"

"Like the master" (meaning Stanley).

"Is he young or old?"

"He is old. He has white hair on his face and he is sick."

Stanley set out immediately. Several days later the expedition reached Ujiji. Stanley describes the meeting in his journal:

> I pushed back the crowds . . . , before which stood the "white man with the beard." As I advanced slowly toward him I noticed that he was pale, and he looked wearied. . . . I would have run to him, only I was a coward in the presence of such a mob— would have embraced him, only, he being an Englishman, I did not know how he would receive me; so I did what moral coward- ice and false pride suggested was the best thing—walked deliber- ately to him, took off my hat and said: "Dr. Livingstone, I presume?" "Yes" said he with a kind smile, lifting his cap slightly.

This was the beginning of a lasting friendship between the two.

Stanley remained with Livingstone for four months learning about his mysterious five-year journey. Livingstone had suffered much— thirty-nine attacks of malaria, six weeks of pneumonia, and constant hunger. He had witnessed massacres and survived ambushes. Yet as he recounted these trials it was without remorse. His underlying determination had remained, and with fervor he reiterated, "I am a missionary, heart and soul. In [God's] service I wish to live; in it I wish to die. Viewed in relation to my calling—the end of the geographical feat is only the beginning of the enterprise."

On April 29, 1873, Livingstone's old servant who traveled with him pulled back the curtain of the doctor's hut and found him kneeling by his bed. He had died in the night while praying. His followers embalmed his body, after removing the heart and carefully burying it in the jungle. They then carried Livingstone's body hundreds of miles to Zanzibar. A year later the body arrived in England and was identified by the first wound Livingstone had received in Africa, the maimed arm from the lion's attack. When he was laid in Westminster Abbey, however, he was remembered more for the heartfelt wounds he had continually endured for the African mission. His life was a noble example of courage and determination in the face of seemingly insurmountable difficulties.

He needs no epitaph to guard a name
Which men shall prize while worthy work is known;
He lived and died for good—be that his fame;
Let marble crumble; this is Livingstone.

Suggestions for Further Reading

David Livingstone. *Livingstone's Travels.* Ed. James I. Macnair. New York: Macmillan, 1954.

C. H. Spurgeon: Light Giver

by Christa G. Habegger

Few men have dominated their respective eras as much as Charles Haddon Spurgeon dominated his. He built the largest church in Europe, preached eloquent sermons that—in printed form—reached tens of thousands of people around the world, and became the head of an array of Christian ministries which reached out to nearly every class of needy people. Charles Spurgeon is, in short, possibly the greatest leader in the history of the free churches of Europe (those churces outside the various state churches). The secret of Spurgeon's success was not his talents, tremendous though they were, but his unflagging dedication to God.

C. H. Spurgeon once recorded his impressions of a London street lit up at night by gas street lights:

I did not see the lamplighter, . . . but I saw the lights which he had kindled, and these remained when he himself had gone his way.

As I rode along I thought to myself, "How earnestly do I wish that my life may be spent in lighting one soul after another with the sacred flame of eternal life! I would myself be as much as possible unseen while at my work, and would vanish into eternal brilliance above when my work is done."

Spurgeon was indeed such a "lamplighter." In more than forty years of untiring preaching, he introduced thousands of souls to the light of the gospel of Jesus Christ.

Charles Haddon Spurgeon was born June 19, 1834, in Essex County to a preacher, John Spurgeon, and his nineteen-year-old wife Eliza. Another baby was born to them the next year, and little Charles, at fourteen months, was sent to live for five years with his paternal grandparents.

His early training at the home of the Reverend James Spurgeon, the Congregational minister of Stambourne, could hardly have been better. Both grandparents were godly, loving caretakers, and Charles received much attention as well from his eighteen-year-old Aunt Ann.

By age three, young Spurgeon had discovered a lifelong passion—books. Aunt Ann had taught him to read by the time he was five, and he began devouring the volumes in his grandfather's well-provided library. The Bible was central in the home, both as a foundation for all education and for family discussion. Young Charles learned to speak and think in the context of Scripture. In addition, he familiarized himself with the writings of the great Puritan authors to such an extent that his precocity was often remarked upon. Robert Schindler wrote that the young boy "would astonish the grave deacons and matrons . . . by proposing subjects for conversation and offering pertinent remarks upon them."

When Spurgeon moved back home with his parents in Colchester, there were three other children. His father secured for them the best local education, and Charles proved himself an eager student. A missionary, Richard Knill, once stayed with the family and recognized immediately the young boy's abilities. Before he left, he took Charles on his knee and announced, "This child will one day preach the Gospel, and will preach it to great multitudes," a prophecy whose fulfillment Spurgeon eagerly awaited.

The boy could discuss the intricacies of theology, but he was unconverted. He felt the weight of sin keenly. One biographer described his predicament thus: "Although he knew as well as anyone that 'Christ died for our sins,' he saw no application of this truth to himself." It was Spurgeon's very knowledge of the majesty and justice of God that, in his own words, "overpowered my soul, and I fell down in utter prostration of spirit." Looking back on his misery, he was assured, though, that "a deep and bitter sense of sin is of great value. . . . It is terrible in the drinking, but it is most wholesome in the . . . after life."

During the Christmas season of 1849, Spurgeon happened upon a service in a small Primitive Methodist chapel. There were only about a dozen people there. The regular minister was snowed in, and a layman went into the pulpit to preach. Spurgeon remembered that the poor fellow was obliged to "stick to his text, for the simple reason that he had little else to say." The text, "Look unto me, and be ye saved," was the right medicine for Spurgeon's sin-sick heart. The preacher pointed out that "lookin' don't take a deal of pain" or a college degree. Spurgeon felt there was hope for him in that. When the stumbling discourse was nearly done, the speaker singled out Spurgeon as a stranger and remarked, "Young man, you look very miserable. And you will always be miserable . . . if you don't obey my text." Suddenly Spurgeon could see his way clear to the Saviour. He looked to Christ and was wonderfully transformed. His joy in sins forgiven could not be contained. He began immediately to witness of his conversion and to lead others to Calvary. He was fifteen when he wrote out the solemn covenant that was his lifelong theme:

I yield myself up to Thee; as Thine own reasonable sacrifice,
I return to Thee Thine own. I would be forever, unreservedly,
perpetually Thine; whilst I am on earth, I would serve Thee;
and may I enjoy Thee and praise Thee for ever!

Whatever men point to as the secret of Spurgeon's phenomenal success in the pulpit hereafter, one fact is to be remembered: Charles Haddon Spurgeon was a man wholly dedicated to his Master's service.

Schooling continued, but it was not long before Spurgeon's gifts of memory and speech fitted him more to be a teacher than a pupil. He taught for a time in a school at Newmarket. Meanwhile, he distributed tracts regularly and began teaching a Sunday school class in the Baptist church which he joined shortly after his conversion. He entered upon his preaching ministry quite without intending to. He was invited to go to a nearby town one Sunday evening because "a young man was to preach there who was not much used to services and very likely would be glad of company." Spurgeon assumed that his companion was the young man in question but found to his consternation that he himself was to be the preacher. During the walk to the meeting place, he decided within himself that he could at least "tell a few poor cottagers of the sweetness and love of Jesus," which he did with such earnestness that the congregation demanded he return as soon as possible.

He accepted the pastorate of the Baptist church at Waterbeach in 1851 and shortly thereafter resigned his teaching position to devote himself full-time to the ministry. The church grew beyond its capacity under his youthful guidance, and the town was entirely transformed because of the gospel he preached.

In December of 1853, Spurgeon received an invitation to preach in the New Park Street Baptist Church in London. Spurgeon, then only nineteen, recalled later, "I felt [at first] amazed at my own temerity, for it seemed to my eyes a large, ornate and imposing structure." However, when he stood to preach, he had no thoughts of his own worthiness but only for the book he preached. He called the attention of the congregation to God as the Father of lights, expounding the divine attributes. The members, who had become accustomed to dry discourses in the past months, rejoiced in his preaching. Here before them was a young man who was wholly in earnest and who possessed a voice of extraordinary range and power. That night the congregation was even larger; and following the service, the majority remained in the building, unwilling to end the meeting. The deacons prevailed on Spurgeon to accept another invitation, this time for three Sundays in January. Accordingly, he returned and was offered the pastorate. He demurred, feeling the awesome responsibility, but agreed to minister on three months' trial basis. "One thing is due," he stipulated, "namely, that in private as well as public, they must all wrestle in prayer . . . that I may be sustained in the great work."

Reluctantly, he resigned his work in the church at Waterbeach and commenced the ministry in London, where he remained until his death forty years later.

One member of the congregation held her pastor in special esteem. Susannah Thompson was present the first time he preached at New Park Street, although she afterward confessed that his country manner and dress at first "attracted most of her attention, and . . . awakened some feelings of amusement." Soon, though, she profited spiritually under his ministry and began to admire the preacher for both his public and private demeanor. A friend of the Olneys, in whose home Spurgeon often visited, Susannah was drawn into his friendship. Spurgeon's first gift to her was an inscribed copy of *Pilgrim's Progress*. In June of 1854 he invited here to the gala opening of the Crystal Palace. Their time together that day cemented their growing affection. Within a few weeks they were engaged to be married early in January of 1856.

When Spurgeon undertook the work at New Park Street, there were under a hundred active members. Within a short time, he was addressing several thousand, and the problem of overcrowding became severe. When the church proved inadequate for the great crowds desiring to hear the gospel, Spurgeon arranged to use the Surrey Gardens Music Hall, a massive auditorium with seating for ten thousand. The opening service was scheduled for October 19, 1856. Capacity crowds filled the hall when Spurgeon rose to bring his message. Then tragedy struck. Troublemakers in three areas of the building called out: "Fire!" "The galleries are falling!" "The whole place is collapsing!" Efforts to calm the panic which ensued failed, as thousands of terrified people rushed for the stairs and exit doors. Under the weight, a stair railing gave way, and several fell into the crowd beneath. Others were trampled. Order was eventually restored when it became apparent that the alarms were false, but not before seven people had died and twenty-eight others had been injured and taken to the hospital.

The effect on Spurgeon was such that he never fully recovered. To the end of his ministry, the sight of a crowded facility caused him visible strain. The catastrophe produced one good result— the New Park Street members began planning in earnest for a large structure of their own.

The first Sunday in the new church, called the Metropolitan Tabernacle, was March 31, 1861. The building, wonderfully planned for comfort, beauty, and efficiency, was opened free of debt. Its young pastor was but twenty-six and had observed his flock grow from about eighty to more than six thousand. His influence upon his own congregation was vast, but even more remarkable was the effect his preaching had on the entire country and beyond. Victorian England was moved from its lethargy and complacency when God's people became stirred about souls. The era's most prominent thinkers—in politics and literature—came to hear Spurgeon in the Tabernacle.

Spurgeon did not limit himself to preparing a few sermons a week. He published messages weekly, each with thousands of subscribers; edited a magazine, *The Sword and the Trowel;* and wrote major works, such as his seven-volume *Treasury of David,* a commentary on the Psalms. When he saw a need in his church or city, he moved to meet it, with the result that within time, the church was responsible for orphanages, almshouses, and a pastors' training college. Mrs. Spurgeon, often an invalid, was not idle and at her husband's suggestion began a ministry of distributing books and tracts all over the world to pastors who otherwise would have no access to them.

As the membership grew, so did Spurgeon's personal commitment. He never became aloof, despite the vast numbers. With his astonishing memory, he remembered the name of nearly every member he interviewed. He reserved Tuesdays for the purpose of speaking with each spiritual seeker who had been converted the previous Sunday at the Tabernacle. In addition, he traveled often, speaking frequently to crowds of over ten thousand in the open air, a feat he scarcely remarked upon, but which seems incredible in our day of sound amplification.

A friend once demanded to know how he kept his killing schedule. Spurgeon smiled and said, "I suppose you think that a man who works twelve hours a day can get through a good deal of work?" "Yes," replied the friend. "Well," said Spurgeon, "I work eighteen!" Significantly, he continued at his accustomed pace not only when he was young and strong but also after he began to struggle with rheumatic gout. His suffering was intense. He learned to rely more heavily upon his Saviour's grace and developed a keen sensitivity to those who, like him, were subject to bouts with pain and accompanying depression.

There were other talented, dedicated preachers in history. Why is C. H. Spurgeon known as the "Prince of Preachers"? Men point to the phenomenal voice with which he was gifted. He once addressed a crowd of 23,654 in the Crystal Palace, with no sign of vocal strain. Others comment on his eloquence and his mental facility. He was never at a loss for the right expression. He absorbed everything he read, with the result that he could always draw from a vast reserve. A voracious reader, he amassed a library of over twelve thousand volumes. Listeners were charmed by his humor, always a vehicle to illustrate a solemn truth. The common man was attracted by the simplicity of his message and the undisputed zeal with which he directed it to him. No one who heard him speak could be impervious to the attraction of his personality. His appearance, while not essentially handsome, was a factor. Of medium height, he was stocky, with a powerful upper body and a large leonine head. His face was eminently expressive, so much so that a portrait painter declared it to be "different every day" and thus unpaintable.

Yet these are all merely contributing elements. At the root of his success was his yieldedness to the Spirit of God. His brother James made the simple statement, "The secret of my brother's success so far as I have solved it, is prayer." D. L. Moody made a similar assessment when asked whether he had heard Spurgeon preach. "Yes," he replied, "but better still, I heard him pray."

Any man who preaches truth fearlessly will encounter controversy, and Spurgeon had his share. When he attacked the error of baptismal regeneration, he bore the scorn of many contemporary preachers; but it was when he had to speak out against unbelief in the Baptist Union that he faced a painful separation from brethren he loved. The issue, which became known as the Downgrade Controversy, arose over pockets of un-Scriptural teaching in England's Baptist churches. Evolution and a process of thinking which denied the authority of Scripture had influenced several Union members. Reports of unbelief among the membership disturbed Spurgeon, who requested that the Union combat heresy by adopting a clear statement of faith for its membership. When

178

the Union authorities refused to take any punitive action, Spurgeon spoke out against "The Downgrade" in his magazine. Eventually, he concluded that his only recourse was to separate from the organization. He presented his reason as follows: "With deep regret we abstain from assembling with those whom we dearly love and heartily respect, since it would involve us in a confederacy with those with whom we can have no fellowship in the Lord."

As a boy, Spurgeon had asked God to allow him to spend himself in service; and God was pleased to grant that prayer, to the salvation of thousands. Spurgeon died on January 31, 1892, at age fifty-seven. It might be said that he died young, but when we realize that he ministered for forty-two of those fifty-seven years, we receive a different perspective. He grew old early, a fact he himself recognized. At forty, he lectured on "Young Men," saying "in all seriousness that he was an old one. 'I might have been young man at twelve, but at sixteen I was a sober, respectable Baptist parson, sitting in the Chair and ruling and governing the Church.'"

Spurgeon addressed his people once, anticipating his own demise: "When you see my coffin carried to the silent grave, I should like every one of you . . . to be constrained to say, 'He did earnestly urge us, in plain and simple language, not to put off the consideration of eternal things.'"

Suggestions for Further Reading

C.H. Spurgeon. *Autobiography.* Vol. 1, *The Early Years,* 1962. Vol.2, *The Full Harvest,* 1973. Edinburgh: Banner of Truth Trust. (An edited but improved edition of a work published shortly after Spurgeon's death.)

Arnold Dallimore. *Spurgeon.* Chicago: Moody, 1984.

R.J. Sheehan. *C.H. Spurgeon and the Modern Church.* London: Grace Publications, 1985. (An excellent short history of the Downgrade Controversy.)

François Guizot and Abraham Kuyper: Statesmen, Scholars, and Saints

by Mark Sidwell

Europe in the nineteenth century often underwent turmoil as new ideologies clashed in the political arena or even on the battlefield. Christians did not ignore these conflicts, and many sought to bring the Scripture to bear on social, political, and economic questions. Two outstanding examples of this tendency were François Guizot and Abraham Kuyper.

Nineteenth-century political history in Europe is studded with great names. Disreali and Gladstone in England and Bismarck in Germany are notable examples. The names of François Guizot of France and Abraham Kuyper of the Netherlands are not as well known today, but their attempts to govern men by the precepts of God are worthy of note.

François Guizot

A historian noted that although François Guizot was often respected and sometimes admired, he was never popular. Guizot's reserved and cold demeanor did not win him numerous friends. Rather, Guizot's unbending honesty and his single-minded devotion to principle made him an important leader in France.

Guizot was born in Nimes, France, in 1787, into a Protestant family. When Guizot's father was executed in 1794 during the Reign of Terror, Guizot's mother then took her family to Geneva for refuge. Guizot returned to Paris in 1805 to study law, and he soon built a reputation as a writer. His annotated version of Edward Gibbon's *Decline and Fall of the Roman Empire* (1813) made him famous and helped earn him a position as a professor of modern history at the Sorbonne in Paris.

After the fall of Napoleon Bonaparte, Guizot became involved in French politics. He held several positions in the French government and in 1830 was elected to the Chamber of Deputies. In 1840, Guizot became Minister of Foreign Affairs and, thereby, the real head of the French government.

In France's parliamentary government, a faction stayed in power only as long as it kept a majority of the legislators on its side. Otherwise, the king would call on another faction to lead the government, or he would call for new elections. From 1830 to 1840, France had several governments, or ministries, as they were called. The Guizot ministry, however, lasted for nearly eight years. Under Guizot's government, France knew peace, prosperity, and stability.

Guizot believed in constitutional government in which written guarantees defined and protected the rights of all citizens. He also believed in limiting the right to vote to property owners. Thus, Guizot thought, those who had the greatest interest in stable government would hold the reins of power. Guizot also thought the government should allow all men the opportunity to rise socially and politically—if they were willing and able. He once said, "The movement of ascension is nowhere stopped. With work, good sense, good conduct, one rises, one can rise as high as it is possible to rise in the social hierarchy."

Guizot had many enemies. On one occasion in 1844, the opposition trumped up a charge of treason against Guizot. In a stormy session of the Chamber of Deputies, Guizot defended himself against the charge. As his enemies tried to shout him down, Guizot said, "You may perhaps exhaust my physical strength but you cannot quell my courage. . . . As to the insults, calumnies and theatrical rage directed against me, they may be multiplied and accumulated as you please, but they will never rise above my contempt."

In 1848, a wave of revolutions swept over Europe and toppled governments in its wake. France was no exception. Opposition forced Guizot out of power, and the king fled the country. Guizot spent a brief exile in England, but he returned to France in 1851 and resumed his teaching.

After 1848 Guizot gave closer attention to the cause of French Protestantism. Even before that time, he had not hidden his faith. For example, when the *réveil* (see pp. 163-67) brought spiritual awakening to French Protestants, Guizot spoke out publicly in 1838 in defense of the revival.

Guizot became concerned about the growth of liberalism within the French Reformed Church, and he joined other orthodox laymen and pastors who wanted the church to adopt a definite statement of faith. Liberal pastors attacked the idea of subscribing to a creed. One leading liberal reportedly said that he was so opposed to the idea of subscription that he would not sign even a declaration that two plus two equals four. The orthodox party pressed on, however. At the National Synod of 1872, the Reformed Church adopted a statement of faith affirming the church's belief in the authority of the Bible, the deity of Christ, His resurrection, and salvation through faith in Him alone. The liberals then left the church, leaving the orthodox party completely victorious. Before his death in 1874, Guizot claimed that his part in this struggle was his last great victory.

Abraham Kuyper

About the time that François Guizot's career was drawing to a close, Abraham Kuyper's was just beginning. He was born in Maassluis, Netherlands, in 1837. Kuyper entered the ministry of the state church, but he began as an unconverted liberal. At his first church in Beesd, Kuyper was impressed by the simple piety of the orthodox laymen in his congregation. As Kuyper talked with these devout if "unlearned" Christians, he realized that they possessed a peace and joy that was alien to him. He later wrote,

> What drew me most to them was that here the heart spoke— there was inner experience. I came back to them again and again. True, I did my best to function as parson but found that I had more inclination to listen than to teach. . . . I thank God that I did not oppose them. Their persistence brought bless- ing to my heart and the dawn of the morning star in my life.

Kuyper's change of heart resulted in a change of mind as well. He rejected the liberal views he had held and became a tenacious defender of orthodoxy. When Dutch universities proved hostile to orthodox theology, Kuyper led a movement to found a Christian school. He refused to be satisfied with a seminary or a Christian liberal arts college; Kuyper wanted a full-fledged university which would educate young people from a Christian perspective in order to prepare them to serve in all walks of life. The culmination of this dream came in 1880 when the Free University of Amsterdam opened its doors with Kuyper as a professor of divinity.

Kuyper opposed liberalism in the state church by protesting vigorously when the church eased its requirements for the ordination of ministers. Instead of having to subscribe to the church's orthodox creed, ministers had only to promise "to promote the interests of the Kingdom of God in general and especially those of the State Church." Then church authorities relaxed standards for admission to the church so that it became easier for the unregenerate to become members. The fight over this latter action led to the suspension of Kuyper and seventy-four other orthodox men. Kuyper and the others then formed their own independent denomination in 1886.

Kuyper's faith embraced all aspects of life, and his broad concerns led him into politics. Kuyper joined the Christian Historical or Anti-Revolutionary party, and in 1867 he became its head. He founded a political newspaper, *De Standaard,* and was elected to the Dutch Parliament in 1874. The climax of Kuyper's political career came in 1901 when his coalition of parties captured a majority of the seats in Parliament and Kuyper became prime minister (1901-1905).

Kuyper took as the basis of his political philosophy the idea of God's sovereignty. In fact, his party's name, "Anti-Revolutionary," derived partly from its opposition to the doctrine of the French Revolution that political power ultimately resides with the people and not with God. "Authority over man cannot arise from man," he wrote. Instead he emphasized that "all authority of governments on earth originates from the Sovereignty of God alone."

Kuyper viewed society in terms of three "spheres of sovereignty": the family, the church, and the state. "Each sphere has its own unique, inviolable, delegated authority," he said. "No sphere . . . may suppress or tyrannize or draw parasitically upon others." In fact, Kuyper viewed the family, not the individual, as the basis of society. When these three spheres worked in proper harmony, Kuyper said, then all three would fulfill their respective purpose.

Kuyper's ideas did not die with him in 1920. His political party survived him and carried on his ideals. His theology proved even more influential as it spread to the United States through Dutch immigrants and won a large following in American Reformed bodies.

Conclusion

Guizot and Kuyper had much in common. Both were respected scholars and writers, both were successful statesmen who governed their countries well, and both were outstanding Christians who fought against theological liberalism. Their lives reveal that these three facets of their lives were interrelated. Guizot and Kuyper were not great politicians in spite of their Christianity; they were men whose faith shaped their lives and indeed made them great.

Suggestions for Further Reading

Douglas Johnson. *Guizot: Aspects of French History, 1787-1874.* London: Routledge & Kegan Paul, 1963.

Frank Vanden Berg. *Abraham Kuyper.* Reprint; St. Catharines, Ontario: Paideia Press, 1978.

"Gipsy" Smith

by Christa G. Habegger

The late nineteenth and early twentieth centuries were the era of the great urban evangelists. These men held huge city-wide campaigns all over the world but particularly in Great Britain and the United States. The best known of these evangelists were usually American—D. L. Moody (1837-1899), R. A. Torrey (1856-1928), J. Wilbur Chapman (1859-1918), Sam Jones (1847-1906), and, of course, Billy Sunday (1862-1935). Rodney "Gipsy" Smith (1860-1947) was one of the few English evangelists of equal stature to the Americans. His career perhaps typifies the ministries of these men who transformed cities and even nations by their preaching of the Word of God.

Rodney Smith was born to Cornelius and Mary Welch Smith on March 31, 1860, in a gipsy tent east of London, England. He was the fourth of six children. The family earned their living making and selling kitchen utensils, baskets, and clothespins. Cornelius Smith supplemented the family's income by playing his violin in local taverns. Often, young Rodney would dance while his father fiddled and collect money after the entertainment.

Real gipsies (not the costumed, palm-reading sort), as Rodney was always eager to point out, were an uneducated but meticulously clean and generally upright race. Rodney often noted the gipsies' strict observance of the Sabbath—despite their inability to read the Bible. Gipsy families were close-knit. Rodney commented once: "The gipsy wagon can be the happiest home in the whole of England."

Rodney's mother Mary was still a young woman when she died of smallpox. Cornelius was heartbroken at her loss and awed by the responsibility of rearing his large family alone. His conscience was awakened, and he began to desire to know God. He met a mission worker who invited him to a gospel service. "I am converted!" he announced to his family afterwards. "Children, God has made a new man of me. You have a new father!"

Rodney, impressed by the transformation of his father's life, was under deep conviction. On November 17, 1876, in a Cambridge chapel, he accepted Christ. Rodney described the exchange between himself and a dear old man who dealt with him after the service. The old man quoted John 1:12 and reminded him, "You must believe that He has saved you." Rodney replied, "Well, I cannot trust myself, for I am nothing; and I cannot trust in what I have, for I have nothing; and I cannot trust in what I know, for I know nothing." The young gipsy therefore put his entire trust in his Saviour.

Rodney was determined to serve the Lord. Above all, he desired to preach, but in order to preach, he needed to learn to read God's Word. He acquired "three mighty volumes"—a Bible, a dictionary, and a Bible dictionary. His brothers and sisters laughed at him for carrying the books around with him, but Rodney replied, "I am going to read them some day, and to preach, too." His self-education continued to the end of his life. He became an avid reader and a polished speaker as a result of his efforts.

At the age of seventeen, Rodney Smith left the gipsy wagon and joined the ranks of the Salvation Army. Rodney was in a meeting one night when William Booth suddenly announced, "The Gipsy boy will sing." As Rodney stood before the crowd, a man called, "Keep your heart up youngster." Rodney, not intending to be overheard, retorted, "Well, it's in my mouth. How high do you want it?"

Rodney was soon sent out as an evangelist, preaching on street corners and in mission halls in various English towns. At first Rodney wondered whether he should ask someone else to read the Scriptures for him before he preached, but he decided against that in favor of another method which served him well until he became more skilled. Whenever he came across an unfamiliar word in the Scripture lesson, he would stop before it and comment upon what he had just read. Then he would continue his reading—on the other side of the problematic word!

At nineteen, Rodney married a new Christian, Annie E. Pennock, at the town of Whitby. Together they were assigned to work at Chatham, where their ministry resulted in many converts. There, the name "Gipsy" Smith first became widely used. There also, the first of the Smiths' three children was born.

In 1882 Gipsy Smith severed his connections with the Salvation Army and set out in evangelism on his own. His ministry, which began on street corners, eventually became worldwide as offers to preach came to him from all over the European continent and from such places as Australia, Africa, and the United States. Although Gipsy was saved in a Primitive Methodist church, he was not intent upon making Methodists of his converts. He worked willingly under the auspices of many different Christian groups. His first trip to America, which began in January 1889, for instance, was suggested by two Congregationalists and a Presbyterian.

Unfortunately, he was not careful to avoid association with theological liberalism, then in its early stages. He seemed to lack spiritual discernment in the matter of ecclesiastical separation. He failed to balance his favorite sermon theme, "The Love of God," with the equally important Biblical theme of separation.

Gipsy once accepted an invitation to preach a campaign in Manhattan under the auspices of early liberals, including Parks Cadman and others like him. His un-Scriptural cooperation with them made it impossible for a strong separatist, Dr. J. Wilbur Chapman, to hold the campaign he had envisioned for New York the following year. Other separatists viewed many of Gipsy's alliances with alarm. Had liberalism been more firmly entrenched in Gipsy's day than it was, his cooperation with it would have been a serious blight on his ministry.

Gipsy Smith, who did not enjoy traveling, nonetheless whole-heartedly enjoyed being with the people of other countries. He found Americans particularly friendly. He said once, "You will see more handshaking after one service in America than after tea in this country. In England, when the benediction is pronounced, we rush for the door; in America they rush for one another."

Gipsy Smith became "the evangelist whom America loved." Even the press complimented him extravagantly, describing his appearance, his manner, and his sermon content in vivid detail. His meetings drew enormous crowds of several thousands, with hundreds of converts. This was the great era of massive evangelism in America, and Gipsy Smith was one of the prime instruments of the God-given revival in the early decades of the twentieth century.

Apart from the obvious blessing of God on Gipsy's ministry, one might say there are human reasons that his meetings were popular occasions. One of these was the spontaneity which characterized any service at which Gipsy presided. He disliked rigid formats for a preaching meeting. Rather, he liked to "get the feel of his audience" by singing with the people or talking casually to them until he felt he had their confidence and could meet their needs. Once, when presented with "an order of service," Gipsy responded: "Well, if you wanted that, you had better go on your holidays. I was born in a field, and you can't cram me into a flower pot." Often, while preaching, Gipsy would spot someone in the congregation whom he recognized as an old friend or a new convert. He never hesitated to stop, acknowledge the friend by name, and give a special greeting before continuing his message.

Gipsy's humor was irrepressible. It originated, perhaps, in his natural exuberance for life and his optimism. He drew from his wide experience with people and from his colorful gipsy past for his humorous anecdotes which were such a delightful and instructive part of his preaching. He liked to tell of an incident in which he was seated next to a proper old lady at a prayer meeting. "Are you a Christian?" Gipsy asked her. "No, sir," the little lady replied. "I'm an Episcopalian."

Gipsy's preaching was emotional, in the best sense of the term. He was never ashamed of his own tears when he was moved by a sad story or a long-awaited conversion. His preaching was always characterized by the warmth of his feelings. His biographer and close associate, Harold Murray, wrote, "I know that Gipsy puts *himself* into all he says; his own experience, his own sorrows, his own joys, his own longings." He went on to say of his power to move an audience, "The scenes Gipsy sees are real and living, and every time they rise up the tears well up too; and seeing the pictures with him the audience is moved and melted. There is heart, not art in it."

Yet, for all the emotionalism in the service, there was little in the inquiry room. There Gipsy demanded quiet, thoughtful prayer and a thorough understanding of what the decision to be saved signified.

Music was another element which was inseparable from Gipsy's campaigns. He loved to sing, and he expected others to join him. Sometimes, during the first hymn, Gipsy would complain of half-hearted participation. He would say: "You are not all singing. Now you have all had a good look at me, and know what I'm like. You must sing—or go home!"

A chorus he heard once became the theme song of many campaigns: "Let the Beauty of Jesus Be Seen in Me." It became as well the topic for many of his sermons. Another of his favorites was the gospel song "Wonderful Jesus." He himself wrote songs which continue to be well-loved. Among them are "Jesus Revealed in Me" and "Not Dreaming."

Follow-up of new converts was vital to the lasting success of Gipsy's campaigns. He knew that the primary responsibility would rest with the congregation. That is why, when a church member commented that he hoped "they will follow up these decisions," Gipsy eyed him sternly and said, "Excuse me, but *you* are 'they.' "

His biographer, Murray, described Gipsy as a humble man, despite well-founded accusations that the evangelist talked too much of himself and his accomplishments. Murray pointed out that Gipsy's boasts, at least as regarded his campaigns, were always of the Lord's goodness and His gifts of grace in revival blessing. Gipsy was well aware that people often mistakenly assumed that he was responsible for success in a campaign. He said once, "Gipsy Smith doesn't matter. If you claim the promises and pray from your heart for revival, God will find His instrument. I'm only the channel, not the source."

As an old man, Gipsy Smith was remarkably youthful and energetic. At seventy-six he could snort at the idea of retirement and surprise onlookers by demonstrating that he could still touch his toes, an exercise he recommended. He continued to accept preaching engagements until the end of his life.

Following the death of his wife, Annie, in 1937, Gipsy made headlines by remarrying. His new wife was Mary Alice Shaw, with whom he was united on June 2, 1938, the bride's 27th birthday. Despite the difference in their ages, the match was a good one. Mary Alice was able to help him when he most needed assistance, particularly in the last years when his health began to fail.

At 87, the old evangelist was keen of mind but weak of voice and heart. The Smiths decided to travel to Florida for the restoration of his physical strength. Three hours from New York harbor, on August 4, 1947, Gipsy Smith died of a heart attack.

Two years later, near his birthplace in England, a memorial was unveiled. At the end of the inscription are these appropriate words: "What Hath God Wrought." Gipsy Smith left behind many memorials in his books, songs, and sermons, but perhaps the most fitting memorial is the tribute of thousands of people across the world who owe their spiritual rebirth to his tireless ministry.

Suggestions for Further Reading

Gipsy Smith. *Gipsy Smith: His Life and Work.* New York: Revell, 1925.

David Lazell. *Gipsy Smith: From the Forest I Came.* Chicago: Moody, 1970.

Harold Murray. *Sixty Years an Evangelist.* London: Marshall, Morgan and Scott, 1937.

I Shook Hands with Hitler

by Edith S. Long

The rise of totalitarian dictatorships challenged the Christian Church in the twentieth century. Modern-day antichrists such as Lenin, Stalin, Mussolini, and Hitler announced their hatred of God and violently persecuted Christians. Some believers suffered because they opposed the ungodly policies of such leaders; others suffered simply for bearing the name of Christ. As the following article shows, these dictators made gods of themselves. Hitler in particular presented himself as a German messiah. Millions of Germans, such as the one who wrote this article, ultimately learned that Adolf Hitler was a false savior. The author also learned, however, that the only true Saviour is Jesus Christ.

Since childhood I have dreamed of freedom. Here in America my dream has come true. For here I have found not only political freedom but also spiritual freedom.

Although I was born in Czechoslovakia, my parents were Germans. We lived in the Sudetenland, which was Austrian until after World War I when it became Czech territory. In the 1930s most Germans in the Sudetenland were without regular work because of their nationality. From 1934 to 1938, however, my father was able to make a living for our family of four by running an insurance, cotton, and candy agency. He was also caretaker of a German-owned factory.

By 1938 our savings were exhausted, and as war approached, all Germans were under suspicion and subject to arrest whenever it pleased the Czechs. Many were hungry and destitute, just as they had been in Germany in 1933 before Adolf Hitler came to power. As the Germans in Czechoslovakia looked across the border, they could not help being a little envious of the prosperity they witnessed. Everyone in Germany had a job (primarily in war industries) and could feed his family. Thus, in October 1938, Hitler was welcomed with open arms in the Sudetenland as the savior of the oppressed. We were sure that because of him everyone would have a job, food on the table, and a better living standard.

One day in September 1938, my mother announced that Hitler was coming to a nearby town, and we were going to see him. How excited we were! Early that morning we eagerly boarded a train to get a glimpse of the great man. After we arrived in Breslau, we got into line to march by the review stand where Hitler was supposed to be. After an hour and only a few blocks of progress, someone announced that Hitler had been detained and would arrive in two hours. Meanwhile, everyone was kept happy by the beautiful marches that were played over the loudspeakers set up all over town. After nearly three hours the voice again announced a delay, and then again and again. Through it all, we were entertained by march music. By the time Hitler finally arrived, everyone had worked himself into a frenzy. "He must be greater than we think. He is so important that people detain him everywhere he goes. He can do everything for us. He is our great, great leader!"

We finally arrived at a large stadium, where we found that we would be so far away from the review stand that we could hardly see Hitler. My mother decided to get closer and broke through the restraining ropes. A young lady saw that I was gasping for air underneath the feet of the grownups and rescued me by lifting me up on her shoulders. Now we were on our way; everyone made room for this unusual pair. Finally we arrived at the review stand. As we came in front of Hitler, he reached down and shook my hand and the hand of the young lady. What a cheering went up from the crowd, and what excitement it was! To see Hitler was absolutely great, but for him to shake my hand was unbelievable. "Don't wash your hand," was the advice everyone gave me. I was asked to repeat the story over and over after we arrived home.

By summer 1939 there was again talk of war. But, of course, Hitler could handle that. Had he not taken care of the Germans since 1933? Furthermore, the war would be over in a few months, and everyone could live in peace thereafter. It was for the good of the people to get rid of the enemies.

My family did not worry about the war since we believed Hitler's propaganda. We were ready to give up some comforts temporarily in order to have a good life in a few months. But the months grew to years, and the war went on and on. By 1944 the enemy was coming closer and closer to the German borders, but we all still believed that Hitler would save us. There was even talk about a secret, powerful weapon that would crush the enemy.

Early in 1945 someone told my family of the horrors of the prison camps. Most people did not know that people died not only on the battlefield but also in the prison camps. Those who did know dared not tell. We simply refused to believe the stories; Hitler was a savior, not a murderer.

But he was no savior. In April 1945 he killed himself so that the Russians would not capture him.

Now began the hardest days for the German people. Everyone tried to flee west to the Americans. They were known as the most humane people—the ones who would give the best treatment and would not torture or misuse us in any way. Those who had come from the east told terrible stories of the Russians, of how they raped, tortured, and killed refugees. So, when we heard one morning that the Russians would be in our town in two hours, my mother and I quickly left with whatever we could carry.

We were picked up by a Red Cross vehicle that carried us and some wounded westward. Only one thought was in our minds: "Let's get as far away from the Russians as we can." On May 10 we came near the city of Chaslau and could hear the sound of machine guns and other weapons. As we came closer to town, everything grew quiet. At the town square, we saw a Czech waving a white flag and calling, "German soldier, please do not shoot. We not want fight. Please, please!" Then chaos broke loose around us. We had been led into an ambush. Had it not been for a truck parked next to the Red Cross bus, we would have been riddled by bullets. We spent the next ten days in Russian-controlled territory but escaped unharmed.

It took a long time to reach the Americans. It was very warm during the days, and we were hungry and thirsty, but there was nothing to eat or drink. We were spit upon, cursed, called all kinds of names, and our lives were threatened. The farmers chased us off their land with their dogs when we begged for water. In several places the water was poisoned. We drank out of every creek and dirty puddle we could find. Each day we thought we would reach the American line, but each day the line was moved farther west to accommodate the Russians, and we had to wait another day to gain our freedom. During those days the Lord protected us from all kinds of harm, and I am deeply grateful. Now, as a Christian, I can see God's hand, but at the time we felt we were just lucky.

Finally we caught up with the Americans. Now we started our journey to Weiden in Bavaria where my father's brother was a refugee. We hoped to find my father and brother there. When we arrived, we found everything completely crowded. There was no place for us to stay since we had to have a job in order to get a room. We finally found jobs in a makeshift hospital. The patients there had typhoid fever, diphtheria, tuberculosis, scarlet fever, and many other communicable diseases. We scrubbed floors, cleaned toilets, and emptied the spittoons. Here again the Lord miraculously protected us and kept us in good health despite our exhausted, starved condition.

West Germany became the home for more than seventeen million refugees. The loved ones of these were either in a hospital or prison camp or were dead. Some found each other after months and years of searching. My family, what was left of it, was no exception. We heard in 1947 from the Red Cross that my brother had died in a French prison camp fourteen months earlier. My father passed away after he came back from a Russian prison. It was then that my mother and I decided to go to Vienna, Austria.

We were always looking for something better—a place where we belonged and, above all, a place where we could be free. So, when we heard that people could immigrate to the United States, we rushed to fill out the forms, for this meant freedom at last.

On June 21, 1950, my dream came true. As I entered the harbor of New York, there was the beautiful lady, the Statue of Liberty, waving to me. I greeted her with tears in my eyes.

The United States was all I had expected it to be. I had the physical freedom I wanted. I had enough good food, nice clothes, and the necessary shelter. And after five years in this country, I became a citizen. After ten years of being a noncitizen, of being unwanted by any country, I was now the citizen of the greatest country in the world, and I had the same rights and freedom as anyone who is a citizen by birth.

It was here in the United States that I met the wonderful Christian man who was to become my husband, and through him I realized that the most important freedom in my life was missing: I did not know Christ. When I accepted Him as my Saviour, I knew a freedom that far surpassed any political freedom I had ever dreamed of.

Looking back, I realize that the tragedy of losing my homeland and loved ones became my biggest blessing. Had we remained in Czechoslovakia, I would be a Communist today. Had my father and brother not died, I would have stayed in Germany and may never have known Christ, for only a few there hear the Word.

The Lord protected me from bullets, starvation, diseases, and the Russians, and He has led me to this great country to make me truly free—free from the bondage of sin and free to serve Him.

With this peace within me and His Word to guide me, I am able to consider prayerfully all decisions I must make. The world can crumble around me, but my Lord will be with me. Through my experiences I have learned that the Lord takes care of us. He punishes us individually or nationally, but He guides in all. Freedom can always be found in Christ, who said, "Ye shall know the truth, and the truth shall make you free" (John 8:32).

Suggestions for Further Reading

J.S. Conway. *The Nazi Persecution of the Churches, 1933-45.* New York: Basic Books, 1968.

Andrew Drummond. *German Protestantism Since Luther.* London: Epworth Press, 1951.

E. J. Poole-Connor:
A Lifetime of Faithful Service

by Mark Sidwell

A major theme in twentieth-century church history has been the conflict between theological liberalism and orthodoxy. In America, this battle was typified by the fundamentalist-modernist controversy which engulfed the major denominations in the 1920s. In other countries, many other Christians have joined the ranks of orthodox believers who oppose liberalism. In Great Britain, C. H. Spurgeon was the forerunner of those who refused to be associated with liberalism. D. Martyn Lloyd-Jones (1899-1981) was perhaps the greatest twentieth-century leader. Standing as a link between these men was the life and ministry of E. J. Poole-Connor.

Edward Joshua Poole-Connor was born in 1872 into a devout English Protestant family. One of Poole-Connor's fondest memories of childhood was his father's long and fervent prayers, particularly for his family. Poole-Connor noted later in life that his father's prayers were answered—all six children were converted.

Poole-Connor did well at school, but he had to drop out at the age of thirteen when his father fell ill and he had to operate the family business. Like many people denied the opportunity to continue their education, Poole-Connor sought to make up for this lack by becoming an avid reader. His family responsibilities did not interfere with his spiritual life, either. His work in his church, his participation in evangelistic campaigns, and his skill in speaking to small gatherings caused a local Baptist pastor to urge Poole-Connor to consider entering the ministry. In 1890, at the age of eighteen, E. J. Poole-Connor began a lifetime of Christian service by taking the pastorate of a small Baptist church.

The years 1890 to 1910 were a period of growth and maturing for the young minister. He pastored four different Baptist churches and in the process learned much about how to lead a congregation and even more about how to depend on God. For example, he called his pastorate at the Balaclava Baptist Church in Surbiton (1900-1910) a time in which he was "very short of money, but very happy." Despite his ministerial duties and limited funds, Poole-Connor also made time to attend lectures at London University while in Surbiton.

In 1910, Poole-Connor began a brief ministry which shaped his later career. He served as assistant pastor to Fuller Gooch, minister of an independent work in Lansdowne Hall. As he contemplated Gooch's successful thirty-year ministry with that congregation, Poole-Connor later wrote, "It gave me a vision of Christian unity, based first upon the fact of the essential oneness of all believers, and second upon a common belief of the fundamental doctrines of the Christian faith."

Great Britain at that time, like the rest of Europe and America, was witnessing the growth and dominance of liberal theology in its churches. The Downgrade Controversy (see pp. 178-79) had been one of the first skirmishes in the battle between the liberals and the orthodox or, to use twentieth-century labels, between the modernists and the fundamentalists. Poole-Connor was growing increasingly aware that this was a battle in which no thoughtful Christian could remain neutral.

Poole-Connor left the ministry at Lansdowne Hall in 1912. Although Gooch had hoped that the younger man might later take over the work, Poole-Connor realized that a faction in the church was preferring him to the pastor. Rather than risk splitting the congregation, Poole-Connor left and took the pastorate of Talbot Tabernacle in London. In this new place of service, Poole-Connor organized a Sunday school which reached one thousand children at its height. He held special monthly missionary prayer meetings which not only offered prayers for the missionaries but also inspired members of the congregation to go as missionaries themselves. During the winter months, the congregation operated a soup kitchen to minister to the needy.

In 1921, Poole-Connor left Talbot Tabernacle to become deputation secretary for a mission board. As he traveled about England on behalf of the board, he observed the situation in the churches closely. He wrote later,

> I naturally took special interest in what I saw of the unattached Churches. I found that the smaller assemblies of this order were often very isolated, some of them being scarcely aware that any others existed. I noted that many of their pastors, although spiritually qualified men, had no general recognition as accredited

"ministers of religion." I observed that others, although being blessed to the conversion of the unsaved, were limited in their ability to "feed the flock of God," for lack of adequate training. . . . I also met a number of denominational ministers who were becoming disturbed at the growth of Modernism in the body to which they belonged, but, being aware of the disagreeable consequences of secession, were uncertain as to the course to pursue. In all these cases there seemed to be either needs requiring to be met, or possibilities that might be developed; and the knowledge of them drove me to thought and prayer. Could not these unattached Churches—so I began to ask myself—be brought together in some association of mutual helpfulness?

Poole-Connor proposed founding a fellowship of independent churches. Although some opposed the idea, others supported it. He wrote, "Many were of the opinion that if some such union as was proposed was formed, with a strong 'Fundamentalist' basis, it would not only lessen the sense of isolation which many experience, but would also strengthen their hands in combating the dangers of Modernism."

The result of these efforts was the founding in 1922 of what became known as the Fellowship of Independent Evangelical Churches (FIEC). The FIEC sought to meet the needs of its members through a variety of functions and outreaches. A Ministerial List and a Register of Churches, for example, gained pastors and churches official recognition so that they could serve as or sponsor chaplains in the military. The FIEC also provided examinations to help validate the sometimes irregular courses of study that independent pastors had to follow—as demonstrated by Poole-Connor himself. For those desiring further study, the body provided a recommended reading list along with a schedule of reading. To provide a source for the reading, the group established the Evangelical Library. Building on a previous collection of twenty-five thousand volumes, the library provided a wealth of resources for pastors and churches. Poole-Connor took a strong personal interest in this library, even to the point of helping assemble bookshelves at its new location in London. In addition to all of this, the FIEC administered funds for charitable causes and sought to establish churches in areas in which no clear gospel witness existed.

In an effort to define the group's opposition to modernism, Poole-Connor drew up an unambiguous Declaration of Faith for the FIEC. Without equivocation, the body affirmed the full inspiration of the Bible, the reality of the Trinity, the deity of Christ, justification by faith alone, and other fundamental doctrines.

As involved as Poole-Connor was with the FIEC, he pursued other avenues of ministry as well. In 1933, he resumed the pastorate of the Talbot Tabernacle. For ten years he maintained this ministry, even through the difficulties caused by World War II and the resulting German air raids.

In 1943, Poole-Connor left the church for the final time. He was seventy-one years old, but he did not retire. The FIEC appointed him "National Commissioner," and he redoubled his efforts to speak and write on behalf of that organization. From 1945 to 1948, he served as principal of a Bible college, helping guide it through the postwar years and teaching classes in church history, Old Testament, and more. In 1952, he helped found the British Evangelical Council (BEC), an alliance of independent bodies such as the FIEC and the Free Presbyterian Church of Scotland "united in their opposition to that form of unscriptural ecumenicity represented by the World Council of Churches."

From the earliest years of his ministry, Poole-Connor had set aside a portion of his time for writing tracts, pamphlets, and books in defense of the Christian faith. In 1951, Poole-Connor published his greatest work, *Evangelicalism in England.* From the Renaissance to the twentieth century, the author traced the history of the evangelical faith in England. With a grace of style and depth of learning that belied his supposedly sparse education, Poole-Connor argued that evangelicalism was simply the expression of the Biblical faith and that only as evangelicalism remained true to the Bible would it remain strong. In the conclusion the author wrote, "Evangelicals who remain in complacent fellowship with those that deny their faith are not only failing to stem the tide of apostasy; they are accelerating its pace."

In 1954, the Bible League, an organization founded in 1897 to defend Biblical inspiration against the onslaughts of higher criticism, invited Poole-Connor to become editor of is periodical, *The Bible League Quarterly.* In the *Quarterly*'s pages, Poole-Connor poured out a series of articles, editorials, and reviews designed to defend the true faith and to oppose the advances of liberalism.

In December of 1961, Poole-Connor fell seriously ill, and he died in January of the following year. Up to within weeks of his death, he continued his labors—making his a ministry of over seventy years. It had not been an easy ministry. In his later years, for example, he once wrote in his personal diary,

> My spiritual activities over a long course of years, preaching, teaching, lecturing, writing, have left no permanent mark on my generation. . . . How little—and *how little*—there is to

show for a lifetime's labour. Yet I have sought to do God's will day by day, and to do His work faithfully.

E. J. Poole-Connor did not need to feel any doubts, however. Many Christians appreciated the work he had done and valued his stand for righteousness. Poole-Connor himself never gave way to despair. To a friend who visited him shortly before his death, the old minister said, "Don't be distressed if you see me in pain. It is purely physical suffering—my faith is stronger than it ever was."

Suggestions for Further Reading

E.J. Poole-Connor. *Evangelicalism in England.* London: The Fellowship of Independent Evangelical Churches, 1951.

D.G. Fountain. *E. J. Poole-Connor: Contender for the Faith.* Worthing, England: Henry E. Walter Ltd., 1966.

R.J. Sheehan. *C. H. Spurgeon and the Modern Church.* London: Grace Publications, 1985. (Pages 80-124 discuss the work of Spurgeon's separatist "heirs," notably Poole-Connor and D. Martyn Lloyd-Jones.)

Duncan Campbell
and the Lewis Revival

by Christa G. Habegger

Revivals since the First World War have not, for the most part, matched in scope those awakenings that shook America and Europe in the past. Arguments differ concerning the reason for this fact. Some say that modern apostasy is so great that revival on a large scale will never occur again. Others reject this idea but agree that the sins of the modern church— prayerlessness, worldliness, and more—hinder the moving of the Holy Spirit in blessing us as He would. Revival has not been unknown in this century, however. Although such awakenings have not been so widespread as before, God has visited His people in profound, soul-stirring power. One such occasion is the Lewis Revival in Scotland in the 1950s.

There are a great many views held by people today as to what revival is, so you hear men say, "Are you going out to the revival meetings?" "We're having a revival crusade," and so on. There is a world of difference between a crusade or a special effort in the field of evangelism [and true revival]. . . . We praise God for such movements. But is it not true that such movements do not as a general rule touch the community? The community remains more or less the same and the masses go past us to hell. But in revival, the community suddenly becomes conscious of the movings of God, beginning with His own people, so that . . . in a matter of hours, churches become crowded . . . and you find within hours scores of men and women crying to God for mercy before they [go] near a church.

Duncan Campbell (1898-1971)

That is a description of the type of revival which swept the island of Lewis during the early 1950s. The man with whom the movement is most often associated is Duncan Campbell, a Scottish preacher whose ministry spanned nearly fifty years of this century.

Duncan was born on February 13, 1898, at Blackcrofts in the Scottish Highlands, the fifth child in a family of nine. His parents, Hugh and Jane Campbell, were saved as a result of the witness of two female "Pilgrims," missionaries sent by Scotland's Faith Mission to the Western Highlands and Islands. Family worship became an important part of the family routine, and Jane Campbell particularly influenced the children for righteousness by her constant prayers and godly example. Duncan, described by a brother as a "wee rascal" with a shock of bright red hair, was an adventurous and independent youngster. Like the rest of the Campbell brood, he was expected to harness his energies to help with household and farming chores.

As a young teen, Duncan discovered a talent for playing the bagpipes. By the winter of 1913 he and a group of other young pipers were providing entertainment for dances and concerts. During one concert Duncan was suddenly seized by great conviction of sin. Even as he tried to retain his composure the thought plagued him: "Is this all that life has to offer a young fellow?" He left the concert after a brief explanation to his companions and made his way home to get right with God. His mother, who had prayed earnestly for him, rejoiced with him at his conversion. From then on, there was no doubt in anyone's mind that Duncan Campbell had been born again. The young man witnessed to everyone he saw about the saving power of Jesus Christ.

In his late teens Duncan was called to serve in the British army. As a machine-gunner in some of the bloodiest battles of the First World War, Duncan was in constant danger. The Lord preserved him physically throughout his time in the service, but Duncan was even more aware of God's grace because of the way He protected him spiritually. Duncan maintained a strong testimony, but he testified later that he had fought tremendous inner battles with sin.

Upon discharge from military duty, Duncan returned to the Highlands and soon embarked upon a ministry to his own village and surrounding districts. Not trained to preach, Duncan simply told the Highlanders the story of his own conversion, read the Scriptures, and prayed with the people whose homes he visited. These "kitchen devotions" were effective in pointing many to Christ.

Duncan became conscious of the need for Bible training if he were to expand his influence for the gospel. In 1919 he enrolled in the Faith Mission in Edinburgh where he received nine months of intensive training to be a missionary. His first assignment as a Pilgrim was to North Ireland. From there he returned to his native Scotland and ministered primarily to remote communities in Argyllshire and Inverness-shire.

In December of 1925 Duncan married Shona Gray, a blue-eyed "lassie" with whom he had fallen in love eleven years before. Shortly after his marriage, Duncan accepted a call from the presbytery in the little town of Ardvasar to serve as pastor of their church.

From then until 1948 he pastored churches—in Ardvasar, then Balintore, and finally Falkirk. In addition to regular church services, Duncan filled his schedule with preaching engagements to other congregations. He was a popular preacher, not because he delivered appealing, soothing messages, but because he was straightforward and passionate. Teen-agers were attracted by his vigorous manner and obvious concern for them. His message was simple. He did not try to argue "theology." His was a theology of working Christianity. "He knew God could save and transform lives. He had seen it happen. It worked. That was enough." Duncan avoided long invitations or appeals following a service. Rather, he announced short prayer meetings afterwards to which Christians were welcomed and also anyone who wished to be saved. He willingly counseled with those needing help following a meeting, "but preferred to hear of men and women having transactions with God without any human involvement."

In 1949 at age fifty, Duncan left a settled ministry of twenty-three years to return to his first love—missionary evangelism with the Faith Mission. He and Mrs. Campbell moved their growing family of five children to Edinburgh, and with that as headquarters, Duncan accepted invitations to conduct "missions" (special meetings) all over Scotland.

It was during a series of meetings in 1949 on the island of Skye that Duncan received an invitation to preach in Lewis, the largest isle of the Outer Hebrides. The Christians of Lewis sensed the growing apathy toward spiritual matters among their church members and among the young people of the island, most of whom avoided church altogether.

In the village of Barvas in Lewis lived two godly elderly ladies, Peggy and Christine Smith. Peggy was blind, and her sister was crippled with arthritis. Because they were not able to attend services in the village church, they met with God in their cottage. There they received the promise: "I will pour water upon him that is thirsty and floods upon the dry ground." One night Peggy sent for the minister, Rev. James MacKay, and told him that God had revealed to her His promise of revival. She asked that he call his elders and deacons together for special prayer. They met for months at night in a barn, pleading with God for an outpouring of His power in their midst. Yet, despite their prayers and efforts to interest the Barvas youth in spiritual things, not a single young person attended services.

During one prayer meeting a young deacon rose to his feet and read from Psalm 24: "Who shall ascend into the hill of the Lord? or who shall stand in his holy place? He that hath clean hands, and a pure heart; who hath not lifted up his soul unto vanity, nor sworn deceitfully. He shall receive the blessing from the Lord." He closed his Bible, looked down at the group of kneeling men, and said, "Brethren, it seems to me just so much humbug to be waiting and praying as we are, if we ourselves are not rightly related to God." There among the straw the men confessed their own needs and received assurance that the Lord would certainly visit Lewis in revival.

Duncan Campbell was the man they invited to conduct meetings in Barvas. Their faith was tested when they received his reply stating that he was obligated to remain in Skye to arrange a holiday convention. The minister took the letter to Peggy and told her Duncan would be unable to come. She replied: "Mr. MacKay, that's what man says; God has said otherwise! Write again! He will be here within a fortnight!"

Meanwhile, the Lord was working in Skye to bring Duncan to Lewis. The tourist board of Skye had booked all accommodations for a special festival during the time the convention was to be held. In consequence, the convention was canceled, and Duncan was free to accept the invitation from Barvas.

On arrival he was met by the office-bearers of the church in Barvas. An old elder approached him by asking, "Mr. Campbell, are you walking with God?" Duncan, aware that here were men among whom revival had already come, replied, "Well, I think I can say this—that I fear God."

Tired and hungry after his journey, Duncan nonetheless agreed to address the Christians who had gathered at the church that night. He never got his supper or his sleep that night. After preaching to a congregation of about three hundred, Duncan closed the service, and the crowd dispersed. As he left the pulpit area, a deacon beckoned him to the church door. There Duncan saw that the entire congregation remained outside. Others had arrived at the church also, drawn by deep conviction. The entire crowd, now about six hundred people, packed the church once again and stayed until the early hours of the morning, so great was their hunger for the Word of God. When Duncan finally left the church, he received the news that there were two to three hundred people from neighboring villages gathered at the police station where they knew there was a God-fearing constable. Duncan went to the station and found there men and women on their knees praying to God for mercy. As Duncan was always eager to point out, this was not man's effort, but "a manifestation of God that moves sinners to cry for mercy before they go near a place of worship."

When Duncan had accepted the invitation to come to Barvas, it was for a ten-day mission; but the revival that broke out in Barvas was occurring simultaneously in other parts of Lewis, and Duncan stayed for three years preaching and strengthening new believers. Duncan asserted, "In revival, time does not exist. You see, the presence of God puts to flight programs." Duncan said that during those years in Lewis you could stop any passerby and find that he was thinking about God and the state of his soul. It was this awareness of God that struck Duncan as one of the outstanding features of the Lewis revival. "Because of this awareness of God," maintained Duncan, "the churches were crowded . . . through the day right on through the night to five and six o'clock in the morning."

The revival had begun because Christians got on their knees, and its continuation was due to their perseverance in prayer. Peggy and Christine Smith sought the Lord unceasingly and as a result enjoyed a special intimacy with their heavenly Father. Once when the movement was at its height, Peggy sent for Duncan and told him she felt burdened that he go to a particular village to preach. Duncan demurred, insisting the he had no particular leading to go there. Men in that town were bitterly opposed to revival and had already stated that they did not wish to be involved in any evangelistic effort. Peggy turned her sightless eyes in Duncan's direction and said, "Mr. Campbell, if you were living as near to God as you ought to be, He would reveal His secrets to you also." Duncan took the rebuke and invited the minister to join him and the Smith sisters that morning in prayer. Peggy began to pray: "Lord, You remember the conversation we had this morning at two o'clock. And You told me You were going to visit this part of the parish with revival, and I've just spoken to Mr. Campbell about it but he's not prepared to think of it. You'd better give him wisdom because the man badly needs it."

The next evening Duncan traveled to the village, and God provided both a meeting place and a congregation. Opposition had been overcome, and the Spirit of God was present in convicting power.

One of the chief concerns of the men who had begun to pray for revival in Lewis had been the spiritual unconcern among the young people. Apathy was so widespread among them that conversion was typically referred to as "the plague." Their interests centered mainly in dancing, the cinema, and the drinking houses. A favorite story of Duncan illustrates how God brought revival to the youth of Lewis, despite their hardened condition.

Duncan was preaching in a house-meeting in Barvas. A minister from neighboring Carloway, Murdo MacLennan, was there with his wife to assist in the services. The two preachers rejoiced to see two pipers converted at the meeting. They were to have played at a concert and dance that night in Carloway. Burdened for the youth of their parish, Mr. and Mrs. MacLennan returned to Carloway while the dance was in progress. Mr. MacLennan entered the hall by a side door. The young master of ceremonies for the evening met him and angrily denounced the intrusion of religion. "If you want to come to the dance," he said, "you should have come through the main door and paid your entrance fee like everyone else!"

Mr. MacLennan replied, "As the minister of the parish I have come here with the authority of my Lord." The young man, suddenly daunted by the minister's reply and penetrating gaze, left the hall abruptly and retreated to one of the buses outside, where he sat weeping, already under conviction. He could not be persuaded to go back into the dance hall, not even to retrieve his coat.

Meanwhile, Mr. MacLennan engaged the attention of the entire party. He prayed for them and related to them what was happening in Barvas and how the two pipers had been converted. When he left the hall, the group dispersed. Many of the young people got on their knees in the buses that had brought them and found the Lord that night.

One of the most remarkable manifestations of the power of revival occurred in the town of Arnol, where many villagers remained aloof to the gospel. Godly men in that town met to devote an evening to prayer. Around midnight, Duncan asked the local blacksmith to pray. He rose and addressed the Lord: "O God, You made a promise to pour water upon him that is thirsty and floods upon the dry ground, and, Lord, it's not happening. Lord, I don't know how the others here stand in Your presence . . . but, Lord if I know anything about my own heart I stand before Thee as an empty vessel, thirsting for Thee and for a manifestation of Thy power." After a pause he continued, "O God,

Your honour is at stake, and I now challenge You to fulfill your covenant engagement and do what You have promised to do."

At that moment the house began to shake "like a leaf." Duncan related that a minister said to him, "An earth tremor." Duncan said, "Yes," but he was thinking of the fourth chapter of Acts where the Christians prayed and "the place was shaken where they were assembled together." Duncan pronounced the benediction and "walked out to find the community alive with an awareness of God." From that night forward, a "movement broke out that is spoken of in Scotland today as the Arnol revival, one of the mighty movements in the midst of this gracious visitation."

Duncan lived to see some of the fruit of the great Lewis revival. During its height the local press recorded that "there are more people attending the prayer meetings now than attended public worship on a communion Sunday." More important to Duncan, however, was the evidence that the results of those meetings were permanent. Years later he could state, "I could count on my five fingers all who dropped off from the prayer meetings. You see, in Lewis and in the highlands generally, they would no more believe that you were a Christian, than they would believe that the devil was a Christian, if you don't attend the prayer meetings." To his great joy at the end of his life, he observed that as a result of the continuing prayer meetings, men and women, both young and old, were "coming savingly to Christ," and many Christians were going into the ministry at home and through foreign missions.

Duncan Campbell died in 1971, having preached up to the last week of his life. A young man converted under his ministry wrote that "it was not so much what he said that gripped me but the man behind the words—his Christ-likeness. Jesus was real to him." It was certainly the reality of Duncan's walk with God which rendered him a powerful preacher and an instrument in revival.

Suggestions for Further Reading

Andrew Woolsey. *Duncan Campbell—A Biography*. London: Hodder and Stoughton, 1974.

About the Contributors

Mark Sidwell (general editor) has a Ph.D. in church history from Bob Jones University and is a member of the editorial department at Bob Jones University Press.

Edward M. Panosian has a Ph.D. in church history from Bob Jones University. He is Chairman of the Division of Social Science at Bob Jones University and is professor of church history in Bob Jones Seminary and Division of Graduate Studies. He is the author of numerous articles and booklets, including *The World Council of Churches.*

Christa G. Habegger is a member of the voice faculty at Bob Jones University and author of the book *Saints and Non-Saints,* a collection of articles on real and fictional characters from church history.

Dan Olinger has a Ph.D. in theology from Bob Jones University and is Product Development Co-ordinator, Secondary Level, at Bob Jones University Press. He has written numerous articles and the booklets *Homosexuality* and *British Israelism.*

Craig Jennings has a Ph.D. in church history from Bob Jones University and is co-author of the booklet *Monuments of Faith.* He is currently pastor of the Word of Life Lutheran Church in LeSueur, Minnesota.

Rebecca Lunceford Foster formerly served as Editorial Assistant of *FAITH for the Family* magazine and was a regular contributor to that periodical. She now resides in Raytown, Missouri.

David O. Beale has a Ph.D. in church history from Bob Jones University. He is a teacher in the School of Religion at Bob Jones University and is professor of church history in Bob Jones Seminary and Division of Graduate Studies. He is also the author of *In Pursuit of Purity: American Fundamentalism Since 1850; SBC: House on the Sand?;* and *A Pictorial History of Our English Bible.*

Stewart Custer has a Ph.D. in New Testament Text from Bob Jones University and is Chairman of the Division of Bible in the School of Religion at Bob Jones University. He is the author of several books, including *Does Inspiration Demand Inerrancy?; Treasury of New Testament Synonyms;* and *Tools for Preaching and Teaching the Bible.*

L. Gene Elliott has a Ph.D. in library science from Florida State University and formerly served as Director of the Library at Bob

Jones University. He is currently Director of Library Services at Greenville Technical College in Greenville, South Carolina.

Donna Hess is a member of the staff at Bob Jones University Press. She is author of the textbook *SPEECH for Christian Schools* and the young people's novel *A Father's Promise*. She is also the editor of *EXCURSIONS IN LITERATURE for Christian Schools* and *FUNDAMENTALS OF LITERATURE for Christian Schools*.

Bob Jones is the Chancellor and former President of Bob Jones University. He is a noted preacher, Shakespearean actor, and art expert. He has written many books, including *Wine of Morning; How to Improve Your Preaching;* and *Cornbread and Caviar*.

Edith Long is a member of the German faculty at Bob Jones University. She regularly leads a summer mission team of college students to perform evangelistic work in Germany.

Jeri Massi is a free-lance writer best known for her young people's novels, including the popular Peabody Adventure Series published by Bob Jones University Press.

George Mulfinger, Jr., until his death in 1987, was a member of the science faculty at Bob Jones University. He wrote numerous articles and pamphlets, including *The Flood and the Fossils* and *How Did the Earth Get Here?* He also co-authored the first textbook published by Bob Jones University Press, *PHYSICAL SCIENCE for Christian Schools* (1974).

Raymond St. John has a Ph.D. in American Literature from the University of North Carolina at Chapel Hill. He is Chairman of the English Department at Bob Jones University and edited *EXPLORATIONS in Literature for Christian Schools* and the two volumes of *AMERICAN LITERATURE for Christian Schools, The Early Tradition: 1607 to 1865* and *The Modern Tradition: 1865 to the Present*.

Topical Index

Scripture Index